Colin Woods.

A CONCISE DESCRIPTION OF THE ENDOWED GRAMMAR SCHOOLS

Lancashire and Yorkshire

by

Nicholas Carlisle

THE RICHMOND PUBLISHING CO. LTD. 1974

Bibliographic Note

This volume consists of extracts relating to Lancashire and Yorkshire reprinted from the 1818 edition of Nicholas Carlisle's *A Concise Description of the Endowed Grammar Schools in England and Wales (2 vols.).* The complete work has also been reprinted and details can be supplied by the publishers on request.

SBN 85546 186 1

Republished in 1974 by The Richmond Publishing Co. Ltd.
Orchard Road, Richmond, Surrey, England.

Reprinted in Great Britain by Kingprint Limited
Richmond Surrey.

LANCASHIRE

(extracted from Volume I of *A Concise Description of the Endowed Grammar Schools in England and Wales)*

BLACKBURN.

THE FREE GRAMMAR SCHOOL in BLACKBURN was founded by Queen ELIZABETH, on the humble petition, as well of the Inhabitants of the Village and Parish of Blackburn, as of other persons resident in the neighbourhood, "for the Education, Management, and Instruction of Children and Youths, in Grammar," and to be called "The Free Grammar School of Queen ELIZABETH, in Blackburn, in the County of Lancaster." To consist of one Master, and one Usher.

And that Her Majesty's design might be the more fully answered, and that lands and revenues to be granted for the support of the School, might be the better directed for the continuation of the same, she ordained that there shall be for ever in the Village and Parish of Blackburn, "FIFTY men of the more discreet, and honest, of the Inhabitants or Freeholders," to be Governors of the possessions belonging to the School: GILBERT GERRARD, the Attorney-General, and Sir THOMAS LANGTON, Knight, being in the number of the first Governors.

The Governors to be a Body Corporate, with perpetual succession,—may plead and be impleaded,—have a Common Seal,—and a legal capacity of purchasing and holding lands and revenues, provided they are not holden of the Crown *in chief*, and do not exceed the clear annual value of £30.

The Governors are further empowered to appoint the Master and Usher, and to make good and wholesome Statutes in writing, concerning the preservation and disposition of the Revenues, and the regulation of the School.

The sum of £4..7..4. is now paid out of the Land Revenues of the Crown to the Master. And the endowment, which is chiefly in land, situate in Dilworth, has been increased by various pecuniary benefactions from the Governors.

The School is "*free to the World*," with the exception of an entrance fee and small perquisite. The present number of boys under the Head Master is nearly 30, and from 30 to 40 attend the Usher. Children are admitted at any age, and may remain until their Education is completed.

The ETON Latin and Greek Grammars are used: there is no particular system of education prescribed.

The present Head Master is, The Revd. WILLIAM BOARDMAN, Clerk, whose Salary is £90. *per annum*, together with perquisites which fluctuate and are uncertain. No Pupils are boarded by him; nor by the Usher.

ROBERT BOLTON, an eminent Puritan Divine, and one of the best Scholars of his time, was educated at this School.

BLACKROD, near BOLTON.

OF the FREE GRAMMAR SCHOOL at BLACKROD the Author is not able to give a description, as no Answer has been received to his Letter.

There is an EXHIBITION of about £70. *per annum* to Pembroke College, Cambridge.

GREAT BOLTON or BOLTON in THE MOORS.

THE FREE GRAMMAR SCHOOL of BOLTON in THE MOORS was founded by ROBERT LEVER, Citizen and Clothier of London,—who, by his Will, dated the 16th of March, 1641, devised certain lands in *Harwood*, in the County of Lancaster, either for erecting and maintaining a FREE SCHOOL, or a CHAPEL, as should be thought meet by his Executors.

This benevolent intention appears to have been afterwards carried into effect. And, in 1784, an Act was obtained for incorporating the Governors, and for enlarging the Trusts and Powers, for the benefit of the School:—

By this Act it is declared, that the School shall be called "THE FREE GRAMMAR SCHOOL of the TOWN and PARISH of BOLTON in THE MOORS, in the County Palatine of Lancaster, of the Foundation of ROBERT LEVER, of London, Gentleman, deceased:"—

That the Right Honble. THOMAS Lord GREY *de* WILTON, JAMES BRADSHAW, and TEN others, should be GOVERNORS of the same,—should be a Body Corporate and Politic, with perpetual succession,—and should have a Common Seal:—

The Governors are empowered to appoint a Head Master, and Usher, "to teach and instruct the Children and Youth who shall be educated at the said School, not only in Grammar and Classical Learning, but also in writing, arithmetic, geography, navigation, mathematics, the modern languages, and in such and so many branches of Literature and Education as shall from time to time, in the judgment of the Governors, or the major part of them, be proper and necessary to render the Foundation of the most general use and benefit:"

The Head Master's Salary not to be less than £80., and that of the Usher £40. a year, to be increased as the Revenues of the School will admit :—

The Governors are further empowered to remove the Master, and Usher, on sufficient cause, and to appoint others, after *three* months previous notice in writing :—

The Usher to be under the direction of the Head Master :—

And no Head Master or Usher to teach any Children, besides those educated in the School, belonging to the Parish of Bolton, without the leave of the Governors.

No answer has been received to the repeated applications of the Author.

Robert Ainsworth, the eminent Grammarian and Lexicographer, was educated at this School,—of which he was afterwards the Master.

BURNLEY.

THE GRAMMAR SCHOOL of BURNLEY, in the Parish of Whalley, appears to have existed in the reign of EDWARD the Sixth, as it is recorded in the life of WILLIAM WHITAKER, D. D., the learned Master of St. John's College, Cambridge, that he received the earlier part of his education here, under the care of Mr. HARGREAVES; but it does not seem to have been at that time endowed, though the House of the last *Popish* Incumbent was reserved for the use of a Schoolmaster.

However, in the Twentieth year of the reign of Queen ELIZABETH, 1578, Sir ROBERT INGHAM, Clerk, Rector of Stocking Pelham, in the County of Hertford, granted a certain messuage or tenement called "*Alfrethes*," situate at Farnham, in Essex, to his Nephew JOHN INGHAM, on condition that he the said JOHN should charge the said tenement with a rent-charge of £3. for ever, for and towards the maintenance of a Schoolmaster to teach young persons freely in the Free Grammar School, founded and established in Burnley.

Accordingly the Nephew granted that Rent-charge to RICHARD, Son and Heir Apparent of JOHN TOWNLEY, of *Townley*, Esquire, WILLIAM BARCROFT, of *Lodge*, JOHN PARKER, of *Extwistle*, SIMON, Son and Heir of EVAN HAYDOCK, of *Hesandforth*, ROBERT WHITAKER, of *Holme*, Gentleman, and JOHN WOODROFF, Son and Heir of JOHN WOODROFF, of Burnley, Yeoman, their heirs and assigns, to stand seized of the same for the use and intent aforesaid.

The next donation appears to have been a Farm at Alverthorpe, near Wakefield, in Yorkshire, by a person now unknown.

By Surrender, dated the 30th of April, 1696, EDMUND

TOWNLEY, Rector of Slaidburn, gave *Ackerley's* tenement on the Ridge, to this School.

By Surrender, bearing date the 4th of October, 1699, NICHOLAS TOWNLEY, of Royle, Esq., gave the tenement called "*Cockridge*," to the Church and School of Burnley; probably in equal portions.

HENRY HALSTED, Clerk, B. D., Rector of Stansfield, in the County of Suffolk, by his Will, dated the 5th of August, 1728, gave to the Master and Feoffees of the Free School in Burnley, all his Library of books at Stansfield: this is now arranged in a room over the School, and contains some valuable Classical books.

Besides these Endowments, there is a rent-charge of 10*s.* a year paid from an Estate situate in the Chapelry of Colne, in this Parish.

Two rent-charges, one 4*s.* and the other 9*s.* a year, were formerly paid from estates in the County of York; but they have not been acknowledged for more than Twenty years last past. It does not appear who were the Donors.

There are no STATUTES.

The School is open, for instruction in the *Classics*, to the boys of the Chapelry indefinitely. Formerly, something was paid on admission, and a *Cockpenny* at Shrovetide: But, in lieu of these, the Master was afterwards allowed to make a charge of Two guineas a year for each boy, for teaching writing and arithmetic. The charge is now Three guineas a year to the sons of Gentlemen and principal Tradesmen, but to the rest not so much; out of which the Master provides an Assistant, to teach English, writing, arithmetic, and the mathematics. The number of Classical boys at present does not exceed Twenty: and from Thirty to Forty more attend.

No age being specified when boys shall either enter, or leave the School, the whole is left to the discretion of the Master, and of the Parents or Guardians.

The Westminster Grammars by Ward, are generally used: But when a boy has previously learned the Eton, the Grammar is not changed. There is no particular system of Education prescribed.

In 1572, Alexander Nowell, Dean of St. Paul's, London, established a maintenance for Thirteen Scholars at Brasen-Nose College, Oxford, from The Free School of Middleton, and from the Schools of Whalley and Burnley, or any other School in the County Palatine of Lancaster.

The Master is appointed by The Trustees of the lands, for the time being. The Revenues of the School are managed by him under their direction; but when a Lease has been granted, it has generally been done by The Trustees only.

The present Head Master is, John Raws, Clerk, whose Salary is about £130. a year. The Stipend of the Assistant and the out-goings of the School being liquidated, the surplus of the School charges also belongs to him, which is more or less according to the number of Scholars. This Gentleman is likewise the Assistant Curate of Burnley.

Neither of the Masters takes Pupils.

BURY.

THE following ADVERTISEMENT appeared in "THE COURIER" Newspaper, on Thursday Evening the 2d of April, 1818,—

"To CLERGYMEN, who are Graduates in one of the two Universities, either of Oxford or Cambridge.

THE MASTERSHIP of the FREE GRAMMAR SCHOOL of BURY, in the County of Lancaster, having become vacant by the death of the Revd. FRANCIS HODGSON, who has been Master thereof 49 years, the Trustees of the said School hereby give notice, that they intend to hold a SPECIAL MEETING within the said School, on TUESDAY, the 7th day of April next, at Ten o'Clock in the Forenoon, for the purpose of ELECTING another MASTER; for whom there is a very good double house, with a stable and garden adjoining, pleasantly situated, and well fitted for the accommodation of a family. The Salary will be Two Hundred Pounds a year, payable by four equal payments quarterly. It is not *necessary* for the Master to be in HOLY ORDERS, but it is required by the Statutes of the Founder "That he be a Graduate in one of the two Universities, either Oxford or Cambridge, well skilled in the Latin, Greek, and Hebrew Tongues, a man of prudence and sobriety, and of a good temper." The most respectable testimonials of the preceding qualifications will be expected by the Trustees, to be produced by each Gentleman who may think proper to offer himself as a Candidate on the day of election; and also that he will give such further proofs of his attainments in the above Languages, as may be requested from him at the same time.

Further information may be received on application to THOMAS NORRIS, Esq., of Bury, aforesaid, one of the Trustees, and Steward of the said School. All letters must be post paid.

Bury, February 12.

N. B. That part of the above quotation from the Statutes of the Founder, requiring that the Master be well skilled in the Hebrew Tongue, *will be dispensed with* at the ensuing election; and it may not be improper further to observe, that in addition to the Salary above-mentioned, the Perquisites will probably amount to Twenty Pounds a year."

CARTMEL, near MILNTHORPE.

THE GRAMMAR SCHOOL of CARTMEL does not appear from the Records of the Parish, to have been founded by any particular Person, or at any stated Period; or to have been originally a *Free* School, bnt merely a Parochial Seminary under the authority and superintendance of The Churchwardens and Sidesmen of the Parish.

For a series of years they hired a Master and paid his Salary from the Interest of small sums of money left by Will, at various periods, for that purpose, or to the Parish for pious uses, which was made up to the sum agreed for by a small Quarterage paid by all who sent Children, *except the Poor*, to whom the School was *free*.

Hence it might take the name of a *Free* SCHOOL, for in 1619 it was agreed by the Churchwardens and Sidesmen in Vestry assembled, that Land, not to exceed the value of £20., should be purchased with the School stock for the use of The *Free* School; no Land, however, was purchased until the year 1680, when £131..10..0. were judiciously expended for that purpose.

In 1635, a Master is stated in the Parish-book to have been hired at the ancient wages, and who was also to have 6*d.* a Quarter for Grammarians, and 4*d.* for *Petties (little ones)*, as they are so called. *Pettetes* occurs in the Statutes of Ewelme.

In 1664, the Master's Stipend was £20.—and if the Interest of the School Stock, together with the Quarterage at the rate above mentioned, exceeded that sum, the surplus was then to be applied in part payment of the Usher's Salary.

In 1674, the Quarterage was raised, by order of the Vestry, from 6*d.* to 8*d.* for Grammarians, but remained at 4*d.* for *Petties.*

In 1711, an election took place, when it was agreed that the Master should have for his Stipend the rents of the lands which were purchased in 1680, together with the Interest of the School Stock not expended and Quarterage, which was then raised to 1*s.*.6*d.* for Latin, and 1*s.* for English, but the poor Children to be taught *free* as before.

At a subsequent Election, in 1714, no stipulated sum is mentioned; the Master is to have the whole Salary of the School, allowing to his Usher £3. *per annum*, out of the same. Nothing is said of Quarterage, which appears to have *now* ceased; the Rents of the lands and the Interest of the money remaining, being deemed sufficient for the support of the Master.

Every future election is entirely unconditional. There are no stipulations in regard to the Children of the Poor, nor are the instructions of the Master confined to the Children of the Parish,—but boys are admitted from every part of the Kingdom, and even now from *The West Indies.*

In 1689, Mr. HENRY BIGLAND, then a Citizen of London, but of an Ancient Family in this Parish, gave by Will £400. to be invested in land at the discretion of the TWENTY-FOUR SIDESMEN: and with which a purchase was made in 1692.

The whole of the Endowments, except £40., are now in land, situate near Cartmel Church-Town.

There are no Statutes. But it appears from the Parish-Book that, in 1671, "Two Deeds in Parchment and one in Paper, concerning The Grammar School, were delivered to the safe keeping of THOMAS ASKEW." And, in 1679, it is ordered by The Vestry, that "a new Deed of Trust of the School be made." *Two* only of the Feoffees named in the old Deed being then living. None of these Documents can now be found.

The School is open to the boys of the Parish indefinitely, as soon as they can read The New Testament in English; and they may remain, if their Parents think proper, until they have finished their education. It is customary for persons of property, who have children at the School, to make a compliment to the Master at Shrovetide of a sum, called "*Cock-pence*."—"*This cannot be demanded of right.*" But a charge, *per* Quarter, is made upon the Parents of those Children who write or cypher, the Poor not excepted.

The WESTMINSTER Grammars are used; but it is now more a School for educating boys for Trade and Commerce, than for Classical Learning.

The inscription upon the Monument of THOMAS PRESTON, Esq., who died in 1696, states the following Exhibition,—"Ecclesiæ pauperibus et pauperum filiis in Scholâ Cartmellensi Collegioque Sti. Johannis Cantab. educandis legavit." It is not known to have been ever obtained.

The present Head Master is, Mr. WILLIAM TAYLOR, whose emoluments are,—Rents of land £150., Interest of money £2., Cock-pence from £20. to £30. He takes Pupils, his terms are 44*s.* *per* month for board; writing, cyphering, &c., being charged separately,—and if they are not Parishioners, a certain sum for *Cock-pence* is also expected.

The Second or Writing Master does not take Pupils.

EDMUND LAW, D. D., Bishop of Carlisle, received the early part of his education at this School. His Father was the Curate of one of the Chapels in this Parish, FORTY-NINE YEARS.

CHORLEY.

THE GRAMMAR SCHOOL of CHORLEY was founded in the year 1611, according to the following Document:—

"The Certificate of WILLIAM HAWKSHEAD and THOMAS AINSCOW, Churchwardens of Chorley, concerning the erection of the School-house,—transcribed out of the Register-book, &c.,—

"These are to certify all whom it may concern in Posterity, that whereas in the year of Our Lord 1611,—

"We, WILLIAM HAWKSHEAD and THOMAS AINSCOW, then Church-wardens of Chorley, in the County of Lancaster, together with the most part of the best Inhabitants of the Parish, taking notice of the many inconveniences that formerly had been, by reason we were utterly destitute of a School-house within the said Parish or Chapelry,—whereby it was the same year, and by the said Inhabitants agreed, that a School-house should be forthwith erected at the Parish charges, and should be set *part* within the *Church-yard*, and part within the *Tythe Barn-yard*,—to this end, that neither the Vicar nor the Minister of the said Church or Chapel, nor the Farmer of the Tythes of the said Chapel, should have power to convert it to any other use, but that it should remain constantly for a School-house for ever:—

"All which was finished accordingly by a general consent aforesaid on all sides, with this further promise, that no Schoolmaster should inhabit therein with his *Wife*, neither Minister that should hereafter be the Minister also enjoy that to inhabit therein with his *Wife*, but every such *Wives*, in both sides, in such like case is *to be kept out* of the same for divers great causes,—and especially, that if either Wife, or their Children begotten in such habitation, might become chargeable to the Parish of Chorley,—and for the future hereof, we hope this agreement will discharge all such as hereafter affect to attempt for their Families in part of performance:—

"Whereof and towards the perfecting of the building aforesaid, ROBERT CHARNOCK, of Astley, now deceased, gave so much *brick* as was necessary to be put in the said erection, as it is now finished, and £6. in *money*,—And every Inhabitant in Chorley, that was liable to a *Fifteenth*, gave and paid 20 *Fifteenths* thereunto.—Accordingly with other charges made only by the said Inhabitants towards perfecting the same for a

School-house.—So whereupon it was erected, according to the same agreement:—

"So in regard We, the said Church-wardens, grown aged, and as we think it proper to have it on record to testify the same in remaining, and for the preventing all Suits and future Controversies thereupon, as also that the Truth in future may appear, we thought good to certify the same under our hands the last day of June, *anno Domini* 1634:—

"And, therefore, to that purpose have inserted this our Certificate into the Register Book of Chorley, the day and year last mentioned, in the presence of these Persons and Parishioners, whose names are subscribed here."

It does not appear that there was any original Endowment,—but there have been the following Benefactions subsequently made, for the support of the Master,—*viz.*,

	per annum.
WILLIAM MASON, who died in 1638, left an Annuity, payable out of an Estate, called "*Ingol,*" near Preston, of - - -	£1.. 0..0
An Annuity, payable out of an Estate, called "*Stump,*" near Chorley, but by whom left, is not known, of - - -	5.. 0..0
The Interest of £50. left by a person named HEALD, - - - -	2..10..0
The Interest of £20. left by JAMES ALLANSON,	1.. 0..0
The Interest of £10. left by a person named BROWN, - - - -	0..10..0
An Annuity payable from *Astley Hall,* but by whom left, is not known, of - -	0..15..0
	£10..15..0

At present there are neither Trustees, Trust Deeds, nor what can properly be called an Endowment.

The Stipend being so small, no boys are taught free of expense; and the Master is at liberty to charge whatever Quarterage he pleases. As this is a manufacturing District, all the Youth educated here at present are intended for business,—and consequently, it may with propriety be styled a "*Commercial School*," the *Classics* being seldom introduced.

The present Master is, The Revd. HENRY BRIERLEY, whose Salary and Emoluments average about £120. *per annum.* His terms for Boarders are £25. a year for boys under 12 years of age, and £30. for those above that age.

Previous to this Gentleman's election, which is now 21 years since, the School had been very indifferently managed for a long time; and, of course, when he came it was at a very low ebb, not *six* boys attending when he opened the School,—but by laudable industry and perseverance it is now constantly full, and has averaged for several years past from 60 to 70, and sometimes 80, Scholars.

CLITHEROE.

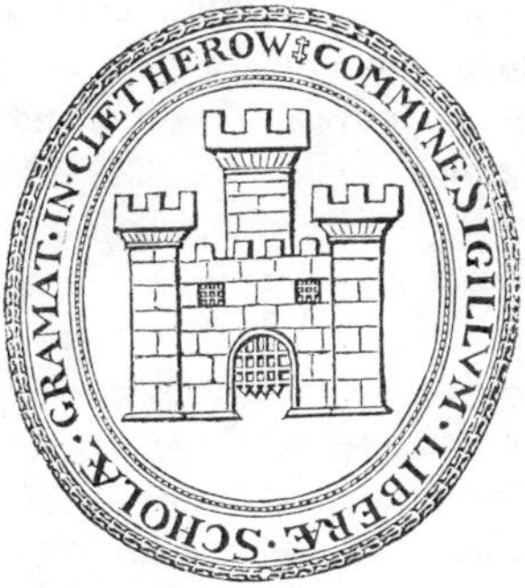

THE FREE GRAMMAR SCHOOL of CLITHEROE was founded by King PHILIP and Queen MARY, and endowed with the Lands and Rectorial Tythes of the Parish of Almondbury, in the County of York.

THE GOVERNORS are SIX in number, and are bound by an Oath for the observance of the Statutes. They are required to have a residence within the Parish of Whalley, which is divided into Parochial Chapelries, of which Clitheroe is one; and the vacancies as they occur, are filled up by the Survivors.

The Head Master, and Usher, are elected after an examination of Candidates by The Governors, subject to the approval of the Bishop of Chester, who is VISITOR of the School.

The Governors have the sole management of the income of the lands and possessions of the School, and appoint the Salaries of the Head Master and Usher, which are at present settled at £200. to the former, and £100. to the latter *per annum*. The surplus of the Revenue arising from the estates, is directed to be applied to the repairs of the School, and sending poor boys educated at this School to the Universities: But there has only been one Exhibitioner within recollection.

The money which has of late accumulated, has been applied to building a house for the Head Master.

This School is exclusively *Classical*, and free without limitation. An annual present at Shrovetide is expected from the Scholars to their Teacher, which is called "*a Cock-penny*;" and it varies, according to the circumstances of the Scholars.

The School possesses no advantages in either of the Universities; nor is it connected with any particular College.

The present Head Master is, The Revd. ROBERT HEATH, M.A., of Brazen-Nose College, Oxford. This Gentleman takes Pupils, his terms for board and education, being £50. *per annum*, exclusive of incidental expenses.

The Vicarage of Almondbury, of which the Governors of the School are Patrons, has usually been presented by them to some private friend.

The Perpetual Curacy of Clitheroe has, of late, been generally presented to The Head Master by the Patron, Lord Viscount CURZON.

FARNWORTH, in *Widnes*, near PRESCOT.

THE FREE GRAMMAR SCHOOL at FARNWORTH, a Chapelry in the Parish of Prescot, was founded by WILLIAM SMYTHE, the good Bishop of LINCOLN, a native of this Parish, and the Founder of Brasen-Nose College, in Oxford, according to an Indenture Tripartite, made the 20th of July, 1507, "betwene WILLIAM SMYTHE, Bishop of Lincolne, and The Dean and Chapter of Lincolne, of the one partie;—JOHN the Prior, and the Convent of *Launde*, in the County of Leycester, of the second partie;—and The Maior and Citizens of Chester, of the third partie,"—

Reciting, That forasmuch as the said Prior and Convent had received of the said Bishop a gift of £300. towards their great charges in procuring the appropriation of the Parochial Church of Rosthorne, in Cheshire, to their Monastery,—They agreed to pay an annual rent of £10., for ever, to the said Mayor and Citizens, who would give the same to "*a sufficyentt and honest Preest,* being a Master or Bachelor of Arte, or *a Master of Grammar* at the least, teaching Grammar freelye, in a Free Schoole at Farneworth, in the County of Lancaster, for ever."

This rent is now paid from Rosthorne, having been fixed to be so paid at the Dissolution of the Abbey.

In 1623, One Hundred and Fifty-five Inhabitants of Farnworth petitioned the Magistrates of Chester in behalf of Mr. HAWARDE, School-master there, whom they highly extol,—Afterwards, "other Masters *had so misused the Children,* that they had been in danger of losing their senses, lives, and limbs."

In 1631, there was a general and joint Petition of the Gentlemen and the Inhabitants of the Chapelry of Farnworth to the Mayor and Aldermen of Chester, praying for "a new Schoolmaster, instead of *old* Mr. HAWARDE, who was *insufficient,*—and *young* WILLIAM who was *idle* and *neglectful.*"

Other gratuitous acts were conferred upon Scholars, natives of the Counties of Lancaster and Chester, by the benevolent Family of SMYTHE.

MATTHEW SMYTH, the first Principal of Brasen-Nose, in 1512, and who died in 1547, left his Nephew, WILLIAM SMYTH, Parson of Barton in The Clay, a tenement and lands in *Sutton*, in the Parish of Prescot, chargeable with 20*s*. to be paid yearly to the Usher at Farnworth. His other land in Sutton he gave to Brasen-Nose College, to pay 20*s*. a year to a Scholar born in the Chapelry of Farnworth, or else in the Parish of Prescot, or near to it. He also disposed of other lands, for the purpose of raising SCHOLARS in the Parish, and supporting them at Brasen-Nose College.

HUMPHREY OGLE, LL. B., gave £100. to Brasen-Nose, to support Two SCHOLARS born in the Parish of Prescot.

There are also payable from an estate in *Rainhill*, in this Parish, annually, - -	£18.. 0..0
KNOWLES's Legacy, placed out on the Wigan and Warrington Turnpike roads, £96. -	4..16..0
Rent of half an estate, in *Penkitt*, in this Parish,	15.. 0..0
House and Garden in Farnworth, purchased with a bequest to the School of £100., -	8.. 0..0

Mr. GREGSON observes, "the beneficent design of the Founders of Brasen-Nose, and the School at Farnworth, could not be executed more advantageously for the future Fellows themselves, and for the Honour of the intelligent and learned Principal and his worthy Associates, the Fellows of Brasen-Nose College, than by the appropriation of a part of their Revenues to the support of an excellent and learned Schoolmaster, to teach freely the Children who are destined to be sent to College from this favourite seat of the Clergy, the Parish of Prescot;—and the Town of Farnworth, from whence so many Lancashire and Cheshire men have risen to the enjoyment of the best Livings in the gift of Brasen-Nose, will do well to continue to nourish such plants as will bring forth fruit that will do credit to the Founders. If the good Bishop had laid out in his days £300. in a landed estate, instead of lending the money, the income, 'ere this, would have been £300. a year. The number of excellent Scholars from this Parish is certainly very great, but it is hoped a hint humbly given by a Layman will be excused; for complaints against the Schoolmaster are not always groundless."

HAWKSHEAD, in FURNESS FELLS.

THE FREE GRAMMAR SCHOOL in HAWKSHEAD was founded in 1585. His Grace EDWYNE SANDYS, Archbishop of York, then obtaining Letters Patent under the Great Seal, dated at Greenwich the 10th of April, in the Twenty-Seventh year of Queen ELIZABETH,—by which Her Majesty granted, that from thenceforth there should be one Grammar School within the Parish of Hawkshead, in the County Palatine of Lancaster,—and that SAMUEL SANDYS, CHRISTOPHER SANDYS, ADAM SANDYS, Gentlemen, WILLIAM SAWREY, BERNARD BENSON, ROWLAND NICOLSON, THOMAS RAWLINSON, and JAMES TAYLOR, Yeomen, should be Governors of the Possessions and Revenues of the School;—should be a Body Corporate, by the name of "THE GOVERNORS of the Possessions, Revenues, and Goods, of the said Free Grammar School," with perpetual succession, and by the same name should be able to receive Manors, lands, &c., as well of Her Majesty, her Heirs, and Successors, as of His Grace The Archbishop, or of any other person, provided they do not exceed the clear yearly value of £30., and be not holden *in capite*;—should have a Common Seal;—might plead and be impleaded;—and that the Archbishop, during his natural life, should make Statutes in writing, concerning the well ordering and government of the Schoolmaster and Scholars, and the Possessions of the School.

By virtue of the Letters Patent, His Grace made the following CONSTITUTIONS, which were duly subscribed on the 1st of April, 1588,—

1. I ordain, constitute, make, establish, and erect, that one Perpetual and Free School of Grammar, from henceforth, be in Hawkshead aforesaid, of one School-master, and his Successors, in one House there, for that purpose by me appointed, and so to continue from one School-master to another, in succession, for

ever, to teach Grammar, and the Principles of the Greek tongue, with other Sciences necessary to be taught in a Grammar School; —the same to be taught in the said School *freely*, without taking any Stipend, wage, or other exaction of the Scholars, or of any of them resorting to the said School to learn;—which said School, shall, from henceforth, be called, for ever, "THE FREE GRAMMAR SCHOOL OF EDWYNE SANDYS," Archbishop of York, in Hawkshead aforesaid, according to the foresaid grant and license from Her Majesty.

2. Also, I do constitute, elect, nominate, ordain, and appoint, PETER MAGSON, Master of Arts, School-master of the said Grammar School, &c.

3. Also, I ordain, will, and declare by these presents, that I, the said EDWYNE, Archbishop of York, during my life, natural, and after my decease, SAMUEL SANDYS, my son, during his life, shall have the nomination, donation, gift, and grant of the said office and room of Schoolmastership or School-master of the said Free School, when and so often as the same shall become void by death, deprivation, or otherwise, to give, grant, and dispose the same to such person and persons as shall be apt and able thereunto, according to the Ordinances herein declared, and hereafter by me to be declared; and after my decease, and the death of the said SAMUEL SANDYS, the Governors of the foresaid Free Grammar School, for the time being, or the most part of them, with the assent of the Bishop of Chester, for the time being, shall, for ever, have the nomination, donation, gift, and grant of the said office and room of School-mastership, or School-master, of the said Free School, in Hawkshead, when and so often as the same shall become void by death, deprivation, or otherwise, to give and grant the same to such person and persons as shall be apt and able thereunto, according to the Ordinances herein declared, and hereafter by me to be declared.

4. Also, I ordain and appoint, that the said School-master shall be well seen, and have good understanding in the Greek and Latin tongues, and shall teach and inform the same to such Scholars of the same School, as shall be most meet and apt for the same, according to the discretion of the said School-master, and that the said School-master before he shall begin to teach the said School, (after my decease), shall be allowed by the Ordinary of the place, for the time being, according to the Statute in that case provided.

5. Also, I ordain and constitute, that the said School-master of the said School, and his Successors, for ever, shall have under him one Usher, in the foresaid School, to be an Usher in the said School, to teach such Children and Scholars in the said School of the Lowest Forms, as to him shall be appointed by the said

School-master and his Successors, and that the said Usher shall be chosen from time to time by the said School-master and Governors of the said School, or the most part of them, for the time being.—And also, that upon any misbehaviour to be committed by the said Usher, it shall be lawful for the said School-master and Governors, or the most part of them, to deprive the said Usher, and at their pleasure to appoint another in his place as foresaid.—And if the aforesaid School-master shall fortune to die, then the Usher of the said School for the time being, shall teach the Scholars in the said School, as Master thereof, until there be a School-master placed in the said room and office to exercise the same, according to the Ordinances and Foundation of the said School: And the said Usher so teaching in the said Vacation time, shall during the same time, appoint one Scholar of the same School, to be an Usher under him, which Scholar, so teaching as Usher, shall have for the said time he shall teach as Usher, the Stipend and Allowance belonging to the Usher; and the said Usher, so long as he shall teach as Master, to have the Stipend and Allowance belonging to the School-master.—The which sums of money, shall be paid to the said Usher teaching as Master, and Scholar teaching as Usher, by the said Governors and their Successors, for the time being, as before is expressed,—Provided always, that after my decease, and the decease of the said SAMUEL SANDYS, my son, if the foresaid Governors of the foresaid Free School, and their Successors, for the time being, with the consent of the Bishop of Chester, for the time being, do not give and grant the said School-mastership within the space of *Thirty* days next after the avoidance thereof, to one apt and able person, according to the Ordinances aforesaid, that then the Bishop of the Diocese of Chester, for the time being, alone shall have the gift, grant, and disposition of the said office and room of School-mastership for that time, so that the said Bishop, for the time being, give and grant the same within *Thirty* days next after the foresaid *Thirty* days appointed to the foresaid Governors of the said School,—And if the said Bishop of Chester, for the time being, do not give and grant the said School-mastership within the said *Thirty* days so limited unto him, as before is said, to one able person, according to the Ordinances aforesaid, that then the Dean and Chapter of Chester aforesaid, for the time being, shall have the gift and grant of the said office and room of School-mastership for that time, and so from time to time, as often as any such default as aforesaid shall happen to be.

6. Also, I ordain and constitute, that the said Schoolmaster and his Successors, for the time being, shall on every Work-day between the Annunciation of the Blessed Virgin Mary and Saint

Michael the Archangel, be in the said School and begin to teach at *Six* of the Clock in the Morning, or at the furthest, within one half hour after, and so to continue until *Eleven* of the Clock in the Forenoon; and to begin again at *One* of the Clock in the Afternoon, and so to continue until *Five* of the Clock at night. —And every Work-day between the Feast of Michaelmas and the Annunciation of the Blessed Virgin, to begin to teach at *Seven* of the Clock in the Morning, or within half an hour after at the furthest, and so to continue until *Eleven* of the Clock before noon;—and then to begin School again at half an hour *before One* of the Clock in the afternoon, and so to continue until *Four* of the Clock at night;—During all which times, I will, that the Schoolmaster shall be present in the School with the Usher, and shall teach all such good Authors which do contain honest precepts of Virtue, and good Literature, for the better education of Youth; and shall once every week at the least, instruct and examine his Scholars in the principles of true Religion, to the end that they may the better know and fear God: —And that the said Schoolmaster and Usher shall not use of custom, to be absent from the aforesaid School during the times aforesaid, nor withdraw themselves from thence, but only for, and upon honest, necessary, and reasonable causes,—And that it shall not be lawful for the said School-master or Usher, to be absent from the said School above *Six* weeks at one or several times in the whole year, upon necessary business, except they obtain the special license of the said Governors, or the most part of them, for the time being, so that the School-master and Usher be not both absent at one time.

7. Certain godly Prayers, as therein set down, to be said every Morning and Evening.

8. The Schoolmaster, Usher, and Scholars, to use and frequent the Church upon the Sabbath-day and Holy-days, to hear Divine Service and Sermons,—and to sit together in some convenient place.

9, 10. The Master to be displaced for misbehaviour by the Governors, with the assent of the Bishop of Chester.

11. Also, I ordain, will, and constitute, that the said Schoolmaster, and his Successors, for the time being, shall *break up* their School and Teaching only at *two* times in the year: that is to say, one full week next before *Christmas*, and to begin to teach again the next Working-day after the *Twelfth* day of Christmas;—and shall break up again one full week next before *Easter*, and shall begin to teach again the Monday Se'nnight after Easter.—Against which several times of breaking up, the chiefest Scholars of the said School, shall make Orations, Epis-

tles, Verses in Latin or Greek, for their Exercises, that thereby the said School-master may see how the said Scholars have profited.

12. The Founder's power in altering the Constitutions and Ordinances.

13. Also, I ordain, will, and constitute, that the Usher of the aforesaid School, shall be obedient to the Master thereof,—and that all Scholars shall be obedient to all good and lawful Statutes and Ordinances now made, or hereafter to be made, touching the good government and ordering of the same School, and shall be of honest and virtuous conversation, obedient to the Master and Usher in all things touching good manners and learning, both in the School and elsewhere, and shall continually use the *Latin* tongue, or the *Greek* tongue, within the School, as they shall be able.—Also they shall use no weapons in the School, as sword, dagger, waster, or other like, to fight or brawl withal, nor any unlawful gaming in the School.—They shall not haunt taverns, alehouses, or playing at any unlawful games, as cards, dice-tables, or such like,—Also they shall keep the hours in coming to the School, before in these Statutes mentioned.—Also in the absence of the Master, the Scholars shall be obedient to the Usher, and to such Prepositors as the Master shall appoint touching good order in the School. All which Statutes now made, and hereafter to be made by me, the said EDWIN, Archbishop of York, they shall inviolably keep and observe, upon pain of Expulsion from the aforesaid School, after *Three Warnings* had and given, concerning the premises, by the School-master of the said School, for the time being;—or by the Usher of the said School in vacation time, when there is no Master of the said School, and the said Scholar or Scholars so expulsed, shall not be received into the said School again without humble suit and earnest Petition, made to the Governors and Master of his or their reconciliation.

14. The Governors, from time to time to preserve and maintain the School and School-house, and all other buildings, and fences of the same, in good repair,—and shall see that all the commodities and revenues belonging to the School, be employed to such uses as appear in the Letters Patent.

15. The Master's yearly Salary to be £20., and that of the Usher £3..6..8., to be paid to them, by even portions, at the Feasts of The Annunciation of the Blessed Virgin Mary, and St. Michael the Archangel.

16. The Governors to visit the School, at the least *twice* every year, and shall make diligent inquiry, from time to time, whether the School-master, Usher, and Scholars, do their duties

as becometh them or not:—" and as they shall find any thing amiss or out of order, they shall redress and amend the same presently, or so soon as they conveniently can."

17. The Governors shall yearly appoint one of themselves to collect and gather the rents and revenues of the School; who, before he enters upon his office, shall give bond, with one or two sufficient Sureties, to make a just and true Accompt, when required.

18. That before any Governor be admitted to the place of Governorship of the School, he shall not only give his consent to the execution of these Statutes and Ordinances; but also shall be *Sworn*, to be true and just towards the School, and to the preservation, government, and faithful sustentation of the same.

19. A strong and substantial Chest to be provided, with three strong Locks and Keys, of three several fashions, for the safe custody of Her Majesty's Letters Patent, and all the evidences and writings concerning the School,—the School-master to have the keeping of one of the Keys, and the *two* first named Governors and their Successors, to have either of them one of the said Keys in their custody,—so as the Chest may not be opened without the consent of all the three Persons so named and appointed.

20. The Governors to pay to the Lord of the Customary tenement such rents, fines, &c., as shall from time to time be due, &c.

21. All the Ordinances and Constitutions to be truly, firmly, and inviolably observed and kept, in every point, by the Governors, Master, Usher, and Scholars.

And to give greater Solemnity and Security for the faithful discharge of the Governor's duty, Doctor JOHN BRIDGMAN, Bishop of Chester, prescribed the following OATH, to be voluntarily taken by such, as are to be elected and admitted Governors of this School:—

"I, A. B., do swear, that I have not given any thing, nor have indirectly laboured, to be made Governor of this School;—and I will diligently and faithfully, to the utmost of mine ability, keep by myself, and cause to be kept by others (as much as I can), inviolably, all these Statutes;—And I will not do any act, at any time, which I shall know, believe, or think, will be prejudicial to the good of the said School;—and I will not appropriate, convert or apply to mine own use, or to the use of any of mine, any part of the profits of the Revenues given to the said School; but will do my best to improve and increase them, to the best advantage of the School, School-masters, and Ushers, in perpetuity, and to such ends only as are set down in the Foundation, and in these present Statutes, and no other use."

This Oath is to be taken in the presence of The Bishop of Chester, and the Schoolmaster.

The pious Founder endowed the School with a Dwelling-house, Out-houses, and a Customary tenement adjoining thereto in the Manor of Hawkshead;—and also with lands and houses in or near Wakefield and Doncaster, in the County of York,—and some Ground-rents in Kendal, in the County of Westmorland.

The principal Estate belonging to the School, is near Doncaster, which was let upon a lease for 42 years; but, it is believed, that this lease will expire in about six or seven years, when a considerable advance of Rent is expected.

The Estate near Wakefield was sold some years since, and the money laid out to greater advantage in the purchase of an Estate in the Parish of Hawkshead.

The School is open to all boys of the Parish indiscriminately, free of expense. The number has sometimes been One Hundred and upwards; but at present there are only about Fifty Scholars, consisting partly of Parishioners, and partly of Strangers.

Children are admitted at any age, provided they can read English tolerably well. If they come out of the Parish, it is expected that they pay about Two guineas Entrance, and a like sum every year at *Shrovetide*, called their "*Cock-penny*," which is all the Charge that is made for their education; except writing and arithmetic, for which they pay about 8 or 10*s. per* Quarter.

The ETON Grammars are now used here: and the system of Education is nearly the same as at all other public Schools.

There are no University advantages, nor Church Preferments, belonging to this School.

The Boys generally continue at the School, until they can be admitted at The University, or are of age to enter into Holy Orders.

The present Master is, The Revd. THOMAS BOWMAN, late Fellow of Trinity College, Cambridge, "which Office he has filled for upwards of THIRTY YEARS." His Salary is about £160. *per annum*, exclusive of Entrance money, and the Cock-penny:—out of which the Governors oblige him to pay the Usher £50. a year, and to keep the School, School-house, and other buildings, fences, &c., in substantial repair.

The Master does not take Pupils into his own house. The boys are usually boarded with some respectable family in or near the Village, and have every necessary comfort and accommodation at Twenty-two guineas a year, including washing, mending of Stockings, &c. An *Extra* charge is made for fire and candles.

On the 19th of August, 1717, The Revd. THOMAS SANDYS, Curate of St. Martin's in The Fields, and Lecturer of St. James's Westminster, by his Will of that date, gave a good Collection of Books to the School. To this collection considerable additions have been made, at different times, by young Gentlemen admitted at Cambridge from hence. The Scholars are allowed the use of these Books, by paying about 5*s.* yearly; which money is judiciously expended in the purchase of new Publications.

In 1816, The Revd. WILLIAM WILSON, Vicar of Moreton, in the County of Essex, and late Fellow of St. John's Cambridge, out of respect to the place of his Education, gave £100. *Sterling*, directing the Interest of it to be distributed yearly in PRIZES, to those who have made the greatest proficiency in CLASSICAL Learning,—to the best DECLAIMERS in English,—or to be laid out in BOOKS for the use of the School, at the discretion of the Master.

There are EIGHT GOVERNORS, who have the general

management of the concerns of the School. The present GOVERNORS are,—

MYLES SANDYS, Esq., Graythwaite Hall.

WILLIAM FELL, Esq., Ulverston.

WILLIAM TAYLOR, Esq., Colthouse.

MATTHEW HODGSON, Esq., Colthouse.

MICHAEL KNOTT, Esq., Water-Head House.

JAMES PENNY MACHELL, Esq., Hollow Oak.

EDMUND WINSTANLEY RIGBY, Esq., Keen-Ground.

The Revd. GEORGE PARK, the present Minister of the Parish of Hawkshead.

The Revd. Dr. WORDSWORTH, Domestic Chaplain to The Archbishop of CANTERBURY, and many other eminent Divines have been educated at this School.

LANCASTER.

IT is not certain when, or by whom, THE FREE GRAMMAR SCHOOL at LANCASTER was founded.

The Town and many of it's Records were three times burnt: Twice by the Scots, on sudden Incursions, in 1322 and 1389; and once by a casual Fire, in 1698. The want of Records, respecting the School, is attributed to the two former disasters.

The Free School is mentioned in some books belonging to The Corporation, so early as the year 1495; and they appear to have repaired it, at different periods, out of their Revenues.

It was in great decay in 1683, when JAMES PILKINGTON, Bishop of Durham, and The Corporation, subscribed liberally, and with the assistance of other benevolent Individuals in the Town and Neighbourhood, raised a sufficient sum of money to rebuild the School, which is capable of holding ONE HUNDRED and TWENTY boys with ease. It consists of two Stories. The Upper Story is appropriated to the Master, who teaches writing and arithmetic: and The Lower one to the Head Master, and Usher. There is also a Room allotted to a Library, in which there are now about 300 volumes, consisting of Divinity, History, British Classics, &c.: this Library was originally established by The Corporation; but, of late years, considerable additions have been made by the laudable example of young Gentlemen, who could afford it, making a donation of an useful book or a set of books, on leaving the School. The Usher has the charge of the Library.

Since about the year 1600, The Corporation have appropriated the Rent of a piece of ground in the Town for the increase of The Usher's Salary; which had most probably been granted originally to them by some Duke of Lancaster, for in the year 1415, King HENRY the Fifth, or his officers, brought a *Quo Warranto* against The Corporation to try by what Title they held it, and they proved a Grant of it which was allowed, but the Proceedings are so injured by time, that it is not now legible by whom the Grant was originally made. This ground was formerly called "*The Deep Carr*," but for many years past "*The Usher's Meadow*;" it contains about two acres, and is now let for £14. *per annum*.

In the year 1615, RANDAL CARTER, a Tallow Chandler, in the Parish of St. Saviour, Southwark, charged certain Houses in White-Cross Street, London, by his Will, with £10. *per annum* for ever, to be paid to The Usher of Lancaster Free School, where he had been educated. This £10. *per annum* was paid until within about Twelve years past; since then it has been discontinued, and cannot be recovered, as it is said the property on which it is charged, cannot be identified. Mr. CARTER also left £10. or £20. *per annum* out of the same estate, to The Free School of Saint Saviour, and which the Trustees thereof have been unable to recover for the same reason. The Corporation of Lancaster have ever since liberally paid The Usher £10. *per annum* in lieu of that which was bequeathed by Mr. CARTER.

The following are the RULES and REGULATIONS of THE SCHOOL:—

Lancaster, 25th Feby. 1802.

Rules and Regulations hereafter to be punctually observed in the Free Grammar School within the Borough of Lancaster, being under the Patronage of The Corporation of Lancaster, *viz.*,

1st, That the School shall be open to any Boy, who is able to read English pretty well.

2nd, That both the Masters shall teach Latin and English promiscuously as they shall be requested; the former to be taught grammatically, as well as the latter.

3d, That Seven shillings and Sixpence be paid for every son of a Non-Freeman.

4th, That the Scholars shall be divided between the two Masters, in such proportions as may be most proper and agreed upon between them.

5th, That the School be ranged into Classes, and that every new Scholar take his place, according to his progress in learning, abilities, &c.

6th, That the Masters shall exchange sides on Tuesday in every week, and that Friday in every week be set apart for hearing over what they have said on preceding Days, and every Saturday forenoon for the repetition and application of Grammar.

7th, That the School hours during Summer (*viz.*, from the first day of April to the first day of October) shall be from *Six* in the Morning until *Eight* in the Morning, from *Nine* in the Morning till *Twelve* at Noon, and from *Two* to *Five* in the Afternoon: And in the Winter, from *Eight* to *Twelve* in the Forenoon, and from *One* to *Four* in the Afternoon. And that Prayers be read (as heretofore hath been accustomed) every morning, the first thing so soon as both Masters are present; and it is expected, that they will be punctual in their attendance.

8th, That Perquisites, called *Cock-pennies* shall be given to the Masters at Shrovetide only; and since there is no Quarterage at all paid by Freemen's children, and only a small one by Non-freemen's, it is hoped these circumstances will be then considered, and also at the entrance of every new Scholar.

9th, That the *Cock-pennies* shall in future be divided between the Masters in manner following, that is to say, seven twelfths thereof to the High Master, and five twelfths thereof to the Usher.

10th, That the vacation times be a week at Shrovetide, a week at Easter, three weeks at Whitsuntide, and a month at Christmas, besides the usual Saints Days, and every Thursday and Saturday Afternoon.

11th, That some part of each Saint Day, and other times occasionally, be set apart for the instructing the Scholars in the Church Catechism, Morality, and the Principles of the Christian Religion.

Revised and Settled by us the undersigned, being a Committee appointed for that purpose.

JAS. PARKINSON, Mayor.
ROBERT ADDISON.
RICHARD JOHNSON.
THOS. BURROW, } Bailiffs.
W. HOUSMAN, }
JN. TAYLOR WILSON.

Added by Order of Council of 3d August, 1803,

RICHARD ATKINSON.

12th, That the Usher for the time being shall be the Librarian, and have the care and management of the Library in this School, which has lately been considerably enlarged, and that he be responsible for the Books belonging to the same, and that the old Usher do deliver the Books and a correct Catalogue thereof to every succeeding Usher.

The Sons of Freemen of the Borough, whether they reside in or out of the Borough, pay nothing for their Education, except that the Gratuity, called a "*Cock-penny*," is expected to be given at Shrovetide. The Sons of Non-Freemen pay 7*s.* 6*d.* *per* Quarter, while under the Second Master; and 10*s.*.6*d.*, while under the Head Master. *All* boys pay 5*s.* on Entrance, which is divided between the two Masters equally. The average number of boys, during the last seven years, has been about Sixty-five; about Forty of whom are taught by the Usher. The Scholars are of a *mixed* sort: the sons of Merchants and Tradesmen of the Town forming a considerable Majority. They stay in the School as long as their Parents please to allow them.

The ETON Latin and Greek Grammars are used: and the System of Education is the same as is followed in other great Schools; with the addition of English Grammar, History, and Geography. Those boys who learn writing and arithmetic, attend the Master a part of each day.

There are no Exhibitions, nor other University advantages belonging to this School; neither is there a Common Seal.

The present Head Master is, The Revd. JOHN BEETHOM, M. A., whose Salary is £70. *per annum*, paid by The Corporation. He also receives Seven twelfths of the *Cock-pennies* collected at Shrovetide, half of the Quarterage money paid for the sons of Non-Freemen of the Town, and half of the Entrance money.

The present Usher is, The Revd. GEORGE MORLAND, whose Salary is £54. *per annum, viz.*, £30. from The Corporation,—£10. from The Corporation, formerly paid out of Mr. CARTER's Estate,—and the Rent of the Meadow £14.; together with Five twelfths of the *Cock-pennies,* half of the Quarterage money, and half of the Entrance money.

The Corporation allow The Writing Master a Salary of £20. *per annum*; and he charges *all* boys 10*s.* *per* Quarter for Arithmetic, and 7*s.* 6*d.* *per* Quarter for Writing.

Neither of the Masters takes Pupils; as they have so many Scholars, that they could scarcely attend to them. They have, however, two or three young Gentlemen occasionally a short time before they go to The University, but not often.

The Author has great pleasure in expressing his gratitude, for the description of this truly respectable and useful Seminary, to the obliging kindness of JOHN TAYLOR WILSON, Esq., the present Mayor of Lancaster.

LEYLAND, near CHORLEY.

THE small GRAMMAR SCHOOL at LEYLAND is entitled to an annual Stipend of £3..17..10., which was granted by Queen ELIZABETH for a Master, and is now paid out of the Revenues of The Duchy of Lancaster; But when, or by whom it was founded is not known.

The whole Stipend at present is under £20., and arises chiefly from Interest of money that has been since given to it.

LIVERPOOL.

THE FREE GRAMMAR SCHOOL at LIVERPOOL was founded on the Dissolution of the Chantries in this Church, and endowed with £10..13..3. *per annum*, now payable out of the Land Revenues of the Crown.

This School has been wholly "*discontinued* since the death of the late Master, Mr. JOHN BAINES, an excellent Scholar," about ten years ago.

But the Corporation have a plan at present under consideration, to revive this ancient Seminary, and thus to give additional splendour to this flourishing Town.

MANCHESTER.

THE FREE GRAMMAR SCHOOL at MANCHESTER was founded, some time prior to the 16th year of HENRY the 8th, by HUGH OLDHAM, a native of *Oldham*, in the County Palatine of Lancaster, and Bishop of EXETER, who died in 1519; and being (in consequence of not abiding by the decision of the Pope, in a dispute in which he had been engaged with the Abbot of Tavistock) excommunicated at his death, was buried in the wall of a Chapel which he had himself built, and annexed to the Cathedral of Exeter.

This eminent Prelate is said to have been as great an enemy to Monkish Superstition, as he was friendly to Learning. Brasen-Nose, and Corpus Christi* Colleges, in Oxford, shared in his bounty, as well as Manchester when he founded this celebrated School; and being himself President of the latter College, he vested the appointment of the Two Masters of the School in his Successors, and in case of a lapse, then in The Warden of the College of Christ in Manchester.

Certain Water CORN MILLS, called "*Manchester Mills*," situate in the Town of Manchester upon the river *Irke*, with the Toll of those Mills,—And also a FULLING MILL there situate upon the same river,—And also certain messuages, lands, and tenements, situate in Manchester, and in *Ancoats* in the County of Lancaster, for the support of THE GRAMMAR SCHOOL, were conveyed to Twelve Trus-

* His effigy is preserved in the Quadrangle of Corpus Christi College. There was formerly one also at the upper end of the School, which, HOLLINGWORTH says, was newly painted and adorned in his time, but was pulled down by some Parliamentary Soldiers, whose rage was excited by the Episcopal habiliments.

tees, on the 1st of April, 1524, by HUGH BEXWYKE, Clerk, and JOHANNE BEXWYKE, widow, from whom it appears they had been leased, or purchased, (for it is not very clear which) by the Executors of the good Bishop's Will.*

The following is a Copy of the Indenture of Feoffment:—

"To all People to whom this present Writing indented shall come, hear, read or see, HUGH BEXWIK, Clerk, and JOHANNE BEXWYKE, WIDOW, sendeth greeting in Our Lord God everlasting. That where the Right Revd. Father in God, HUGH OLDOME, late Bishop of Exeter deceased, considering that the bringing up of Children in their adolescency, and to occupy them in good learning and manners from and out of idleness is the chief cause to advance knowledge and learning them when they shall come to the age of virility, or whereby they may the better know, love, honour and dread God and his laws.—And for that, that the liberal science or art of Grammar is the ground and fountain of all the other liberal arts and sciences, which source and spring out of the same, without which science the other cannot perfectly be had, for science of Grammar is the Gate by the which all other been learned and known in diversity of tongues and speeches.—Wherefore the said late Revd. Father, for the good mind which he had and bore to the Country of Lancashire, considering the bringing up in learning, virtue, and good manners, Children in the same Country, should be the key and ground to have good people there, which hath lacked and wonted in the same, as well for great poverty of the common people there, as also, by cause of long time passed, the teaching and bringing up of young Children to School, to the learning of Grammar, hath not be taught there for lack of sufficient Schoolmaster and Usher; then so that the Children in the same Country having pregnant wits, have been most parte brought up rudely and idly, and not in virtue, cunning, erudition, literature, in good manners, and for the said good and charitable deeds by the said late Bishop, purposed and intended as is before said, in the same Shire, hereafter to be had, seen, used, and done,—that is to say, for Grammar there to be taught for ever, the said late Bishop of his good and liberal disposition, at his great costs and charges, hath within the Town of Manchester, in the County of Lancaster, builded an House joining to

* The original Conveyance from HUGH and JOHANNE BEXWYKE exists both in Latin and English, and is now in the possession of the present High Master.

The College of Manchester in the West party, and the Water called *Irke* of the North party, and the Way going from tne said College into a Street called "*Mill Gate*" in the South party, and a Stone Chimney of GEORGE TRAFFORD of the East party, for a Free School there to be kept for evermore, and to be called "MANCHESTER SCHOOL."—And over and above that, for the same intent and purpose, he, as well at his more further expenses and charges, purchased a certain Lease of many years which are yet to come of the CORN MILLS of Manchester, with all the appurtenances,—and also caused other Lands and Tenements in Manchester before said, called "ANCOTES," and a Burgage in Mill Gate, to be disposed and converted to and for the use of the continuance of teaching and learning, to be had, taught, and continued in the same School for ever, as hereafter is declared and specified.—And also for the further and sure continuance and maintenance of the same School and Learning therein to be taught and had, We, the aforesaid HUGH and JOHANNE, and at our cost and charges, have purchased to the same use and intent, and conveyed a state to us and our heirs, and to one RALPH HULME now deceased, all the Mills, lands, tenements, rents, reversions, services, and hereditaments contained and specified in the Charter to this Schedule indented, annexed, expressed, contained, declared, and comprised,—Whereupon, We, the said HUGH BEXWICK and JOHANNE, for the accomplishment of the said good and ghostly purpose before expressed, have, by our said Charter indented, hereunto annexed, given and granted all and singular the same Mills, lands, tenements, and other the premises, with their appurtenances, to the within named LEWIS POLLARD, Knight, ANTONY FITZHERBERT, Justice and Knight, WILLIAM CARTENEY, Knight, THOMAS DENYS, Knight, ALEXANDER RADCLIFF, Knight, JOHN BERON, Knight, EDMUND TRAFFORD, RICHARD ASSHETON, THURSTAN TILDESLEY, ROBERT LANGLEY, RICHARD HOLLAND of *Denton*, JOHN REDDICHE of *Reddiche*, Esquires, and to their heirs and assigns, to the use and intent hereafter declared and specified,—that is to witt That they, their heirs and assigns for ever, as long as the World shall endure, shall stand and be thereof seized to the use and intent herein specified, and shall perform, execute, fulfil, and observe, and cause to be performed, executed, fulfilled, and observed, all and every acts, ordinances, provisions, constitutions, articles, appointments, and agreements, hereafter ensuing, by us the said HUGH BEXWYK and JOHANNE, and our Council, made and devised, specified and contained in the said Schedule indented, for the good maintenance, sustentation, and sure continuance of the same Grammar School to endure for evermore,—that is to say,—

First, The said LEWIS and other his Feoffees before said, their heirs and assigns, of the issues, revenues, and profits coming, rising, and growing of the said Mills, lands, tenements, and other the premises contained and specified in the said Deeds indented, the said School-house, called "MANCHESTER SCHOOL," sufficiently shall repair, sustain, maintain, or cause to be repaired, sustained, and maintained for evermore in covering, walling, and such other, as by the discretion of The Warden of the said College of Manchester or his Deputy and the Church Wardens of the said College Church, for the time being, shall be thought necessary:—

Item, within the same School nor Library of the same, by night, or by day, any other arts, things, plays, or other occupacions be had or used in them, or any of them, but all ways kept honest and cleanly, as it beseemeth a School or a Library;—and that after the cleanest manner, without any lodging there of any School-master, or of any Usher, or other of them, or of any other person or persons:—

Item, that the said School be weekly, once in the week, made clean by Two poor Scholars of the same house, thereunto assigned by The High Master for the time being, or, in his absence, by the Usher. The same poor Scholars therefore to have of every Scholar, at his first admitting, *One Penny* Sterling;—and therefore to write in a several Book all the names of Scholars that do come into the same School, as Scholar,—and that book and books thereof always to be kept, and every *third year* to be delivered to The Warden of the said College of Manchester or his Deputy, to the intent that therein may and shall always appear, which have been brought up in the same School, and so they to have Exhibitions to Oxford or Cambridge, as hereafter is expressed:—

Item, if there be Sickness infective, as Pestilence universal, the School to be left for the time being, by the discretion of the Warden of Manchester College for the time being, or his Deputy.—And if such sickness continue by the space of Twelve weeks whole, so that the Master and Usher there teach not usually by the same space, then the Master and Usher, every of them, to have but half the said wages for that time.—And if it continue the half year, they to have in like manner.—And if it continue by the space of Twelve months so, then they to have £6..13..4., and no more, that to be divided between them, according to their portions of wages.—And the rest of their said wages then to go to the Store Chest, set and ordained to keep the money and receipts of the said lands, tenements, and acts, concerning the naming of the School-master and Usher, and their Ordinances:—

Item, the said HUGH BEXWYK and JOHANNE BEXWIKE, during their life and the longer liver of them, shall name, chuse, and elect a convenient person and School-master, *single man,* Priest or not Priest, so that he be no Religious man,[a] being a man honest of his living and whole of body, as not being vexed or infect with any continual Infirmity or disease, and having sufficient Literature and Learning to be a School-master, and able to teach children Grammar, after the School use, manner, and form of the School of BANBURY, in Oxfordshire, now there taught, which is called " STANBRIDGE *Grammar,*" or after such School use, manner, as in time to come shall be ordained universally throughout all the Province of Canterbury :—

Item, the said HUGH and JOHANNE, during their life as before said, shall name, chuse, and elect a convenient Usher, in like manner as they do elect and name the above said High Master :—

Item, after the death of the same HUGH and JOHANNE, and either of them, The President of CORPUS CHRISTI COLLEGE of Oxford for the time being, and his Successors, shall within *One month* after the death or departure of every Schoolmaster and Usher, and either of them, name, able, elect, and chuse School-master and Usher, and either of them, as before is expressed, being a man honest and literate, not *Regular,* as he shall think convenient.—And if the said President do not name, elect, and chuse the Master and Usher within the said Month, as is after expressed, that then the said Warden or Deputy of the College of Manchester, for the time being, shall, within *One other Month* then next ensuing, name, able, elect, and chuse such Master and Usher, and either of them, as before is in the first Chapter of the Master, being a man honest and literate, as they shall think convenient :—

Item, that every Schoolmaster and Usher for ever, from time to time, shall teach *freely* and *indifferently* every Child and Scholar coming to the same School, *without any money* or *other rewards taken therefore,* as "*Cock-penny, Victor-penny, Potation-penny,*"[b] or any other whatsoever it be, except only his said Stipend and Wages hereafter specified :—

Item, that the High Master and his Usher, for the time being,

---

[a] Of none of the Religious or Monastic Orders.

[b] Pretexts for perquisites to the Master.

It was the barbarous custom at *Shrove-tide,* for those boys in THE MIDDLE SCHOOL to throw at a *Cock,* which was buried in the ground up to the neck,—hence "*Cock-penny*" was of great importance to the Second Master, every boy making him a preif they be within Holy Orders, at every Festival day and double Feast, being kept Holy-day in the year, yearly, be at Divine Service in their Surplice, in the Choir of The College of Manchester aforesaid, and be there at the Commandment of The Warden of the said College, or his Deputy, for the time being :—

Item, the High Master and the Usher, for the time being, every Wednesday and Friday weekly, for ever, with their Scholars, being and going two and two together, shall go in procession solemnly before The Warden of the same College or his Deputy, for the time being, and Fellows of the same, and their Successors for ever, if they have any Procession for the day, and every Scholar to say, if he able of learning, the common Litany, with the suffrages following, and *de Profundis* for the Soul of HUGH OLDOM, late Bishop of Exeter and Founder of their School, his Father and Mother Souls, and for the Soul of Sir RICHARD ANDERON, HENRY TRAFFORD and THOMASIN his wife deceased, and for the souls of GEORGE TRAFFORD of *The Garrett,* and MARGARET his wife, then next and immediately ensuing, when and what time it shall please God Almighty of his Mercy and Grace to call for the said GEORGE and MARGARET, or either of them, and for the Souls of HUGH BEXWYKE, Clerk, and JOHANNE BEXWIKE, widow, special Benefactors of the said School, when and what time it shall please God Almighty of his Mercy and Grace to call for the said HUGH and JOHANNE, or either of them, and for the Souls of all the Feoffees and Benefactors to the maintenance of the same School at that day departed, and all Christian Souls, and for the good prosperity of the Feoffees and Benefactorers then being in life :—

Item, that no High Master, or Usher, be expelled or removed against his will from the said School, and office of High Master or Usher, except it be for his or their miss living, or insufficient attending or teaching the Scholars there, or having any sickness or disease incurable, as Pox, Leprosy, or such other great offences or sicknesses, which be and shall be reserved to the discretion and order of the Warden of the College Church of Manchester aforesaid, for the time being, or his Deputy :—

Item, every Schoolmaster, and Usher, in form aforesaid elect

---

sent at that time: A dinner was given upon this occasion by him to the Scholars and some of their Friends.

Nutt Money was in like manner presented at Michaelmas to The High Master.

But all these Perquisities were abolished, when the present Two principal Masters were appointed.

and chosen, within One month of his said election or putting in to the said office, *shall*, before The Warden of the said College of Manchester, or, in his absence, before his Deputy of the same College, *swear* upon the Evangelist, that he shall diligently and indifferently teach, and correct all and every the said Scholars of the same School, for the time being, all fraud, guile, and deceit in that behalf only laid apart :—

Item, the Master, or Usher, which of them cometh first into the School in the Morning, say openly with the Scholars there, this Psalm, "*Deus miseratur nostri*," with a Collect, as they use in Churches Dominical days,—and every Night, in such like manner, the Master or Usher to sing Anthem of Our Blessed Lady, and say "*de Profundis*" for the soul of the late Bishop of Exeter, HUGH OLDOM, Founder of that School, his Father and Mother, and for the souls of Sir RICHARD ARDERON, HENRY TRAFFORD, THOMASSYN his wife deceased, and for the souls of GEORGE TRAFFORD of *The Garrett*, and MARGARET his wife, then next and immediately ensuing, when and what time it shall please Almighty God of his Mercy and Grace to call for the said GEORGE and MARGARET, or either of them, and for all the souls of the Feoffees and Benefactors of the same departed, and all Christian Souls,—and to say in audible voice in the School, before the beginning of "*de Profundis*," in this manner, for the soul of HUGH OLDOM, late Bishop of Exeter, Founder of our School, and his Father and Mother souls, and for the souls of GEORGE TRAFFORD and MARGARET his wife, and for all the souls that they be bounden to pray for, and for all the Benefactors souls, and all Christian souls "*de Profundis* :"—

Item, that no High Master, nor Usher, leave or depart from the said School, except he thereof give openly knowledge to the Warden or his Deputy, and openly in the School before the Scholars, by the space of *Fourteen weeks* before his or their departure, or else to leave and lose his or their Quarter wages that so departeth :—

Item, the said High Master, nor his Usher, shall grant no licence to the Scholars there to play, or depart from their School and Learning, except it be by the consent of the Warden or Deputy of the said College of Manchester, for the time being, and then to play honest games, and convenient for youth, and all together and in one place, to use their *Latin* tongue :—

Item, the said High Master, and Usher, to continue teaching in their Schools before every Feast, unto four days next before every Feast, as Easter and Christmas :—

Item, every High Master, and Usher, shall take yearly only Twenty days to sport them, at one time or sundry times, as they be not both absent at one time :—

Item, that if the High Master be sick of sickness incurable, or fall into such age that he may not conveniently teach, and hath been a man that long and laudably hath taught in the said School, then he to have of the Surplusage and Store belonging to the same School, yearly, £4. Sterling:—

Item, in like manner the Usher to have, yearly, Four marks:—

Item, if the High Master be sick of sickness curable, the Usher to help him, and to take the more pain upon him,—and also to have for his said pain, by the discretion of the said Warden or Deputy of the said College of Manchester, of the wages of the said High Master.—And in like wise, if the said Usher be sick, then the High Master to take more pain in teaching the Scholars, and to have part of the wages of the said Usher, by the discretion of the Warden of the said College, or his Deputy:—

Item, the High Master, for the time being, shall always appoint one of his Scholars, as he thinketh best, to instruct and teach in the one end of the School, all Infants that shall come there to learn their A B C Primer, and sorts till they being in Grammar, and every month to chuse another new Scholar so to teach Infants.—And if any Scholar refuse so to teach Infants at the commandment of the said High Master, or, in the absence of the High Master, at the commandment of the Usher for the time being, the same Scholar so refusing, to be banished the same School for ever:—

Item, the Usher being well literatured, and honest of his living, shall have the High Master's room and office whenever it is void, before any other, if he be able in learning:—

Item, if it happen the High Master and Usher to be both sick at once, and of sickness curable, as Agues and such other, then they to hire one sufficient after the use aforesaid, to teach for them, and they to pay his wages, that is to say, portionably after their wages, the High Master more than the Usher or Sur-Master, after the discretion of The Warden, or his Deputy.

ACTS and ORDINANCES concerning THE SCHOLARS.

Item, There shall be no Scholar ne Infant OF WHAT COUNTRY OR SHIRE SOEVER HE BE OF, being man child, BE REFUSED, except he have some horrible or contagious infirmity infective, as Pox, Leprosy, Pestilence for the time being, or such other Infirmities, which be and shall be always remitted to the discretion of the Warden or Deputy of Manchester College, for the time being:—

Item, every Scholar within the same School shall be obedient to help the Schoolmaster and Usher, for the time being, for the correction lawfully of any Scholar or Scholars of the same

School, at the commandment of the Schoolmaster or Usher for the time being:—

Item, no Scholar there being at School wear any dagger, hanger, or other weapon invasive, nor bring into the School, staff or bat, except their meat knife:—

Item, that no Scholar there make any affray within the same School upon the Master, the Usher, or upon any other Scholar of the same School, upon pain of leaving off his said School by one month,—And if any Scholar there make two frays as above is said, then to leave the same School by the space of two months,—And if any make the third, he to be banished the same School for ever without any favour:—

Item, The Scholars of the same School shall use no Cock-fight, nor other unlawful games, and riding about for Victors or other Disports had in these parts, which be to the great let of learning and virtue, and to charge and costs of the Scholars and of their friends:—

Item, that every Scholar of the same School be at the said School in the Morning, betwixt Michaelmas and Easter, before *seven* of the Clock, and between Easter and Michaelmas, at *six* of the clock, except such as come daily far to their learning, which shall come to the School at such an hour as shall be limited to them by the Master, according to the distance of the place that they come from:—

Item, that the Master, or Usher, be in the School at the hour limited to the Scholars:—

Item, every Scholar pay at his first admitting, and writing in of his name in the Book of Scholars, *One Penny* Sterling, and not above, that always to be paid to the Two poor Children for the time being, which keep the Book of Scholars' names, and make clean the School, as is before rehearsed:—

Item, that no Scholar shall bring meat or drink into the School, nor there to use their meat and drink, but always, if any such poor Scholars there be, that for their great poverty bring their meat and drink with them, they to go to some house in the Town, and there to eat and drink, and so to resort again to the School.

Item, that if any Scholar of the same School go from and forsake the same, and repair to any other School, and after return again to the same School, he to be taken again for one time, —but, at the second departure, he to be excluded and banished the same School for ever without any favour.

Item, that the Schoolmaster, and Usher, shall cause all Scholars, being learned in Grammar, at all times to use to speak their *Latin* tongue within the School, and all other places convenient.

ACTS for the WAGES of THE SCHOOLMASTER and USHER.

Item, the said HUGH and JOHANNE, and either of them longest living, with the issues and profits of the above named Mills, lands, tenements, reversions, and services, called "MANCHESTER MILLS," shall by them, or their sufficient Deputy, pay or cause to be paid yearly, without fraud, guile, delay, or deceit at the Feasts of Easter, the Nativity of Saint John Baptist, Saint Michael the Archangel, and the Nativity of Our Lord, by equal portions, £10. Sterling,—that is to say, at every of the Feasts aforesaid, 50s. to the High Master there for the time being teaching:—

Item, that the said HUGH and JOHANNE in like manner shall pay or cause to be paid of the issues and profits aforesaid, yearly, £5. Sterling to the Usher, Sur-Master there, for the time being teaching,—that is to say, at every of the Feasts aforesaid, 25s. Sterling:—

Item, after the death of the same HUGH and JOHANNE, the within named LEWIS POLLARD, Knight, ANTONY FITZHERBERT, Justice, WILLIAM COURTENEY, Knight, THOMAS DENYS, Knight, ALEXANDER RADCLIFFE, Knight, JOHN BERON, Knight, EDMUND TRAFFORD, RICHARD ASHTON, THURSTAN TILDESLEY, ROBERT LANGLEY, RICHARD HOLLAND, and JOHN REDDICHE, and their heirs, by them or by their sufficient Deputy, shall with the issues and profits aforesaid pay, or cause to be paid the Wages yearly of the High Master and Usher, in manner and form as is aforesaid, for ever:—

Item, that if any man being High Master, or Usher Sur-Master, for any time being, happen to die before the Quarter payment, as is aforesaid, then the same Master, or Usher Sur-Master, his executors or assigns that so shall happen to die, shall be paid after the rate and time of his death, as the same Quarter wages will amount:—

Item, in like manner the High Master, or Sur-Master, that happen to come and teach in the same School before the Quarter, he to have after the rate of his Quarter wages, for his coming and teaching before the Quarter:—

Item, the Wages of the Receiver of the lands, concerning the same school, shall be 20s. yearly, to be paid at Michaelmas, when he maketh his accompts, and not otherwise.

ACTS for THE FEOFFEES.

Item, when it shall happen the said Feoffees to die to the number of *Four*, then the same Four to make like Feoffment and Articles in manner as this is, to TWELVE honest Gentlemen and honest Persons within the same Parish of Manchester; and so they in like manner to make, from time to time, for ever, when it cometh to the number of *Four*, to the use aforesaid:—

Item, the Feoffees, for the time being, shall make no manner Lease or Estate of the said Mills, lands, or tenements belonging to the same School, or any parcel thereof, above *Ten years*:—

Item, The Abbot of Whalley, for the time being shall name from time to time one substantial person dwelling within the Parish of Manchester, putting in surety to be bounden to Two of the said Feoffees, to make true accompts, and pay Quarterly the Master and Usher, as is aforesaid,—And also paying to the Lords their rents due and accustomed, which shall receive the rents and profits of all the whole lands concerning the same School, which Receiver shall make his accompts for the said receipt, and for all necessary reparations and payments done there, once in the year at Manchester before the Warden of the College or his Deputy, Two of the Feoffees, and the High School-Master for the time being, if they can be at it, or Two of these persons at the least, there to make a true accompt of every thing, and true allowance ask upon his Oath, and bring and deliver yearly the Surplusage above all wages, reparations, and such other necessary expenses, the same Surplusage to be by the Auditors aforesaid, there being present, put into a Chest therefore made, remaining in the Vestry of the said College of Manchester, whereof the Feoffees for the time being shall have one key, and the Master of the College for the time being another, the Abbot of Whalley for the time being the third, the High Schoolmaster for the time being the fourth key, so that the said Chest in no wise may be opened, except all four keys come together :—

Item, the said Warden or Deputy, the Two Feoffees, and the High Schoolmaster for the time being, for their pain in hearing and viewing the said Recievor's accompts, shall have a Dinner of 5s. charge among them that be present at the said Audit, yearly :—

Item, when it shall happen the Chest to be at Surplusage the sum of £40. Sterling, the rest to be given to the Exhibition of Scholars yearly at Oxford or Cambridge, which hath be brought up in the said School of Manchester, and also only such as study Art in the said Universities, and to such as lack Exhibition, by the discretion of the said Warden or Deputy and High Master for the time, so no one Scholar have yearly above 26s..8d. Sterling,—And that till such time as he have promotion by Fellowship of one College or Hall, or other Exhibition, to the sum of seven marks :—

Item, the Feoffees, for the time being, shall pay of the Stock being in the said Chest, all charges in the Law, if any happen to be, for the defence of the lands of the said School or any part thereof,—And also shall pay the costs and charges of making of new Feoffments and Acts, Ordinances, for the good maintenance of the same when need shall require, as well to substantial learned Counsel in the Law, Temporal and Spiritual, as also for writing and engrossing of the same, with all other necessary expenses belonging to the same:—

Item, the Master and Fellows of the said College shall have yearly for their good and safe looking to the same Chest, and because it shall stand in their Vestry, the sum of 3*s*..4*d*. every Michaelmas, yearly, to them and their Successors, for ever, be truly contented and paid:—

Item, notwithstanding those Statutes and Ordinances before written, yet because in time to come many things may and shall survive and grow by sundry occasions and causes which, at the making of this present Acts, Ordinances, was not possible to come to mind;—

In consideration whereof, we the said LEWIS, ANTONY, WILLIAM, and other our Co-feoffees, trusting greatly to the fidelity of the above named Feoffees and other hereafter to come, will, that they hereafter from time to time when need shall require, calling to them discreet learned Counsel and men of good Literature, they to have full power and authority to augment, increase, expound, and reform all the said Acts, Ordinances, Articles, Compositions and Agreements, only concerning the Schoolmaster, Usher, and the Scholars for their and every of their offices concerning the said Free School, for ever."

The Water Corn Mills were ancient Soke Mills, at which the Inhabitants of the Town of Manchester were bound by immemorial custom to grind their Corn, Grain, or Malt, and to pay a twenty-fourth part thereof as a toll for grinding the same, for the support of the School.

But, by an Act of Parliament passed in 1785, which recites the custom, and that divers Suits had been commenced and Decrees obtained in confirmation of it, the Inhabitants were *discharged* from the obligation of grinding their Corn and Grain, except *Malt*, at "*The School Mills;*" and the same discharge was confirmed, and put under certain regulations.*

---

* During the dispute in 1737, the following Epigram was written by Mr. BYROM,—

These Mills, *three* in number, are situate upon the river *Irke*, not far from it's confluence with the *Irwell*,—The HIGHEST of them is a *Corn Mill*,—The LOWEST has been employed in the manufacture of *Snuff* and *Pins*, and for the purpose of *Fulling* woollen cloth,—both these Mills are let to respectable Tenants,—But the MIDDLE Mill, which is used for grinding *Malt*, is retained in the hands of the Feoffees of the School. According to the Act of 1785, it grinds all the *Malt*, which is used in the Township of Manchester,—the Inhabitants being obliged to send it there for that purpose, paying 1*s*. *per* load of Six bushels.

This sum having been fixed at a time, when money was much more valuable than it is at present, now bears no proportion to the labour effected; so that the Mill, originally intended to be of benefit to the *School* only, is now of far greater consequence to the Inhabitants of the *Town*. It is this Tax upon grinding *Malt*, however, which has induced the Public *Brewers* to settle themselves in the adjoining Townships of Salford, Chetham, Ardwick, Chorlton Row, and Hulme; none of the Breweries being actually situate in Manchester.

In addition to the Endowment it is said, that MARTIN BERON, a Clothier, who realized a large property in Manchester, left a considerable sum towards the erection of The Free School.

There is also an Annuity of £4..1..9. payable out of the Duchy Rents to the Master, which was first granted when his Salary was only £10. *per annum*.

From the profits of the Malt Mill,—from the Rental of the two other Mills, and several Houses,—and from the In-

---

" *Bone* and *Skin*, two Millers thin,
" Would starve the Town, or near it;
" But be it known to Skin and Bone,
" That *Flesh* and *Blood* won't bear it."

terest of money vested in the Funds, an Income of upwards of £1600. *per annum*, is now received.

The property for the support of the School is vested in, and is under the management of Twelve Trustees,—Gentlemen of the highest respectability, who have the satisfaction in matured life, of testifying by their honourable attention to the interests of the Establishment, the invaluable benefits which they themselves may have derived from it in their early days.

The following are the names of The Trustees, from the 15th of October, 1685:—

Sir Raphe Asheton.
Edm. Traiford, Esq.
J. Hulme, Esq.
William Hulme, Esq.
James Chetham, Esq.
James Lightborn, Esq.
Jo. Arderne, Esq.
Joshua Hordon, Esq.
Earl of Warrington.
James Holte, Esq.
Henry Hulton, Esq.
Jo. Atherton, Esq.
Peter Egerton, Esq.
Samuel Chetham, Esq.
P. Legh, Esq.
Sir John Bland, Bart.
Richard Arderne, Esq.
John Warren, Esq.
Alexander Radclyffe, Esq.
William Ashton, Esq.
Sir Thomas Grey Egerton, Bart.
Earl of Barrymore,—who sat in the English Parliament from 1714 to 1747, for Wigan.
Robert Booth, Esq.
Revd. James Banks.
Robert Radclyffe, Esq.
The Right Honble. James Lord Strange.
Sir Edward Egerton, Bart.
John Parker, Esq.
John Arderne, Esq.

1749.

Robert Gwillym, Esq.
Edward Greaves, Esq.
Miles Lonsdale, Esq.
From 1760 to 1772 are wanting.
R. V. Gwillym, Esq.
Lord Grey de Wilton, afterwards Earl of Wilton.
P. Ainscough, Esq.
William Egerton, Esq.
John Houghton, Esq.
Samuel Egerton, Esq.
William Banks, Esq.
Charles Ford, Esq.
Samuel Clowes, *Junr.*, Esq.
Revd. Croxton Johnson.

The present Trustees are,—

John Arden, Esq., of *Pepper Hall*, Yorkshire.

Sir Joseph Radcliffe, Bart., of *Mills-Bridge House*, Yorkshire.

Revd. Thomas Foxley, M. A., *Ratcliffe*.

Sir Robert Holt Leigh, Bart., M. P. for Wigan, *Leigh Place*, Lancashire.

Thomas Parker, Esq., *Astle*, Cheshire.

John Ford, Esq., *Abbey Field*, Cheshire.

Revd. George Heron, M. A., *Daresbury*, Cheshire.

William Fox, Esq., *Manchester*.

Revd. John Clowes, M. A., Fellow of Christ's College, *Manchester*.

Wilbraham Egerton, Esq. M. P. for Cheshire, *Tatton Park*, Cheshire.

Thomas William Tatton, Esq., *Withinshaw*, Cheshire.

There is at present one vacancy, occasioned by the death of John Entwisle, Esq., of *Foxholes*, Lancashire.

The Revd. Thomas Blackburne, LL.D., as Warden of Christ's College, is the present Visitor.

The present School, which was erected in the years 1776 and 1777, upon the old foundations, is situate near The

College Gates, in *Long Millgate.* It is a plain brick building, with a large stone Medallion in front, upon which is carved in *alto relievo*, an OWL, the Crest of THE FOUNDER, whose Arms are placed at one end of THE UPPER SCHOOL-ROOM, which is 96 feet in length, and 30 feet in breadth. It contains four fire-places,—is extremely well lighted by 26 large windows,—and is furnished with desks and seats, that bear evident marks of long service, by the numberless initials of names which succeeding boys have carved upon them. The Ceiling of this room is between 20 and 30 feet high,—a circumstance greatly favourable to the health of the Masters and the Scholars. This room is appropriated solely to instruction in the higher Classics. The number of Scholars in it has for the last ten years been about 140, after the annual Remove.

THE LOWER SCHOOL is literally *lower*,—being under a part of the former, and about half it's size. English, and the first rudiments of Latin, are taught in this School; and the boys are prepared in it for their reception into THE UPPER SCHOOL. Before the establishment of the NATIONAL and the LANCASTERIAN Schools in Manchester, there were frequently 70 or 80 pupils in this room: but at present the number is between 30 and 40.

The ETON Latin and Greek Grammars are used; but the system of Education is not in all respects similar to that of ETON COLLEGE.

This School is remarkably rich in it's University advantages.

There are ELEVEN EXHIBITIONS for Scholars from this School at any College in either of the Universities, of £40. a year each, which are paid from the School estate; and such of them as enter at BRASEN-NOSE COLLEGE, Oxford, or ST. JOHN'S COLLEGE, Cambridge, have always a good chance of obtaining other valuable appointments.

The young men, who have been educated at this School,

in turn with those of HEREFORD and MARLBOROUGH, have a claim to SIXTEEN SCHOLARSHIPS in BRASEN-NOSE COLLEGE, Oxford, and to SIXTEEN SCHOLARSHIPS in ST. JOHN'S COLLEGE, Cambridge, of different values, from £18. to £26. *per annum*, on the Foundation of SARAH Duchess of SOMERSET, in 1679, and who died in 1692 :—

The following is an Extract from Her Grace's Will, dated the 17th of May, 1686, in the Registry of the Prerogative Court of Canterbury :—

Also, I do will, direct, and appoint, that the before named Sir SAMUEL GRIMSTON, and his Heirs, shall Settle, convey, and assure by such lawful ways, means, and assurances as the said HENRY Lord DELAMERE and Sir WILLIAM GREGORY, and the survivor of them and his heirs, shall think necessary and convenient for the doing thereof firmly and legally unto and upon the Principal Fellows and Scholars of BRASEN-NOSE COLLEGE, in the University of Oxford, and their Successors, for ever, All that my Manor of *Thornhill*, with it's rights, members and appurtenances, in the said County of Wilts, and all Messuages, Farms, Lands, Tenements, Meadows, Pastures, Woods, Rents, Commons, Advantages, and Hereditaments whatsoever, unto the said Manor belonging or any wise appertaining, or reputed or taken to be part, parcel or member thereof, to be for ever used and employed for the founding and maintaining of a further number of SCHOLARS in the said College for ever, over and above those that I have already founded there, in such sort, manner and form as is hereinafter directed :—

And also, I do likewise will, direct, and appoint, that the said Sir WILLIAM GRIMSTONE, and his heirs, shall convey, settle, and assure, in such manner and form, and by such lawful ways, means, and assurances as the said HENRY Lord DELAMERE and Sir WILLIAM GREGORY, and the Survivor of them and his heirs, shall think necessary and convenient for the firm and legal doing and establishing thereof unto and upon the Master Fellows and Scholars of ST. JOHN'S COLLEGE, in the University of Cambridge, and their Successors, for ever, all that the Manor of *Wootton Rivers*, with the Rights, members and appurtenances thereof, in the County of Wilts, and all and singular Messuages, Farms, Lands, Tenements, Meadows, Pastures, Woods, Commons, Rents, and Hereditaments whatsoever unto the said Mannor belonging, or in any wise appertaining, or accepted, reputed, or taken part parcel or member thereof, To be for ever used and employed, for the founding and maintaining a further number of SCHOLARS in the said College, over and above those FIVE SCHOLARSHIPS which I have already founded in the said College, in such sort manner and form as is hereinafter directed :—

And for the better increasing both of the number and maintenance of the said additional Scholars in either of the before mentioned Colleges, I do direct and appoint, and I do desire that it may be so provided for in the Settlement thereof, That the said Manors and Hereditaments, to the said Colleges respectively appointed, may be ordered and managed in such sort and manner as is hereinafter directed ;—that is to say, I do will, direct, and appoint, that no Lease or Leases shall be granted or renewed of any the Leasehold Messuages, Farms, Lands, Tenements or Hereditaments within the said Manors hereby by me given or appointed to the said Colleges, or either of them respectively, for any longer or greater term than One and Twenty years in possession only :—And that upon every such New Lease there shall be reserved the best improved Rent that can be gotten for the same Farm so to be leased ;—And that there shall not be directly or indirectly taken for the making of any new grant of any Copyhold Estate or Estates, any Fine or Fines for more than after the rate or proportion of one third part of the improved Value or Rent of the said Tenements or Farm so letten ;—And that full two third parts of the improved yearly value of the said Tenement or Farm shall be reserved in Rent, and made payable half yearly, for the same to be from time to time employed and applied as is hereinafter mentioned ;—And that in every such new lease or grant to be made of the said Premises or any part thereof, the Tenant or Lessee thereof shall be bound to pay all manner of Taxes, and to keep the Messuages and Buildings upon the same in good and sufficient repair :—

And I do further will and appoint, that the said additional Scholars, in each of the said Colleges respectively, shall be called by the name of "SOMERSET SCHOLARS," and that their allowance for their maintenance and other things shall be equal and proportionable, saving only to those SIX SCHOLARS in each of the said Colleges, concerning whom I have hereinafter given particular directions, with those I have already founded there ; and that the Election, management, ordering and government of all the said additional Scholars shall be in the same manner, and according to the same rules, as are given and settled by me for and concerning the "SOMERSET SCHOLARS" by me founded already in the said respective Colleges, with this alteration only as to the Election of the Scholars into the said additional Scholarships : for my will is, and I do appoint, that the said additional Scholars that shall be chosen in BRASEN-NOSE COLLEGE, in Oxford, shall, from time to time, for ever be elected out of MANCHESTER SCHOOL, in the County of Lancaster, and THE FREE SCHOOL of HEREFORD, and THE FREE SCHOOL of MARLBOROUGH, in the County of Wilts, by turns; the *first* of them to be chosen out of MANCHESTER SCHOOL, the *second* out of HEREFORD FREE SCHOOL, and the *third* out of MARLBOROUGH FREE SCHOOL; and that the said additional Scholars, that shall be chosen into ST. JOHN'S COLLEGE, in Cambridge, shall, from time to time, for ever be elected out of MARLBOROUGH FREE SCHOOL, HEREFORD FREE SCHOOL, and MANCHESTER FREE SCHOOL, by turns, the *first* of them to be chosen out of MARLBOROUGH FREE SCHOOL, the *Second* out of HEREFORD FREE SCHOOL, and the *third* out of MANCHESTER FREE SCHOOL; and to keep the same course and turns for ever:—

And I do further will and appoint, that if any of my said Scholars shall be absent from his said respective College above three Calendar Months in any one Year upon any pretence whatsoever, that then his place in the said College shall be *ipso facto* void:—

Provided always, and my will and mind is, that upon any vacancy of any of my said Scholarships, by reason of undue absence or upon any other account or cause whatsoever in either of the said Colleges respectively, If the Principal Fellows and Scholars of BRASEN-NOSE COLLEGE, in Oxford, or the Master Fellows and Scholars of ST. JOHN'S COLLEGE, in Cambridge, or either of the said Colleges respectively, shall neglect by the space of *thirty days* to give notice of such avoydance unto the Master of the School out of which the next of the said Scholars is to be chosen into the said College, That then the College so neglecting shall lose the privilege of electing any of the said additional Scholars for *seven years* next after such neglect:— And that during that seven years they, the said HENRY Lord DELAMERE, Sir SAMUEL GRIMSTONE, and Sir WILLIAM GREGORY, and the Survivors and Survivor of them, and his heirs, shall and lawfully may, from time to time, nominate and present a Scholar or Scholars out of the aforesaid Schools respectively, (and qualified, as in the foundation of my said Scholarships is directed) unto the said College or Colleges respectively, where such place shall be void, to be settled and placed in all or any such of the said Scholarships as shall happen to be void within the said seven Years;—

And I do further will and appoint, that, at the first settlement thereof, there shall be one additional SOMERSET SCHOLAR placed and settled in each of the said Colleges with provision to be made, That when the Rents of the Manor and Hereditaments given to BRASEN-NOSE COLLEGE, in Oxford, shall be so improved that they shall come to Thirty Pounds *per annum,* then there shall be one other SOMERSET SCHOLAR placed in the said College, and so from time to time upon every increase and advancement of Fifteen pounds *per annum* in the rents of the said Manor and Premises to them appointed there shall be ONE Scholar *more* added to the SOMERSET SCHOLARS in the said College; and that in like manner, when the Rents of the Manor and Hereditaments hereby given or appointed to ST. JOHN'S COLLEGE, in Cambridge, shall come to be Thirty pounds *per annum,* there shall be ONE other additional SOMERSET SCHOLAR settled in the said College; and so in like manner, from time to time, upon every increase or advancement of Fifteen Pounds *per annum* in the rents of the said Manor and Premises to them given or appointed there shall be ONE Scholar *more* added to the SOMERSET SCHOLARS in the said College:—

And, as touching the Fines that shall according to the Rents afforesaid be taken or received upon the granting or renewing of Copyhold Estates in the said respective Manors, I do will and appoint, that *three parts out of four* thereof shall go and be to the use and benefit of the said respective Colleges, to whom such Manor is hereinbefore appointed, in recompence for their providing *Chambers* for the said additional Scholars, and *Studyes, Gowns,* and *Caps;* and the other *fourth* part of the said Fines to go and be to the use and benefit of all the SOMERSET SCHOLARS in that College, to buy them *books,* which advantage by the said Fines, although it can be but small at first, in regard that all the Farms within the aforesaid Manors are at present in Lease or Grants under small old Rents, yet as the present Leases and Estates shall determine they will, I hope, prove considerable, for by the account I receive from my Officers I find, that the Manor appointed to BRASEN-NOSE COLLEGE will, when the present Lease and Estates are expired, be worth about Five Hundred and Sixty pounds *per annum;* And that the Manor appointed to ST. JOHN'S COLLEGE will then be worth about Five Hundred and Thirty pounds *per annum:*—

And I do further declare my will and mind to be, and I do appoint, that the Term now in being of the Leashold-Farm and Lands lying in the Manor of *Thornhill,* which Leashold-Farm and Lands at the full and improved value is worth One Hundred and Sixty Pounds *per annum,* shall expire or determine, Then SIX SOMERSET SCHOLARS shall in manner afforesaid be chosen and settled in BRASEN-NOSE COLLEGE, and that the said SIX SCHOLARS shall have for their allowances, for their maintenance the whole rent of the said Leashold-Farm and Lands in *Thorn-*

hill, and that none others of the additional SOMERSET SCHOLARS, in that College, shall have any share or part thereof with them; and that the said SIX SCHOLARS, or any of them, shall not have any share or part with the other additional SOMERSET SCHOLARS of that house of any other Rents, Revenues, or Profits of the said Manor of *Thornhill*:—

And my Will and Mind further is, and I do appoint, that when the term now in being of the Leashold-Farm and Lands lying in the Manor of *Wootton Rivers,* which Leashold-Farm and Lands at the full improved value is likewise worth One Hundred and Sixty Pounds *per annum,* shall expire or determine, Then SIX SOMERSET SCHOLARS shall in manner and form aforesaid be chosen and settled into ST. JOHN'S COLLEGE, in Cambridge, and that the said SIX SCHOLARS shall have for their allowances, for their maintenance the whole Rent of the said Leashold-Farm and Lands in *Wootton Rivers,* and that none others of the SOMERSET SCHOLARS, in that College, shall have any share or part thereof with them; and that the said SIX SCHOLARS, or any of them, shall not have any share or part with the other SOMERSET SCHOLARS of that House, or any other Rents, Revenues or Profits of the said Manor of *Wootton Rivers*:—

And my will is, and I do hereby appoint and direct, that such Youths shall be chosen into the said TWELVE last mentioned SCHOLARSHIPS, whose parents and friends *are not able* to contribute any thing considerable towards their maintenance in the University, and therefore I have given and appointed for them the large allowance; and my will is, that the persons that shall be chosen into the said TWELVE SCHOLARSHIPS, or any of them, shall be such as design or intend to take upon them *the Ministery;* and that they shall in order thereunto, so soon as they shall be fit for it, incline and dispose themselves to the study of *Divinity;* but in all other things relating to the said additional SOMERSET SCHOLARSHIPS in former rules and directions shall stand and be observed, and these last mentioned TWELVE SOMERSET SCHOLARS to differ from them in nothing, save only in their maintenance as is hereinbefore expressed.

On the 12th of January, 1703, Administration with the Will and Codicil annexed of the Goods of the Right Honourable SARAH Duchess Dowager of SOMERSET was granted to WM. STAUNTON, the Curator or Guardian lawfully assigned to the Honble. LANGHAM BOOTH, Esquire, a Minor, the Residuary Legatee, named in the said Codicil for the use and benefit of the said Minor, until he attains the age of one and twenty years, having been first sworn by Commission duly to administer. The Right Honble. HENRY *Comes,* Sir SAMUEL GRIMSTON,

Baronet, and Sir WILLIAM GREGORY, Knight, the Executors dying without taking upon them the Probate and Execution of the said Will and Codicil.

On the 19th of February, 1705, Administration with the Will and Codicil annexed of the goods of The Right Honble. SARAH Duchess Dowager of SOMERSET was granted to The Honourable LANGHAM BOOTH, Esquire, the Residuary Legatee named in the said Codicil, He having been first sworn by Commission duly to administer the Letters of Administration of the goods of the said Deceased, granted in the Month of January, 1703, to WILLIAM STAUNTON, Esquire, for the use and benefit of the said Honble. LANGHAM BOOTH, Esquire, then a Minor, having ceased and expired, by reason of the said Minor having attained his age of twenty one years; And The Right Honble. HENRY *Comes*, Sir SAMUEL GRIMSTON, Baronet, and Sir WM. GREGORY, Knight, the Executors named in the said Will having departed this life without taking upon them, or either of them, the Probate and Execution of the said Will and Codicil.—

GEO. GOSTLING,
NATH. GOSTLING, } Deputy Registers.
R. C. CRESSWELL,

See, *Hereford*.

WILLIAM HULME, Esq., of *Broadstone*, descended from a respectable Family in the County of Lancaster, by his Will,* dated the 24th of October, 1691, most munificently left estates at Heaton-Norris, Denton, Ashton-under-Lyne, Reddish, Manchester, and Harwood, all in this County, (subject to an estate for life, in part of the premises, to ELIZABETH his Wife, and to certain Annuities, which have been long since determined), to maintain as EXHIBITIONERS†

---

* Mr. HULME was buried in a small Chapel adjoining The Collegiate Church of Manchester,—which, having become greatly dilapidated, was restored by order of the Feoffees of his Trust Estates in 1810. On his grave-stone is the following Inscription,—

"Hic jacet corpus Gulielmi Hulme de Hulme Armigeri, qui obiit vicesimo nono Octobris anno Domini 1691. Ætatis suæ 61."

† The Exhibitions founded by Mr. HULME, in Brasen-Nose College, are not connected with The Free Grammar School in Manchester,—but, as they are frequently bestowed upon Scholars

"*Four* of the poorest sort of Bachelors of Arts, taking such Degree in BRASEN-NOSE COLLEGE, in Oxford, as from time to time should resolve to continue and reside there by the space of *Four* years next after such Degree taken,"—to be nominated and approved of by The Warden of the Collegiate Church of Manchester, the Rectors of the Parish Churches of Prestwich and Bury for the time being, and their Successors for ever."*

At the time of the Testator's death these Exhibitions amounted only to £15. *per annum* each; but, in the 10° *Geo.* III., 1770, an Act was obtained, which enabled the Trustees to grant building leases of the Estates for 99 years, and to increase the number of EXHIBITIONERS to *Ten*, whose Stipends should be never less than £60., nor more than £80. a year.

By another Act passed in the 35° *Geo.* III., 1795, the Trustees were enabled to convey in fee or grant leases for lives, or for long terms of years, with or without Covenants for renewal or for perpetual renewal, under reserved yearly rents the Trust estates; and were empowered to increase the number of EXHIBITIONERS to *Fifteen*, whose Stipends should be never less than £60., nor more than £110. a year.

In 1814, by reason of the great increase in the value of the Trust estates, the annual proceeds then amounting to the sum of £2502..16..8., over and above the interest of the sum of £23,700., which the Trustees had saved out of the rents, a third Act was obtained, intituled, "An Act for amending Two several Acts of the 10th and 35th years of

---

belonging to it, and as Mr. HULME was a Feoffee of the School and probably received his education in it, no part of the present work appears more suitable than this to notice his splendid benefaction.

* A Prize of £10. in *Books* is annually given for the best Oration delivered at Brazen-Nose College by one of the Exhibitioners, in memory of so great a Benefactor.

the reign of His present Majesty, relating to the Estates devised by WILLIAM HULME, Esq.; and to enable the Trustees thereof to apply the Trust Monies in making an allowance to and provision for the Exhibitioners of certain Exhibitions, founded by the said Testator in Brasen-Nose College, Oxford; and also in founding and supporting a Lecture in Divinity in the said College; and to incorporate the said Trustees; and for other the purposes therein mentioned."—

By which it was enacted, "That it shall be lawful for the said Trustees, and their Successors, to make unto each of the said present Exhibitioners, and to each of the Exhibitioners who shall be hereafter nominated to take the benefit of Mr. HULME's Estate, such allowance, stipend, or yearly sum, as the Trustees shall think meet and reasonable; never to exceed the sum of TWO HUNDRED and TWENTY POUNDS in any one year; and that the same shall not be paid to any of such Exhibitioners, who shall not regularly reside in the said College from the beginning of Michaelmas Term to the end of Act Term in every year, unless such Exhibitioner shall have obtained such permission as is hereinafter mentioned from the Trustees of the said estates, dispensing with his or their residence at the said College, and no such permission shall extend beyond the power given for that purpose to the Trustees by this Act."

As the College of BRASEN-NOSE was not able to accommodate the EXHIBITIONERS with rooms in the College, and the rent of lodgings in Oxford, and the necessary expenses attendant thereon, having materially increased within a few years past, and the then allowance being inadequate for procuring the benefits intended for the Exhibitioners,—The Trustees were empowered to provide rooms and lodgings in Oxford, or to purchase or build convenient Houses for their residence and accommodation,—

Provided, "That no Exhibitioners shall be allowed to reside in or occupy any such houses, for any longer time than they shall enjoy and receive their Exhibitions, or during only such term, or part thereof, as the said Trustees shall from time to time appoint or determine upon, pursuant to the provision in that behalf hereinafter contained: Provided also, That no greater sum shall be expended or laid out by the said Trustees, in the actual purchase of any such houses, buildings, land, or hereditaments, than the sum of £5000, in the whole."—

The Trustees were also empowered to pay to a Lecturer, to be nominated by the Principal of Brasen-Nose College, for the delivering Lectures in Divinity to the Exhibitioners therein, an annual Salary not exceeding the sum of £150.,—such Divinity Lecture to be called "HULME'S *Divinity Lecture*,"—and "that no person shall be appointed to such office of Lecturer, save and except he shall be in Priest's Orders, and shall have taken the Degree of Bachelor of Divinity or Master of Arts in the said University, and be a Member of the said College:"—

The Trustees, then EDWARD Earl of DERBY, THOMAS Earl of WILTON, JAMES STARKY, ROBERT GREGGE HOPWOOD, ROBERT MARKLAND, JOHN ENTWISLE, RICHARD ATHERTON FARINGTON, WILLIAM FOX, and WILBRAHAM EGERTON, Esquires, and their Successors, were constituted a Body Corporate, by the name and style of "THE TRUSTEES of the ESTATES devised by WILLIAM HULME, Esq.," with perpetual succession; may plead and be impleaded, and have a Common Seal, on which shall be engraven the Coat of Arms borne by WILLIAM HULME, and round it shall be inscribed "*Sigillum Hulmianum*." And the number of the Trustees was to be increased to TWELVE:—

THE NOMINATORS of the EXHIBITIONERS, as often as vacancies shall arise, are empowered "to nominate to the said Exhibitions UNDER-GRADUATES in the said College of Brasen-Nose, who shall have then entered upon the thirteenth term from their matriculation, and who shall resolve and continue to reside there by the space of *four years* next after the commencement of such thirteenth term, and who shall also resolve to take their Degree of Bachelor of Arts in the University of Oxford, as soon as they are of Academical standing for such Degree;—And that the Under-graduates so to be nominated, and residing according to the regulations of this act, shall, from time to time, have, and be entitled to the allowances, stipends, and yearly payments in and by this act authorized to be made to the said Exhibitioners for the space of four years, to be accounted from the commencement of the said thirteenth term: Provided that they, the said Under-graduates so to be nominated, shall, if prevented from taking their Degree of Bachelor of Arts as soon as they are of standing for the same, be actually admitted to such Degree within *eight months* afterwards; but in case the Under-graduates so to be nominated, or any of them, shall not within the same space of eight months duly take their said Degrees, then and from thenceforth their respective Nominations shall cease and be void, and they shall respectively absolutely forfeit and lose all further right, title, and claim to the said allowances, stipends, and payments to be made to the said Exhibitioners, and all benefit and advantage thereof:—

And it was further enacted, "That it shall be lawful for the Trustees, from time to time, by any orders, at any General Meeting of the Trustees, *to dispense with the residence* at or in the said College of Brasen-Nose, of the Exhibitioners who are or shall be hereafter nominated to take the benefit of Mr. HULME's trust, for any time (which shall not be in full term) in each year, as they the said Trustees shall deem most adviseable: Provided, That no such orders shall be contrary to or interfere with the Rules or Discipline of the said College, nor shall such Rules or Discipline be any ways affected by any acts of the said Trustees or their Successors, in the exercise of the powers given to them by this Act."

The present NOMINATORS of the EXHIBITIONERS are,—

The Revd. THOMAS BLACKBURNE, LL. D., Warden of the Collegiate Church of Manchester.

The Revd. Sir WILLIAM HENRY CLERKE, Bart., Rector of the Parish Church of Bury.

The Revd. JAMES LYON, Rector of the Parish Church of Prestwich.

The great celebrity which this School hath justly acquired, has been owing not only to the Splendour of the Foundation, but in a still greater degree, to the talents and assiduity of THE HIGH MASTERS, in whom it has been singularly fortunate.

The present High Master is JEREMIAH SMITH, D. D., under whose able management the School preserves the reputation, which it has long so deservedly enjoyed. This Gentleman was appointed, on the death of the late CHARLES LAWSON, M. A., who, after filling the Chair for more than FORTY-THREE YEARS, with the greatest credit to himself, and the advantage of his Pupils, many of whom became shining Luminaries of the Pulpit, the Bar, and the Senate, died on the 19th of April, 1807, in the 79th year of his age. The Salary of the High Master is £420. *per annum*, with a good House, free of rent and taxes, and kept in good repair. This house, it appears, was bought from the family of the BESSICKS in Salford by the Trustees, in 1698, for the use of The High Master. His accommodations for

Boarders are very extensive, but at present he receives only a limited number, upon the following Terms:—

Entrance Fee, Four guineas.

Board and Tuition, in which Writing, Arithmetic, and Mathematics are included, Fifty guineas *per annum*, until the Pupil enters into his Sixteenth year, and Sixty guineas afterwards.

Washing, Four guineas *per annum*.

French, Drawing, Dancing, &c., on the usual terms.

Two Parlour Boarders may be accommodated,—for whose Board and Tuition 120 or 140 guineas each will be charged, according to the distinction of age stated above.

An Assistant Master resides constantly in the house to give instructions in Writing, Accompts, and Mathematics, on the Tuesday, Thursday, and Saturday Afternoons, and to assist in the general Superintendence of the Boarders.

A Quarter's Notice, or a Quarter's Payment, is required.

The following are the Names of some of THE HIGH MASTERS of this School,—

In 1575. THOMAS COGAN, B. A., and afterwards M. D., of Oriel College, Oxford. He also "practised his Faculty with good success. He wrote "*The Haven of Health*," and "*A Preservation from the Pestilence*," and edited some of CICERO's works. He died at Manchester in 1607, and was buried in the Church there on the 10th of June, "leaving behind him the character of an able Physician and Latinist, a good Neighbour, and an honest Man."

RALPH BRIDEOKE, D. D., of Brasen-Nose College, Oxford. He afterwards became Chaplain to The Earl of DERBY; and when *Latham House* was besieged by the Forces belonging to Parliament, "he was all the time in it, and did good service." In 1651, by his eloquence in favour of his unfortunate Lord, JAMES Earl of Derby, he was made Chaplain to LENTHALL, the Speaker, and soon after Preacher of the Rolls. He successively filled several rich Benefices; and in 1674, "he was by the endeavours of LODOISA Duchess of PORTSMOUTH *(whose hands were always ready to take bribes)* nominated by the King to be Bishop of CHICHESTER, on the translation of Dr. P. GUNNING from thence to Ely. He died suddenly, as he was visiting his Diocese, on the 5th of October, 1678: and was buried in *Bray's* Chapel at Windsor, where a fair Altar monument was erected over his grave, with a suitable Latin inscription. He wrote an Elogy on the death of BEN. JONSON.

In 1661. JOHN WICKES, M. A., of Corpus Christi College, Oxford.

1676. WILLIAM BARROW, M. A., of Corpus Christi College.

1721. JOHN RICHARDS, M. A., of Corpus Christi College, elected on the 7th of March.

1721. HENRY BROOKE, M. A., of Oriel College, Oxford, elected on the 30th of April. In 1744 he published a Speech on the usefulness and necessity of studying the Classics, which is dedicated to The Warden (PEPLOE) and the Feoffees of the School; and in which he observes with regard to attendance, "though I was absent some years ago upon necessary business, and when I had thoughts of quitting the School and put in a *Substitute*, as I was informed with consent and to the satisfaction of all parties concerned, yet being now at free liberty, I shall keep close to the School and the business thereof, as I have done for near three years last past, &c." At the period here alluded to, the Feoffees disapproving of his neglect of the School, had reduced his Salary, as Master, from £200. to £10. the original Endowment. He wrote a Latin work, intituled, "*Medicus Circumforaneus*," and an Essay on "Peaceableness." He was also Fellow of Christ's College, Manchester.

In 1728. WILLIAM PURNELL, M. A., of Oriel College; he died in 1764.

1753. CHARLES LAWSON, M. A., of Corpus Christi College, who taught here as First and Second Master, more than HALF a CENTURY.* His grateful Pupils erected a beautiful Mural Monument of marble, designed and executed by BACON; and which is fixed up over the door leading into the Chapter-House in the Collegiate Church, with an elegant Latin inscription, commemorative of his Excellence and Virtues.

1807. JEREMIAH SMITH, D. D.

---

* In 1749 he was appointed Second Master by Dr. RANDOLPH, then President of Corpus Christi College, and upon the death of Mr. PURNELL, he was nominated his successor. In this arduous situation, for a period almost unprecedented, Mr. LAWSON uniformly displayed a dignity and propriety of conduct, and a fixed principle of action that could not fail to conciliate the esteem and affection of his Pupils, and the warm admiration of his Fellow Townsmen. The extensive literary abilities which he possessed, were of a higher class than are usually met with even in the most distinguished of our Preceptors, and the depth and

The High Master, and the Second Master, have Two Stalls in the Collegiate Church,—over one of which is inscribed "*Archididascalus*,"—and over the other, "*Hypodidascalus*."—A mark of respect, but no source of emolument.

The present Second Master is, The Revd. ROBINSON ELSDALE, M. A., whose Salary is £220. *per annum*, together with a house, free of rent and taxes, and kept in good repair. This Gentleman also takes Pupils, at Forty guineas *per annum* for boys under the age of 14 years, and 45 guineas after that period.

In addition to these Gentlemen whose Official situations are recognized and established in the Statutes, there are also THREE ASSISTANT MASTERS, who have been added by the Trustees,—have Salaries from the School estate,—and are liberally allowed by The High Master to take Boarders.*

The First Assistant Master is, The Revd. GEORGE HOLT, whose Salary is £120. a year; and who has upwards of Twenty boarders in his house.

The Second Assistant Master is, Mr. JOHN JOHNSON, whose Salary is £110. a year. He teaches also writing, accounts, and mathematics.

The Master of The Lower School is, The Revd. THOMAS GASKELL, whose Salary is £130. a year.

The business of the School begins and closes with PRAYERS, which are read by one of the Senior boys, when all the Masters attend,—In SUMMER, from 7 to half after 8 o'Clock,—return at half after 9, and remain until 12,—

---

assiduity with which he constantly pursued his erudite researches, rendered him eminently qualified for that station wherein he was judiciously placed.

* In the original Establishment there were only The High Master and the Usher. In progress of time, a *third* Master was appointed: But the Two Assistant Masters were not appointed, until Mr. LAWSON had been at the head of the School for some years. Then from the great increase of the number of Scholars, additional Teachers became indispensibly necessary.

return again at 3, and remain until half after 5.—In WINTER, it commences half an hour later.

The afternoons of Tuesday,* Thursday, and Saturday are Holidays, and are devoted to Mathematics.

The Vacations are *five* Weeks at CHRISTMAS,—and *five* Weeks at MIDSUMMER.

A PUBLIC SPEECH-DAY was judiciously established by the present High Master in 1811, which is attended by The Trustees, and by numbers of the most respectable Inhabitants of the Town and Neighbourhood. It is holden on the first Tuesday in October.

Among the distinguished Characters who have received their Education at this eminent Seminary of Learning, may be enumerated,†—

JOHN BRADFORD, one of the most eminent of the PROTESTANT DIVINES who suffered Martyrdom in the cruel reign of Queen MARY.

WILLIAM GWYN, Principal of Brasen-Nose College: he died in 1770.

The late REGINALD HEBER, M. A., a learned and amiable Clergyman, the second son of THOMAS HEBER, Esq., of *Marton-Hall*, in the Deanery of Craven, one of the oldest Families in that District of Yorkshire. He died on the 10th of January, 1804.

The late ROBERT THYER, Chetham's Librarian, Editor of BUTLER's Remains.

The late Earl of WILTON, a Trustee.

The late GEORGE LLOYD, Esq., Barrister at Law.

---

* It was the custom for Tuesday Afternoon not to be Holiday, unless some one petitioned for it, and gave either *Five Shillings,* or a *Book,* for the School LIBRARY. And in this way the greater part of the Books have been collected.

† The Register of the Scholars is kept by the Two Senior Boys, to whom one shilling is paid for every entry.

The late WILLIAM EGERTON, Esq., M. P. of Tatton.

CYRIL JACKSON, D. D., late Dean of Christ Church, Oxford.

WILLIAM JACKSON, D. D., late Bishop of Oxford.

The late GEORGE TRAVIS, Archdeacon of Richmond.

The late Lord ALVANLEY, Master of The Rolls.

The late Sir NIGEL BOWYER GRIESLEY, Bart.

The late Colonel STANLEY, M. P. for Lancashire.

THOMAS PATTEN, D. D., Fellow of Corpus Christi College, and afterwards Rector of Childrey, in Berks.

JOHN WHITAKER, B. D., the late very learned Divine, and Author of "The History of Manchester."

SAMUEL OGDEN, D. D., late Woodwardian Professor at Cambridge, and Author of two volumes of Sermons.

The late THOMAS WHITE, M. D.

The late Rev. THOMAS BANCROFT, M. A., Vicar of Bolton.

JOHN PORTER, D. D., the present Lord Bishop of Clogher.

THOMAS BRAITHWAITE, D. D., Fellow of Brasen-Nose College, Rector of Stepney, and Chaplain to Bishop CLEAVER.

THOMAS WINSTANLEY, D.D., CAMDEN's Professor of Antient History, in the University of Oxford.

HOUSTONE RADCLIFFE, D. D., Fellow of Brasen-Nose College.

Revd. T. AINSCOUGH, M. A., of St. John's College, Cambridge.

Colonel JOHN DRINKWATER, Author of the History of the Siege of Gibraltar.

Revd. JOHN CARR, B. D, late Fellow and Tutor of St. John's College, Cambridge.

Revd. HENRY PORTER, Vicar of Enfield, late Fellow and Tutor of Trinity College, Cambridge.

FOSTER BOWER, Esq., Barrister at Law, Recorder of Chester.

JOHN LATHAM, M. D., of London.

JAMES HAWORTH, M. D., formerly Radcliffe's Travelling Fellow.

Sir DANIEL BAYLEY, Knt., Consul General in Russia.

Revd. JOSEPH ALLEN, late Fellow of Trinity College, Cambridge, and now Prebendary of Westminster.

JOHN BACON SAWREY MORRITT, Esq., of Rokeby Park, M. P. for Northallerton.

The Right Honble. FREDERICK FORBES, Son of the Earl of GRANARD.

FRODSHAM HODSON, D. D., Principal of Brasen-Nose College.

JOHN DEANE, D. D., Principal of St. Mary Hall, Oxford.

Major General HERON, late M. P. for Newton, Lancashire.

DAVID LATOUCHE, Esq., M. P. for Dublin.

EDMUND OUTRAM, D. D., the present Chancellor of the Diocese of Lichfield and Coventry, Archdeacon of Derby, and Rector of St. Philip's Birmingham,—formerly Fellow and Tutor of St. John's, Cambridge, and Public Orator of that University.

T. FALCONER, M. A., late Fellow of Christ Church College, Oxford, and Bampton Lecturer.

JOHN WILLIAMS, Esq., Barrister at Law.

The Revd. JOSEPH HODGKINSON, B. D., late Fellow and Tutor of Brasen-Nose College.

The Revd. THOMAS CLAYTON, B. D., late Fellow and Tutor of Brasen-Nose College, Rector of Cottingham, in Northamptonshire.

ASHHURST TURNER GILBERT, M. A., one of the present Tutors of Brasen-Nose College.

MIDDLETON, near MANCHESTER.

THE FREE GRAMMAR SCHOOL at MIDDLETON was founded, by Charter dated the 11th of August, 1572, by ALEXANDER NOWELL, D. D., Dean of St. Paul's, London; who, at the same time founded Thirteen Scholarships in Brasen-Nose College, Oxford, of which he was Principal.

As these Benefactions were both of them established by Royal Patent, he chose that the School should be called "Queen ELIZABETH's School," and the Scholars "Queen ELIZABETH's Scholars." Her Majesty having most graciously given £20. yearly for ever towards it's endowment; of which £14..10..0. *per annum* are now paid to The Head Master by The College, and £5..10..8. out of the Land Revenue of the Crown.

How much he had this good work at heart, for the encouragement of Religion and Learning, appears by a Letter of his to the Lord Treasurer BURGHLEY, dated the 24th of June, 1572, while the Patent of Foundation laid in his hands; in which, by the advice of Sir WALTER MILDMAY, a blank was left for the *Mortmain*, upon good hope, that it would please Her Majesty to license a large sum, for such goodly uses. He, therefore, "in Her Majesty's name humbly prayed His Honour to finish the good work, which he had so happily begun; and to move Her Majesty to license the sum of £100., or so many marks at the least, by him and others to be purchased in Mortmain, for the increase of the Stipends of the Schoolmaster and Usher, and of the number and exhibition of the said Scholars, and the better relief of the great Company of that poor College; and all to be done in Her Majesty's name."

Mr Archdeacon CHURTON, in his Life of Dean NOWELL,

observes, that, by the Charter of Foundation, certain Rent-charges, in London and elsewhere, are vested in THE PRINCIPAL and FELLOWS of BRASEN-NOSE COLLEGE, who are Incorporated GOVERNORS of this Free School, on condition that they pay to The Upper Master Twenty marks, and to The Under Master or Usher Ten marks, yearly; and Five marks a piece to Thirteen Scholars, chosen from this School, or from the School of Whalley, or Burnley, or, in defect, from any other School in the County Palatine of Lancaster.

But the liberal Donor having shortly afterwards bought of Sir HENRY CHENEY, Lord CHENEY, and the Lady JANE, his Wife, the Manor of Upberry, and the Rectory of Gillingham in Kent, with the Advowson of the Vicarage, he bestowed these Estates also on the College, in Trust, to augment the Stipend of the Master and Usher, and the allowance of the Scholars, as well as to improve the weekly Commons or Allowance of The Principal and Fellows.

The Manor of Gillingham and the Estates thereto appendant were part of the Endowment of the See of Canterbury in the time of The Conqueror, as appears by certain grants of Archbishop ANSELM, remitting to the Monks of St. Andrew's in Rochester part of the Rent, which they used to pay for the right of fishing in the sea, a Privilege belonging to the said Manor.

The Archiepiscopal Estates in the Parish of Gillingham were alienated to the Crown in the time of HENRY the Eighth; and by him granted to the Family of CHENEY, who re-sold them to NOWELL.

A part of the Estate, on a commanding spot in Upberry, by recent purchase from The College of Brasen-Nose, has been re-invested in The Crown, for the purpose of constructing Barracks and other Public Works, "in these days when the proud menaces of a neighbouring *Usurper* have served only to rouse, with redoubled ardour, the ancient spirit of BRITONS."

There is also belonging to The Head Master a small Field in which the School is situate, being about One acre of *customary* measure.

A Stipend of £10. *per annum* is also paid to The Under or English Master by Brasen-Nose College: The Principal and Senior Fellows whereof appoint the Masters: And they are likewise the Visitors.

There are no Statutes or Ordinances.

The School has always been open to Boys of the Parish of Middleton, free of expense, when taught the *Classics* only. But for many years past, a *Commercial* Education, particularly in this manufacturing part of the Country, has been preferred; and consequently more attended to, for which *6s.* Quarterage for each boy is paid, otherwise the Salary being so small, the School might remain without a Master.

There is no particular form of Admission, nor routine of Education prescribed.

The Scholarships at Brasen-Nose College are so very small, that they have not been claimed, for a Century past, by any Scholar from Middleton School.

In later days the Master's place has usually been given to the Curates of Middleton; one of whom, RICHARD DEAN, was the Author of an ingenious Essay on an unpromising subject, "The future Life of *Brutes*, introduced with Observations upon Evil, it's nature and origin," printed at Manchester, in 1767. Mr. DEAN died and was buried at Middleton, on the 10th of January, 1778.

He was succeeded by The Revd. JAMES ARCHER, the present Head Master, who has filled that Office, with the greatest respectability, for the last THIRTY-NINE YEARS; during which time he has been constant and regular in his attendance, having seldom fewer than from Forty to Fifty Pupils under his care, who are boarded and lodged in the Village.

Mr. JAMES HEYWOOD, lately appointed Under-Master, has generally a greater number, having been instructed to teach upon Dr. BELL's Plan. He receives 2*d. per* week for each child, whether Boy or Girl.

Girls have been received into both Schools.

The School was new roofed and ceiled in 1781.

PRESCOT.

The old SCHOOL at PRESCOT, now part of the Master's House, and the House itself with the one adjoining, were established at a period now unknown, by the Township of Prescot, and that part of the Parish called "*The Parish Side*," and supported by contributions or rates from each Township, for the benefit of education to the Inhabitants of those Districts.

But such Parochial support ceased above a Century since, when the Funds consisted of

Old Stock,	- -	£50..0..0
Mr. GREEN's gift,	-	3..1..3

which, together with about £4. *per annum* arising from several properties in Prescot, and the above-mentioned School and Dwelling, constitute the whole Endowment, worth about £40. *per annum.* At an annual Parish Meeting on *St. Luke's* day, FOUR WARDENS are chosen to elect a Master, and to do other necessary business.

Subsequently several Benefactions in land and money have been made to other Trustees, *viz.*, The Steward and Officers elected at the annual Court of the Copyholders, for the instruction of poor boys in the Town, where and in what manner they think proper. These Trustees have built a new and enlarged School, and by common consent about Forty years since, joined with the Wardens chosen by the Parish, in the Election of the Master on their having determined to unite the two Schools, and send the poor boys according to the extent of the new Funds, to THE PUBLIC SCHOOL.

The pecuniary Legacies have been employed in building Houses in Prescot, and in the purchase of a small estate in *Rainhill;* and the Lands bequeathed, lie in the Townships of Widnes and Whiston, all in the Parish of Prescot. But all these estates are also subject to the support of other Charities, besides the education of poor boys, so that the surplus only is applicable to that purpose, and is now about £65. *per annum.*

A Legacy of £200. has recently been received from the Executors of the late Revd. SAMUEL SEWELL, Vicar of Prescot, the interest of which is to be appropriated to the education of poor Boys.

No STATUTES prevail beyond the election of a Master belonging to the Established Church, and the instruction of the poor boys in the Church Catechism. The boys are to be selected from the Inhabitants of Prescot, and consequently are nominated by The Steward and Officers of the Manor-Court of Prescot.

Boys from this School, if born in the Parish, are sent to Brasen-Nose College, in Oxford, where they have a preference to SEVEN FELLOWSHIPS. Lancashire men also have the preference to several good Exhibitions in the same College.

The number of boys upon the Foundation is now THIRTY-THREE :—*Three* having been added in consequence of Mr. SEWELL's legacy, but the admission of these was optional with the Master. There are no data by which the determinations of the Trustees are regulated beyond occasional usage, in the number of free boys. The number of Day-scholars is now also about THIRTY. It was formerly much greater ; but owing to very gross mismanagement during the Mastership of the present Gentleman's immediate Predecessor, who, soon after his appointment, rendered himself independent of the Trustees by procuring a License to the School from the Bishop, and the consequent establishment of other Schools in the Town, it is probable that the number will not much increase. It must also be added, that the Town is poor, and that the terms for instruction in the other Schools are lower than in this.

It is expected that the Boys, at the time of Admission, should be able to read in a Class. They are admitted at the age of *Eight*, and at *Fourteen* are superannuated: but these are points not very scrupulously adhered to. The education of the Free Boys is confined to Reading, Writing, and Arithmetic. The selection of Books is left to the Master.

The ETON Latin and Greek Grammars are used.

The present Head Master is, Mr. JOHN HAMNETT, whose Salary, in consideration of the Free Boys, is £90. *per annum*, together with the interest of Mr. SEWELL's legacy, and the rent of the House, making in the whole about £113. *per annum*. This Gentleman takes Pupils, his terms being Thirty five guineas *per annum*. The terms for Day-scholars average about a guinea *per* Quarter.

Several of the most respectable Merchants in Liverpool have been educated in this School.

PRESTON.

THERE are no Documents now remaining to show when, or by whom, THE GRAMMAR SCHOOL in PRESTON was founded. But, as the Corporation of Preston are the Patrons of the School, and pay the principal part of the Salaries to the Masters, it is probable that it was founded and endowed by that Body; from whom the Head Master receives £45., and the Second Master £40. *per annum.*

At a subsequent period, a Mr. BARTHOLOMEW WORTHINGTON of this Town left a field adjoining to it, for the benefit of The Head Master; which has lately been built upon, and now produces in Ground rents, a little more than £50. a year.

There are no written STATUTES or ORDINANCES.

The School is open to boys from all parts, without any restriction or limitation, except the following, *viz.*, that those boys, who are not the sons of Freemen of the Borough of Preston, have usually paid a small sum, as Quarterage; but this distinction is not now insisted upon. Boys are admitted, at the discretion of the Masters, about the age of *Seven*, and are not subject to superannuation. The number of Scholars at present is about Forty.

The ETON Grammars are used; and the system of Education is the same as is established in most of the Grammar Schools in this County.

There are no Exhibitions, nor other University advantages belonging to this School; neither are the Students sent to any particular Colleges.

The present Head Master is, The Revd. ROBERT HARRIS, B. D., whose Salary is about £100. *per annum*, exclusive of the compliments that are usually made to him at *Shrovetide*, by the boys under his immediate care. This Gentleman has generally Two Pupils in his house upon liberal Terms; but he has not accommodation for a larger number.

The Under-Master has not been in the habit of taking any Pupils.

It is gratifying to observe, that there is an excellent LIBRARY, consisting of several Thousand volumes in various languages, in a room adjoining to the School. The Town of Preston is indebted for this Benefaction to a Gentleman of the name of SHEPHERD, who was long an eminent Physician here, and died about 60 years since. At his death, he bequeathed his own valuable Library to certain Trustees, with a Fund of about £50. a year for it's future augmentation, and a small Salary to a Librarian. The Mayor and Aldermen are perpetual Trustees, and the Master of the Grammar School is the Librarian. The Public very liberally have access to this Library, under certain regulations prescribed by it's Guardians.

JOHN PRESTON, D. D., was educated here.

RIVINGTON, near BOLTON.

THE FREE GRAMMAR SCHOOL of RIVINGTON, in the Parish of Bolton le Moors, called also "THE FREE GRAMMAR SCHOOL of Queen ELIZABETH in ROVINGTON *alias* RIVINGTON," was founded by Letters Patent, dated the 13th of May, in the Eighth year of the reign of Queen ELIZABETH, 1566, by JAMES PILKINGTON, Bishop of Durham, "for the bringing up, teaching, and instructing of Children and Youth in Grammar, and other good Learning, to continue for ever:" and endowed by His Lordship with lands, then of the annual value of £30., situate in the County Palatine of Durham; some of which have lately been sold, and others purchased in their stead, in the Parish of Bolton le Moors, near to the School.

The present rental of the estates is about £400. *per annum.*

By the Sixth Chapter of the STATUTES it is ordered,—

That "every Governour shall his year about in course, beginning at the Eldest first, take charge of all the goods, tenements, and lands belonging to the School,—He shall also receive the rents and other money due for that year,—and further shall pay the Schoolmaster and Usher their wages, and such other charges as shall go out for that year,—And for the true dealing therein, he shall at his entering put into the rest of the Governors' hands, an Obligation of double the value of that he shall receive;—which Obligation shall be laid up with the Common Seal,—and he shall not receive his Obligation again, until he have made a full accompt and payment of his receipts and laid into the common chest, what money soever shall remain unspent of that his year,—And if he be proved not to have dealt truly toward the School, the forfeit of his Obligation shall be taken:"—

"And because the other Governours may the better spie his upright dealing, they shall call for and he shall make afore them, twice in the year, at Midsummer and Christmas, or within ten days next following, a true accompt, both of what he hath received and paid,—and if he be found to have paid any thing, without all the Governours' consent, or *four* of them at the least, besides himself,—except it be the Master and Usher wages,—or otherwise to deal untruly with the Tenants, or elsewhere touching the School matters,—he shall be put out of the number of Governours for ever, and one other chosen in his roome:"—

"They shall never seal any thing with their Common Seal, except Four of the Governors agree to it at the least.—And if it be for putting away any lands, they shall not seal any thing without the consent of all the SIX GOVERNOURS,—and that only on this condition, to buy as much good land or better as they put away, and that not to be done *without the advice of Six other* of the discreetest men dwelling within the Towns of the Corporation, or the other Towns next adjoining:"—

"The Governors shall not make any lease of any lands belonging to the School, for more years than *Twenty one,* or for three lives at the most,—nor let more leases forth at once than one,—nor renew any leases, until the old leases be forfeited or surrendered, or expired within four years."

The Governors, within Six weeks after the vacancy of a Master, are to recommend to The Master and Fellows of

ST. JOHN'S College, Cambridge, two persons who have been Students in either of the Universities for Four, or Three years at the least, of the age of Twenty-four years; one of whom the said Master and Fellows are to elect.

On the vacancy of an Usher, the Governors are within one month to nominate "a learned and honest man," whom they are to present to the Bishop of Durham or Chester, and if after examination he be found sufficient, he shall then be admitted.

The School is open to all "our faithfull and leige people *whosoever they be*," indefinitely, free of expense. But a preference is given to boys residing within the Six following Townships, which, in the Statutes, are called "THE CORPORATION OF THE SCHOOL," *viz.*, Rivington, Anglezarch, Fowlds, Anderton, Heath-Charnock, and Horwich. There are no limitations as to age, or number; and no particular form of Admission.

The Latin and Greek Grammars in use, are those improved by WARD; and the routine of Education pursued, is the same with that of Grammar Schools in general.

The present Head Master is, The Revd. J. WHITAKER, M. A., who was appointed on the 20th of June, 1815. His Salary is £100. *per annum*, together with a house, &c. This Gentleman does not take Pupils at present.

The Salaries of the Usher, and Writing Master, are £50. *per annum* each, together with Houses, &c. They have no Pupils at present.

The School has of late years been very much reduced. The Trust is now in the hands of SIX GOVERNORS, *who are all Socinian Presbyterians!*

The following is a List of the HEAD MASTERS,—

In 1625. HENRY BODURDA.
1633. —— KENWORTHY.
1635. JOHN CROOKE.
1646. HENRY FIELDEN.

In 1678. John Bradley.
1727. John Norcross.
1765. John Norcross, M. A.
1789. Richard Hargreaves, M. A.
1799. Joseph Coward, M. A.
1801. Thomas Jenner Hogg, M. A.
1805. William Heaton, B. A.
1815. Joseph Whitaker, M. A.

ROCHDALE.

THE GRAMMAR SCHOOL of ROCHDALE was founded by MATTHEW PARKER, D. D., the Second PROTESTANT Archbishop of CANTERBURY, by Indenture bearing date the 1st of January, in the Seventh year of the reign of Queen ELIZABETH, 1565, the School being built upon a piece of ground near the Church-yard, which was given for that purpose by RICHARD MIDGLEY, then Vicar; and endowed with £15. *per annum* for the Head Master, and £2. *per annum* for the Usher, payable by The Archbishop from the Tythes, which were sold in the year 1813. And the Purchasers of the Tythes of the Township of *Castleton*, in this Parish, are subject in future to the payment of the said sums annually.

The original Deed is in the Library of CORPUS CHRISTI COLLEGE, Cambridge, the great deposit of Archbishop PARKER's Manuscripts, and is attested by ROBERT HORNE, Bishop of Winchester, RICHARD COX, Bishop of Ely, ALEXANDER NOWELL, Dean of St. Paul's, THOMAS WATTS, Archdeacon of Middlesex, and JOHN HAMONDE, Chancellor to the Bishop of London. They were present also at the delivery of the Charter and Title Deeds to JAMES WOULDFENDEN, Clothier, and JOHN WARBARTON, Merchant, both of Rochdale, Proxies for the Parish, on the 18th of June, 1571.

The School Chamber is let for £4..4. *per annum*, to which sum the Master is entitled.

A messuage, with certain lands and premises situate in *Ardesley*, in the County of York, are subject to the payment of £3. annually to the Master; but this sum *has not been paid* for the last Seventeen years!

The Master receives £2. annually from CHARLES CHADWICK, Esq., of *Healey Hall*, in the Parish of Rochdale; and also £13..10..0. annually from an estate, called "*Newfield Head*," in the Township of Butterworth, in the same Parish; being subsequent Endowments.

The School is open to the Boys of the Parish, to be instructed in the *Latin* language and true Piety, free of expense. About Thirty Scholars are educated at the School. None are admitted at present upon The Foundation; but several are taught the Latin language, free of expense; yet all pay a guinea and a half *per* Quarter, as they are instructed in other branches of Literature besides what is required upon The Foundation.

Boys are admitted so soon as they are capable of receiving instruction, paying a guinea entrance; and may continue until their education be completed.

The ETON Latin Grammar, and the WESTMINSTER Greek Grammar, are in use. And, in addition to the Classics, writing, arithmetic, history, geography, &c., are also taught.

SAMUEL RADCLIFFE, D. D., Principal of Brasen-Nose College, Oxford, from 1614 to 1648, bequeathed in the latter year lands in Harrowden, in the County of Bedford, amounting to the yearly value of £40. for Two SCHOLARS, from the Schools of Steeple Aston, in the County of Oxford,—of Rochdale or Middleton, in the County Palatine of Lancaster, —or any of the Undergraduates of Brasen-Nose College, who are unpreferred.

The present Head Master is, The Revd. WILLIAM HODGSON, whose Salary arises from the Endowment, and the Quarterage already mentioned. This Gentleman does not take Boarders.

The Revd. THOMAS DUNHAM WHITAKER, LL.D., Author of the "History of the original Parish of Whalley," and other much approved Publications, received the early part of his Education at this School, under The Revd. JOHN SHAW, whom he gratefully describes, as being "an industrious and able Master, and to whom he still feels himself daily indebted."

WHALLEY, near CLITHEROE.

THE FREE GRAMMAR SCHOOL at WHALLEY was founded by King EDWARD the Sixth. The original Endowment was *Twenty marks* (£13..6..8), payable out of the Rectory of Tunstal in Lancashire, and is now paid by the King's Receiver General out of the Duchy Rents.

Subsequently, Eighty Pounds belonging to the School were laid out in a purchase of lands in the Township of Great Harwood, for which the Master now receives £4..14..0. *per annum.*

And, in the year 1814, Mr. JOHN READ, of Knightsbridge, London, left by Will, dated in September 1813, the sum of £468., which is vested in the 5 *per* Cent. Navy Annuities; the Dividend being paid half yearly or yearly. This Gentleman also left by his Will to Mr. ADAM COTTAM, of Whalley, one of his Executors, a Legacy of £50.; which sum Mr. COTTAM was generously pleased to give to the School, and it is now vested in the same 5 *per* Cents, and the Dividend thereof is paid at the same time, and in the same manner.

There are no Statutes belonging to this School; neither is there a Common Seal.

The School is open to the Boys of the Parish at large indefinitely, free of expense, *for Classics.* And about Thirty Boys are educated at the School, upon an average. It is at the discretion of the Master, at what age Children shall be admitted.

The ETON Latin and Greek Grammars are used; and the routine of Education is similar to what is pursued in other Classical Schools.

In 1572, ALEXANDER NOWELL, the excellent Dean of St. Paul's, left certain Rent charges to The Principal and

Fellows of Brasen-Nose College, in Oxford, upon condition, that they paid *Five marks* a piece to THIRTEEN SCHOLARS, from the Free School of Middleton, or the Schools of Whalley and Burnley, or any other Schools in the County Palatine of Lancaster.

Boys have been sent from hence to both the Universities of Oxford and Cambridge.

The present Head Master is, The Revd. RICHARD NOBLE, who makes about £70. or £80. *per annum* of the School. This Gentleman takes Pupils, his terms for Board and Education being £30. a year.

There is no Second Master. Neither are there any Church Preferments, or advantages, belonging to the School.

The principal Inhabitants of the Township of Whalley have the appointment of the Master.

WIGAN.

THE FREE GRAMMAR SCHOOL of the THE BOROUGH of WIGAN appears to have been founded prior to the 16th of King JAMES the First, but by whom is not known, and it is presumed that a small Cottage standing upon "*The Old School Common*," was the original School.

JAMES LEIGH, Gentleman, by Indenture dated the 11th of January, 1619, gave to certain Trustees an annual Rent of £6..13..4., issuing out of the messuage, lands, and tenements in Orrell, in the County Palatine of Lancaster, called "*The Ackhurst*," and all other his lands and tenements, for the maintenance of a FREE GRAMMAR SCHOOL in WIGAN, for the bringing up of poor Scholars of the Parish and Town of Wigan.

By an Indenture of Feoffment, dated the 1st of February, in the 16th of King Charles the Second, 1665, several messuages and lands situate in Aspull, in the County of Lancaster, called "*Blackshaye* or *Backshaye*," and their respective appurtenances,—and two other Closes situate in Wigan and Wigan Woodhouses, called "*The White Rydeings*," or "*Browne Meadows*;"—And also one Annuity of £20. issuing out of a messuage in Thames Street, London, called "*The Chalice and the Shepherd*," and out of other messuages and lands situate in Mincing Lane, London,—were conveyed to Sir ROGER BRADSHAIGH and other persons, as Trustees, for the maintenance of the FREE GRAMMAR SCHOOL.

And by another Indenture of Feoffment, dated the 22d of January, 1723, the revenues of the School were further augmented with a messuage and croft, containing about half an acre, called "*Cockerham's House and Croft*," situate in a Street in Wigan, called the "*The Mill Gate*,"—

upon which the Trustees soon after erected a handsome School of stone.

It being afterwards presumed that the Foundation would be much improved and become of general benefit, if certain persons were INCORPORATED as GOVERNORS of the School and it's Revenues, and invested with such other powers as might be reasonable and proper,—An Act of Parliament was accordingly obtained, which received the Royal Assent on the 9th of June, 1812.

By this Act it is enacted,—

That the present School shall be, and at all times hereafter shall be deemed and taken to be, and shall be called and known by the name of "THE FREE GRAMMAR SCHOOL of THE BOROUGH of WIGAN, in the County Palatine of Lancaster:"—

That THE MAYOR of Wigan, and JAMES BARTON, JOHN BLINKHORN, JOHN WALMSLEY, JOHN HODSON, WILLIAM CLAYTON, THOMAS BARTON, HENRY UNSWORTH, JOHN VAUSE, and ROBERT LATHAM, which last named Nine persons are the present Feoffees and Trustees of the said School, and are also Aldermen or Burgesses of the said Borough, shall from thenceforth be Governors of the said School, and Feoffees and Trustees of the Messuages, Lands, &c., thereof; and that from thenceforth The Governors of the School, and their Successors, shall be a Body Corporate by the name of "THE GOVERNORS of THE FREE GRAMMAR SCHOOL of THE BOROUGH of WIGAN, in the County Palatine of Lancaster," have perpetual Succession, and a Common Seal: and they are also empowered to increase the number of Governors to FIFTEEN:—

The Governors are to elect such Masters, to teach and instruct the Children and Youth who shall be educated at this School, not only in Grammar and Classical Learning, but also in the modern Languages, Writing, Arithmetic, Geography and Mathematics, and in such and so many other Branches of Literature and Education as shall from time to time, in the judgment of The Governors, be proper and necessary to render this Foundation of the most general use and benefit, and as the state of the Revenues of the School will admit, "nevertheless, there shall be always ONE HEAD MASTER, and ONE USHER, at least." Who are to be paid such annual Stipends as to The Governors shall seem meet, so as the Salary of The Head Master be not less than £100. *per annum*, clear of all deductions; and that of the Usher be not less than £40. a year, clear of all deductions:—

That when in the judgment of The Governors, it shall be thought necessary that the Head Master or Usher ought to be removed by reason of Immorality, Neglect of Duty, Incapacity, or other just or reasonable cause, it shall be lawful for them so to do; so as that Three Calendar Months previous notice in writing under the hands of The Governors, or any Three or more of them, shall be given to the person so to be removed :—

But in case it shall happen that any Head Master or Usher shall be displaced for Incapacity (through the Visitation of God), it shall then be lawful for the Governors to allow out of the Revenues of the School, to such person, having been Head Master or Usher during the term of *Fifteen* years, during his natural life, or for so long as they shall think proper, such yearly sum of money as shall seem reasonable, not exceeding in the whole the clear yearly sum of £15. to such Head Master, and £10. to such Usher; and so as the Salary of the succeeding Head Master, and of the Usher for the time being, shall not, by reason of such allowance, be reduced to less than as before mentioned :—

The Head Master or Usher shall not teach or accept any payment whatsoever, for teaching or instructing any person whatsoever besides the Children belonging to the Borough of Wigan, without the leave of the Governors :—

Neither shall the Head Master or Usher officiate as Curate or Lecturer of the Parish Church of Wigan; nor perform any Clerical duty in any Church during the usual hours appointed by The Governors for teaching at the School, without their leave in writing :—

The Under Master or Ushers shall be under the direction of the Head Master, with regard to the Children and Youth to be instructed :—

The Governors are empowered to make Statutes and Bye-Laws, for the general regulations of the Establishment :—

The annual Meeting of The Governors to be on the *Second Wednesday* in June, between the hours of 10 and 12, in the School, or in the Old or New Town-Halls, or some public place within the Borough, as the Mayor for the time being shall appoint by notice under his hand, to be posted on the South door of the Parish Church of Wigan, and in two conspicuous places in or near the Market-place, on the Sunday next preceding any such Meeting :—

All the business of the School to be done at regular Meetings of the Governors, at which at least *Five* shall be present :—

The Proceedings of the Governors are to be entered in Books, which may be produced and read in Evidence in all Courts whatsoever.

By the Act the Governors were empowered to sell the property at Aspull, and to lay out the purchase money in other hereditaments,—and they have accordingly sold it and purchased an Estate, called "*Dennow*," in the Township of Appleton, in the County Palatine of Chester, containing 18 acres.

The following is a copy of THE STATUTES, which were made by THE MAYOR of the Corporation of Wigan, by the advice and consent of all THE TRUSTEES of the School, on the 9th of August, 1664;—

1. It is limited and ordained, that no person whatsoever shall be capable of being admitted to be principal or head Master of the said Free Grammar School, but such as have taken the degree of Master or Bachelor of Arts, in one of the Universities of Oxford or Cambridge, or some Protestant University elsewhere; or if such cannot be procured, some Undergraduate of the Universities aforesaid, or other sufficient well qualified Scholar, who is to be sober, discreet, and also well skilled and experienced in School Learning, and in the Original Languages, wherein they are to instruct their Scholars: and to the end that they be certainly thus qualified, it is ordained, that before the election of any Master, his abilities aforesaid, shall be tried by the Right Reverend the Lord Bishop of Chester, for the time being, or such other learned orthodox persons as the said Mayor of WIGAN for the time being, and the greater number of Trustees shall desire or appoint; and being very well assured of his sufficiency and integrity, the said principal or head Master, shall first be and remain six months upon trial in the said School, and then upon further approbation, shall be confirmed principal Master of the said Grammar School, under the hands of the said Mayor of WIGAN for the time being, and the greater number of the said Trustees, at which time the said Master shall subscribe a bond of £100. that he shall submit to the rules and orders of the School, and quietly depart from and leave the possession of the same, when the said Mayor of WIGAN, and the greater number of Trustees shall require.

2. It is ordained, that no person shall be capable of being Usher or under Master of the Free-School of WIGAN, but such as are of competent knowledge and learning both in the Latin and Greek Tongues, and so well qualified in School learning as may enable them to instruct their Scholars in case of the head Master's absence, and that shall be fit and capable by reason of

their learning and abilities to be received and entertained in either of the Universities of Oxford or Cambridge, and the trial hereof, to be before the said Reverend Lord Bishop of Chester, for the time being, or such other learned orthodox persons, as the said Mayor of WIGAN for the time being, and the greater number of Trustees, shall desire or appoint.

3. It is ordained, that if any person or persons so elected and appointed as Master or Usher, shall afterwards be found insufficient, or remissly negligent, or upon just occasion be detected of notorious licentionsness, such as common swearing, drunkenness, a common haunter of ale-houses and taverns, or otherwise scandalous, or shall take upon him any other charge or employment to the hindrance of his or their employment of the duty of the said places: that then the said Mayor for the time being, and the greater number of the said Trustees, upon assured evidence, or their own knowledge thereof, shall remove him or either of them, found so obnoxious to good rule and government, and cease all further payments to him or them, (save for the time he or they shall serve) and in their room, elect or settle such other sufficient Master and Usher in the said places and employments, qualified as before mentioned, as the said Mayor and Trustees shall think fit.

4. The Schoolmaster and Usher, elected and appointed as aforesaid, shall be constantly resident and attendant upon their trust, and if either be observed to be absent from the School at the times hereafter mentioned for his attendance without the Mayor of WIGAN's consent, and to neglect his due performance in the instructing of the Scholars, so that upon complaint, inquiry, and examination, it be found to be true by the said Mayor for the time being, and the greater number of the Trustees, and thereupon the Master or Usher being admonished and no amendment immediately follow, then the said Mayor and Trustees, upon three months warning, shall remove them, and proceed to elect and settle other sufficient persons, qualified as beforesaid in their place and office. And if the Master or Usher at any time desire to depart for their preferment or otherwise, they shall give three months warning to the Mayor of WIGAN, upon pain of forty shillings, to be deducted out of their wages, that so the School may not be disappointed of constant teaching.

5. No Schoolmaster or Usher shall keep any ale-house or tavern, or house of gaming, or other unthriftiness, or evil rule.

6. The Schoolmaster and Usher shall not be absent from the School at one and the same time, that so the School may not be neglected.

7. It is ordained, that the Schoolmaster for the time being,

shall have and receive the sum of £30. per annum, and the Usher £10. per annum, standing wages, to be paid quarterly, and the first payment to commence on the 29th Day of September next ensuing the date hereof.

8. The Master shall take special care of the LIBRARY now belonging to the School, or that shall hereafter be bought for the School, to have a perfect catalogue of them written in a book to be fixed to the desk, there always to remain, of all such books, as are or shall be bought, together with the names of the authors, title, and edition, together with the number of the volumes of the said books, with the names of any future Donors, and shall be ready to give a true and perfect account of the said Library, when the said Mayor for the time being, and the greater number of Trustees shall require it, and that none of the said books (upon any pretence whatsoever) shall be lent out or removed out of the said Library at any time; and the Master and Usher for the time being, shall, from time to time appoint such or so many Scholars as he or they know fit to make use of the said Library books, or so many of them as shall be useful for their better profiting in their respective way of learning, and that none whosoever, shall be suffered to write in, or scratch, or deface with pen, or otherwise, any of the said books, and that once in a week by the care and appointment of the Master or Usher, the dust shall be beaten and put off the said books, and the like care to be taken by them for the preservation and good usage of them, as by experience they shall find best, or otherwise shall be advised.

9. The Master may grant part of a day, for recreation in a month, and no more, except it be by the consent of the Mayor of WIGAN for the time being, provided it be not on Friday, market day; and also, each Thursday in the afternoon, from three o'clock in the summer half year, and the whole afternoon in the winter half year shall be a *remedy* for recreation, and for the winter half year, the School shall be continued as now it is accustomed, till twelve o'clock.

10. If the Master or Usher be visited or inflicted with an horrible loathsome or contagious disease, he shall be removed by the Mayor and Trustees for the time being, with some charitable relief out of the revenues of the said School, to be extended towards him at the discretion of the said Mayor and Trustees, and another meet person be chosen in his stead that shall be removed.

11. The Master or Usher upon the first meeting every morning, after a solemn prayer for God's blessing, shall cause a chapter to be read by any Scholar he pleaseth to appoint; and before their departure in the evening, they shall sing one of

David's psalms, or a part thereof, as the Master or Usher shall appoint, and then conclude with prayers and thanksgiving; and hereof the Master and Usher are enjoined to take care that these religious duties be duly and diligently performed and attended by the Scholars, as becometh such holy performances, to which end, the Master is to have a roll of all the Scholars, which is to be orderly called over twice or thrice every week, that the absent Scholars may be punished for their negligence, according as the Master and Usher judge meet.

12. The Master and Usher shall take special care that the Scholars do constantly repair to the Church every Lord's day, morning and afternoon, and other days set apart for God's worship, and to be placed together in the Church, with, or near the Master or Usher, if so there be, or hereafter shall be any conveniency procured so to do, and that they decently and reverently behave themselves during the time of public prayers and sermons, and submit themselves to be publicly catechised as the Rector of WIGAN or his Curate shall from time to time appoint: and that one or more Scholars be appointed to view and take notice of such Scholars as shall be absent, or not decently behave themselves during the time of public prayers and sermons, and that every Monday morning, account shall be required by the Master or Usher of any so offending, who shall be corrected as the nature of the offence shall deserve. And it is further ordained, that every Monday morning after reading of the chapter, some short convenient time shall be spent by the Master or Usher, or both, in calling some Scholars at one time, and some at another, to give an account of their profiting on the Sabbath day before; and to the end that catechising being of such singular use for the training up of youth in the knowledge of the oracles of God, and may be the better carried on, the Master or Usher, or both, shall spend one hour at least, every other Saturday throughout, in catechising the Scholars.

13. The School shall break up six days before the feast of our blessed Lord and Saviour Jesus Christ, and three days before Easter and Whit-Sunday, and not sooner, and the Master shall begin to teach, after Christmas, upon the next week-day after the 12th day, and after Easter, on the Monday next after Low Sunday, and after Whitsuntide, upon Monday after Trinity-Sunday, Saturdays in the afternoon, with all holidays used in the Church of England, are to be allowed for the Scholars' refreshments as is accustomed.

14. The Master shall teach and read classical authors, chaste and clear, in order to grammatical learning and knowledge of the tongues, with a special regard to the Protestant religion, morality, and pure language, such as Tully, Cæsar's Commen-

taries, Sallust, and Livy, with what others are most used in the best Free Schools for Prose; and for Verse, Virgil, Ovid, Horace, and Terence; for Greek, the Greek Grammar, Greek Testament, Isocrates, or Xenophon his Cyrus, with such other authors for Verse or Greek, as are usually taught in the best Schools.

15. The hours of coming and departing from the School from the 10th of March to the 10th of September yearly, shall be from seven o'clock to eleven o'clock, and from one o'clock until five o'clock in the afternoon, and from the said 10th day of September to the said 10th day of March, from half an hour after seven o'clock (save about two months when the days are shortest, from eight o'clock) till eleven o'clock, and from one o'clock till three, four, or five o'clock in the afternoon, according as convenient day-light may fall out for the Scholars going home, it being ordained, that no candles shall be used in the School for teaching at any time.

16. That no children that have upon them any noisome, or infectious diseases, shall, during the same time be admitted, and if after admission they shall fall into such maladies, they shall be absent until they are perfectly cured.

17. The Master and Usher shall have a special care to the good manners and decent deportment of the Scholars towards all persons, and shall exemplarily punish all misdemeanors, especially the crimes of swearing, cursing, lying, drunkenness, filthy or obscene talking, or acting, reproaching or miscalling persons by foul language, gaming for any thing of price, and in an especial manner, shall diligently endeavour to see the Lord's Day kept free from any profanation, (as much as in them lieth) as well after, as during the Scholars being in the Church.

18. All Scholars of what degree soever, are to submit to due correction from the Schoolmaster or Usher, which shall be promised by their parents at their admission, and referred to the Schoolmaster's discretion; and all stubborn and disobedient Scholars that are pertinatiously and exemplarily bad, by resisting the Master or Usher, or offering to struggle with, strike, spurn, and abuse the Master or Usher, when he or they are orderly correcting them for their fault, after two admonitions, wherewith their parents or friends shall be acquainted, shall the third time be expelled the School, after due proof thereof made before the Mayor of WIGAN and the greater number of Trustees for the time being: and those parents that molest the Schoolmaster, against reason and order, for correction of their children, their children shall be utterly expelled the School for ever, unless they can prove the correction unreasonable; and all the Scholars shall be obedient and ready to help the Master or Usher, for the

due and lawful correction of any stubborn Scholar that resisteth.

19. No Scholars shall bring to the School, or wear any weapons, neither shall any Scholar make any affray on his fellow Scholar, upon pain of severe correction from the Master or Usher, and if any Scholar be a common quarreller and setter of debate and fightings amongst the Scholars, and will not amend after correction and admonition by the Master or Usher, upon complaint of the Master or Usher to the Mayor of WIGAN for the time being, and the greater number of Trustees, and due proof made thereof, he shall be expelled the School.

20. No Scholar, being in health, shall be absent above six days together, and that with the Master's allowance, and if he shall be absent longer, after admonition of the Scholar, or notice given to the parent or friends, unless in some extraordinary case, and the Master approving the cause, shall forfeit all privelege or priveleges in the School, unless the said Mayor of WIGAN, and greater number of Trustees for the time being, upon hearing the cause, do order re-admission, upon promise from parents or friends, that there shall be more constant attendance for the future upon the School for their better profiting in learning.

21. All Scholars that have attained to such progress in learning as to be able to speak Latin, shall neither within School or without, when they are among the Scholars of the same or a higher rule, speak English; and that the Master shall shew which are the forms that shall observe this order of speaking Latin, and shall take care that it be observed, and due correction given to those that do neglect it.

22. Each Scholar shall be placed according to his progress in learning, and without partiality preferred by the Master according to his desert; and in case of injury offered herein by the Master, there shall be appeal to the Mayor of WIGAN, and greater number of Trustees for the time being.

23. That once in six weeks, or in two months at the furthest, throughout the year, Saturday in the forenoon shall be spent by many of the upper forms as shall be fitted for it, in such exercises as the construing of such authors of themselves, as the Master shall appoint, proposing of grammatical or historical questions one unto another, and making declamations, and such like exercises as may tend to the begetting of an emulation in learning amongst the Scholars.

24. No Scholars shall at any time, with a knife, or otherwise, cut or break the windows, wainscot, forms, seats, tables, desks, doors, or any other materials belonging to the School or Library, the Master upon conviction of such offender or offenders, shall give him or them exemplary punishments.

25. The Usher shall stand to the Master's direction for method and order of teaching, also the Master shall often examine the profiting of the Scholars, and the Usher's teaching, and by himself (or if need be) by advice of the Mayor of WIGAN and Trustees for the time being, take course for regulating of what shall be amiss.

26. The Scholars' play shall be shooting the long bow, running, leaping, and other harmless sports, but to avoid cards, dice, and other unlawful games, betting openly or covertly, upon pain of extreme punishment.

27. These Statutes and Orders, fairly written, shall be fixed upon a convenient place, publicly in the said School, and the Master shall cause them to be read or shewed to all such persons as offer their children to be admitted Scholars, and also, they shall be openly read in the School, once in a quarter of a year, from time to time, that so none may plead ignorance; and if any parents or friends refuse to have their children or relations to observe these Statutes and Orders, or any of them, they are not to be admitted into the School.

28. The Mayor of WIGAN, and greater number of Trustees for the time being, apprehending defects in any Statutes and Orders, herein comprised, and that other Orders are necessary, and may further tend to the good of the said School, shall meet so often as shall be requisite, (at the least twice in every year) to enlarge, alter, and change in substance or words, what by experience and prudent counsel shall appear to be beneficial to the furtherance of literature and education of youth.

11th June, 1760.—ORDERED further, by THE TRUSTEES of the said School,—

First, that the Head Master shall not for the future have under his care and instruction, any Scholar or Scholars who shall not be then fit to be instructed in the Grammar: and that *no Schoolmaster or Usher shall hereafter teach or instruct any Scholar or other person, Writing or Arithmetic, in the School hours:* and the Scholars shall not for the future, be allowed to be absent from the School in order to go home to Breakfast.

2nd October, 1711.—That the Usher shall not hereafter take upon him to teach and instruct any Scholar or Scholars but what are in the Testament and Books above.

There was originally no limitation as to the number of Scholars, but the TRUSTEES have found it necessary to restrict the number to EIGHTY. They are admitted at any age, provided they can read in the English Testament, and they are allowed to remain as long as they please.

The ETON Grammars are used ; and the System of Education is in a great measure left to the discretion of the Master.

There are no Exhibitions, nor other University advantages, belonging to this School.

The present Head Master is, The Revd. THOMAS COLLETT, whose Salary is £130. *per annum*. This Gentleman takes Boarders at Fifty guineas a year each.

The Second Master does not take Boarders.

WINWICK, near WARRINGTON.

THE FREE SCHOOL at WINWICK was founded by GWALTER LEGH, Esq., and endowed with £10. *per annum.*

In 1618, Sir PETER LEGH, of *Lyme*, in the County Palatine of Chester, Knight, and great Nephew of the Founder, re-built the School-house, and added £14. *per annum* to the Endowment, making the whole £24. chargeable upon lands in *Haydock*, in the Parish of Winwick.

Lord LILFORD who married Miss ATHERTON, the heiress of the *Atherton* estate, pays the Master £5. *per annum* from that Estate.

And Mr. ROTHWELL, of *Hoole*, pays £5. *per annum* also from an Estate in Hoole.

The School is open to the boys of the Town and Parish of Winwick, and has been distinguished for a Century past as a *Classical* School. The House is well calculated for the reception of Boarders,—the late Dr. PRINCE having had at least FIFTY,—and the present Master, The Revd. ROBERT BARLOW, having now about the same number.

There are no Exhibitions, nor other University advantages, belonging to this School.

The family of LEGH, of *Lyme* and *Haydock*, is Patron of the School, and it's present Representative is, THOMAS LEGH, Esq., M. P. for Newton.

The whole Township of Winwick belongs to the Rector of Winwick as Rector, except the School-house and a small quantity of land adjacent to it.

Mr. LEGH is also Patron of the School at NEWTON, in the Parish of Winwick, the Endowment of which is about £50. *per annum.* That, however, is merely an *English* School.

The present Master is, The Revd. JOHN SEDGWICK.

YORKSHIRE

(extracted from Volume II of *A Concise Description of the Endowed Grammar Schools in England and Wales)*

ACASTER SELBY, near Selby.

The Free Grammar School at Acaster Selby has a Stipend of £8. *per annum*, payable out of the Land Revenues of the Crown.

According to Bishop Tanner, a College for a Provost and two or three Fellows, one of whom was *to teach School*, was founded here by Robert Stillington, about the year ———. It was dedicated to St. Andrew, and, in the 26th of Henry the Eighth, was valued at £33..10..4. in the whole. It was granted, in the 2d of Edward the Sixth, to John Hulse, and William Pendred.

No answer has been received to the Author's Letter.

ARKSEY, near DONCASTER.

Of the FREE SCHOOL at ARKSEY the Author is not able to give a description, as no answer has been received to his Letter. See, *Doncaster*.

BATLEY, near LEEDS.

THE FREE GRAMMAR SCHOOL at BATLEY was founded in the 10th of King JAMES the First, 1613, by WILLIAM LEE, Vicar of Stapleford, in the County of Cambridge, a native of this Parish,—and endowed with 30 acres of land, and a messuage with it's appurtenances, in the Township of Gomersall, then producing £15. *per annum.*

It appears that there was a subsequent endowment, as there are lands and houses in the Township now let for £27..8..0., and in the Township of Horbury for £32..5..0., —The present amount of all the School estates being £133..10..0. a year.

The School is open to the boys of the whole Parish indefinitely, free of expense, and the average number is about Fifty. Very few Extra-Parochial Scholars attend, the number seldom exceeding 10 or 12,—but at present, not even that number. Boys are admitted, on application to the Master, as soon as they are capable of reading the New Testament in English, and may remain as long as their Parents choose.

LILLY's Latin Grammar improved by WARD, and the ETON Greek Grammar, are those in use: And the system of Education is such as is generally followed in Grammar Schools, except that the Master is required by the Foundation Deed to teach *English* and *writing*, and also *arithmetic* by a particular agreement with the Trustees of the School.

But *Classical* learning here is now, and for some time past, has been little regarded—the Inhabitants being persons engaged in business, and almost entirely of the lower class of labouring people. Reading, writing, and arithmetic are, therefore, all that they wish for in the education of their children, with very few exceptions. And even these branches of Instruction they are far from regarding with that concern, which might be desired.

There are no Exhibitions, nor other University advantages, belonging to this School.

The present Master is, The Revd. Matthew Sedgwick, whose Salary is £110. *per annum*, and a house. This Gentleman does not take any Pupils to board and educate, having declined that important task for a few years past; when he did take Boarders, his Terms were 35 guineas *per annum*.

There is no Usher or Assistant provided for, or appointed by the Foundation Deed; but the present Master employs one constantly at his own expense, to whom he pays 35 guineas a year.

No Register of Scholars educated here, has been kept,—but it is credibly stated, that Dr. Priestley had the early part of his education in this School.

BEDALE.

THE GRAMMAR SCHOOL at BEDALE is very ancient; but neither the time when, nor the person by whom, it was founded, can now be ascertained. It is supposed to have existed before the Dissolution of the Monasteries, as a Stipend of £7..11..4 is paid annually at the Audit holden at Richmond, out of the land Revenues of the Crown.

FRANCES Countess of WARWICK, by deed, in the reign of CHARLES the Second, gave a rent charge of £13..6..8. *per annum*, issuing out of certain lands at *Collough Grange*, in the County of Lincoln.

Mr. WILLIAM HEATON, by his Will left £100., the interest thereof to be given to a Schoolmaster, for teaching *Eight* poor boys of the Township of Bedale, *gratis*. This Sum having been laid out in the purchase of land in the Township of Crakehall, now produces an annual rent of £10..10..0. It has for many years been combined with the Grammar School.

The ETON Latin and Greek Grammars are used, when required.

The Rector of Bedale and the Select Vestry of Twenty-four nominate the Master, and elect the eight Scholars.

The present Master is, Mr. JOHN WEAVER, whose emoluments are the endowments already stated. But about a year and a half since, his Salary was augmented by subscription to £52..10..0. *per annum*, and Sixty boys of the Parish of Bedale are now admitted, free of expense, and educated upon Dr. BELL's system.

BEVERLEY.

THE FREE GRAMMAR SCHOOL at BEVERLEY, which is of ancient date, is probably co-eval with THE COLLEGIATE SOCIETY of SAINT JOHN,—for it does not appear when or by whom it was founded. The Patronage is now in The Corporation of the Town.

The old School, of brick, stood in The Minster Yard within the Close, South-West of the Church,—on the site of the Cloisters and Conventual buildings, all destroyed. About two years since it was pulled down to improve the Church, and was re-built by the Corporation in a commodious and handsome style in an adjoining street. They also liberally provide a large and convenient House for the residence of the Master.

There are no STATUTES or other REGULATIONS than such as are made by the Master, with the approbation of the Patrons.

The School is open to sons of Burgesses indefinitely, on the payment of £2. *per annum* for their instruction in the Classics, and £2..2..0 for writing and arithmetic. The sons of Non-Freemen, and Day-Scholars, pay £6..6..0. for the Classics, and £3..0..0. for writing and accompts. There are now about 10 free boys,—30 other Scholars,—and 12 Boarders,—and the School is increasing under the conduct of the present Master.

The ETON and CHARTER-HOUSE Latin Grammars, and VALPY's and MOORE's Greek Grammars, are used,—and the general system of Classical instruction is pursued.

In 1626, Mrs. MARGARET DARCEY gave to St. Mary's in Beverley £40., to be put out at interest by the Minister and Church-wardens for the time being, towards the maintenance of a Scholar at Cambridge, born in that Parish, and towards binding of some poor children apprentices.

Robert Metcalf, D. D., and one of the Senior Fellows of Trinity College, Cambridge, by his Will, dated the 9th of October, 1652, devised to The Mayor, Aldermen, and Burgesses, as Trustees, the yearly sum of £40., charged upon a large barn and divers closes or parcels of land adjoining each other, lately inclosed, and containing by admeasurement 90ª..1ʳ..30ᵖ., which are freehold and tythe free, situate at *Gilden Morden*, in the County of Cambridge,—of which, £10. a year are to be paid to the Preacher or Lecturer of the Town of Beverley,—£10. a year to the Schoolmaster of The Free School,—and £20. a year to Three poor Scholars of the same School, naturally born in this Town, such Scholars to be appointed and approved by The Mayor, Aldermen, and Burgesses, and by the Lecturer and Schoolmaster, for their better maintenance at The University of Cambridge,—and the said maintenance to be continued until they shall take the Degree of Master of Arts, if they so long continue Students at the University, and upon condition that they take the said Degree at the due time within *eight years* after their admission into the University;—But should there not be such Three poor Scholars at the University, or ready to go there, who should stand in need of that maintenance, and be *poor men's sons* (and not the sons of any of the Aldermen, or of any other that are of sufficient ability) who should not be able otherwise to maintain their children there,—then what can be spared of the said £20. (no poor Scholar having above £6..13..4. yearly) shall be distributed amongst the poorest people of the Town of Beverley, on the 20th of December yearly, or the day before or after, as may be thought most convenient by the Mayor and Lecturer.

In 1669, Mrs. Margaret Farrer, a native of Beverley, by her Will gave £150., with which lands were bought by The Corporation,—£2. of the annual amount of which were to be paid for the education of "an honest man's son" of Beverley at The Free School,—and £3. towards his maintenance at The University, 'till such time as he shall commence Master of Arts.

William Lacie, D.D., of *Thornhill*, in the County of York, by his Will, dated the 7th of September 1670, devised to the Mayor, Aldermen, and Burgesses £350., as Trustees, which is secured by an Indenture, dated the 26th of June, 1688, upon certain closes belonging to The Corporation, situate at Beverley, called "*Saint Gyles's Crofts,*" and charged with the annual payment of £16.—to Two Scholars that shall be born in Beverley, and educated at The Free School there, and sent from thence to The University of Cambridge, and entered Students in St. John the Evangelist's College,—each to have £8. a year, until they go out Masters of Arts, provided they go out Masters of Arts within *eight years* after their admission,—and so successively to such Two Scholars as shall be sent from this School for ever,—But, if there be no such Scholars sent from this School to that College, then the Mayor, Aldermen, and Burgesses shall distribute to the Poor of the Town of Beverley, *during such vacancy and no longer,* the said £16. every year upon *St. Andrew's* day, being the last day of November, or upon the day before, or the day after.

Mr. WILLIAM COATS, one of the Capital Burgesses, by his Will previous to 1697, gave £100. to The Corporation to be put out to Interest, six months after the decease of his mother Mrs. ELIZABETH COATS, for the use of one poor Scholar, born in St. Mary's Parish, and educated in the Grammar School, towards his maintenance in The University,—and for want of such, to be given to the Poor.

ROBERT CLERK, a native of Beverley, B. D. and Senior Fellow of St. John's College in Cambridge, gave to that College £200. to the founding of a Scholarship for a native of Beverley, with respect first to his kindred of the name of CLERK, and then of JOHNSON.

JOHN GREEN, late Lord Bishop of Lincoln, by his Will, dated the 17th of August, 1778, devised to The Mayor, Aldermen, and Burgesses, £1000. Stock in the 3 per cent. Consolidated Bank Annuities, the gross annual income of which is £30.,—the objects of which Charity are, in the first place, such Scholar, being the son of a Freeman of Beverley, as the Mayor, Aldermen, and Burgesses shall, from time to time, nominate and appoint to be sent off from the Free School here to Bene't or Saint John's College in the University of Cambridge, and who shall have been educated at this School at the least *three years* immediately preceding such nomination, as to the sum of £10., —which shall be continued to be paid to the person so nominated, for *seven years* after he shall be admitted into either of the said Colleges, in case he shall so long live and continue a Member thereof, or until he shall have taken, or be of sufficient standing to take the Degree of Master of Arts,—yet upon this condition, nevertheless, that he shall proceed regularly to the Degree of Bachelor of Arts, and after that time shall continue to reside in one of the said Colleges for *two months* at the least in every succeeding year, during the time above specified,—And after the said Exhibitioner shall have enjoyed the benefit of this Exhibition for the term of Seven years, or in case he shall die or cease to be a Member of either of those Colleges within that time, and before he shall be of sufficient standing to take the degree of Master of Arts, or shall lose the benefit thereof, by not residing within the College of which he shall be a Member, after he shall have taken the degree of Bachelor of Arts, then and in any or either of those cases, the Mayor, Aldermen, and Burgesses shall nominate and appoint another Scholar, sent off from this School, qualified as aforesaid, to succeed to this Exhibition, who shall hold and enjoy the same for the like term, and upon the like conditions as the person first mentioned,—And in case no person shall at any such vacancy be ready to offer himself, or be judged by the Mayor, Aldermen, and Burgesses, to be a proper candidate for such Exhibition, then all arrears of the said £10. which shall accrue until a person qualified as aforesaid shall be found, or during any vacancy, shall be paid to the person next offering himself, and who shall be chosen, over and above the said £10. a year, and as an augmentation thereof.

Lady ROKEBY founded One Fellowship in St. John's College, to be enjoyed by a person born in Beverley, and brought up at this School,—and for want of such, one born in the County of York,—provided he be a Priest at his election, or be one within Six months after.

Mr. HALITRY-HOLME founded One Fellowship in St. John's College, Cambridge, to be enjoyed by one born in the Town of Beverley, or some other Town near it, and educated at this School,—and that he be also a Priest at his election, or be one within Twelve months after.

The present Master is, The Revd. JOHN ORMAN, M. A., a Scholar of the celebrated Master, Mr. TATE, of Richmond, —whose Salary is,—

Dr. Metcalf's endowment, - -	£ 10.
An annual gift from the two Representatives in Parliament - - -	20.
Annual payment by The Corporation, -	70.
	£100.

with an excellent Dwelling-house, at a trifling Quit-rent. This Gentleman's terms for Boarders are,—

Entrance, - - -	£ 2..2..0
Board and lodging, with instruction in the Greek and Latin languages, English Grammar, and Geography, - - -	42..0..0
Mathematics, - - - -	6..6..0
Writing and Arithmetic, - -	3..0..0

There are no Church Preferments,—but the Parishioners

of St. MARY's usually give the Lectureship of their Church to the Master.

Among the Eminent men who have been educated here, may be mentioned,—

JOHN ALCOCK, D. D., Bishop of Ely.

JOHN FISHER, D. D., Bishop of Rochester.

JOHN GREEN, D. D., Bishop of Lincoln.

ROBERT INGRAM, a worthy Divine.

HENRY REVELL REYNOLDS, a late eminent Physician, in London.

There is an excellent LIBRARY, including STEPHENS's *Thesaurus*, and several *Aldine* editions, &c.

BINGLEY, near BRADFORD.

Of the FREE GRAMMAR SCHOOL at BINGLEY the Author is not able to give a description, as no answer has been received to his Letter.

BOWES, near GRETA BRIDGE.

THE FREE GRAMMAR SCHOOL at BOWES has an endowment of £339..13..0. *per annum.*

There are SIX SCHOLARSHIPS at PEMBROKE HALL, Cambridge, founded by The Revd. CHARLES PARKYN, formerly Rector of Oxburgh, in Norfolk, for Superannuated Scholars from Merchant Taylors' School, and for ONE SCHOLAR educated at The Free School of Bowes,—they are each of the value of £40. *per annum*, and may be holden *seven* years.

No answer has been received to the Author's Letter.

BRADFORD.

THE FREE GRAMMAR SCHOOL at BRADFORD was founded as early, if not earlier than the Sixth of Edward the Sixth, 1553,—And was incorporated by King CHARLES the Second, in the 14th year of his reign, by Letters Patent dated the 10th of October, 1663:—

By which it is ordained, that there shall be a Free Grammar School here, to be called "THE FREE GRAMMAR SCHOOL of King CHARLES the Second at BRADFORD," for the teaching, instructing, and better bringing up of Children and Youth in Grammar and other good Learning and Literature,—to consist of one Master or Teacher, and one Usher or Under Teacher:—

That there shall be THIRTEEN men of the most discreet, honest, and religious persons of the neighbourhood, whereof the Vicar of Bradford shall always be one,—who shall be Governors, and be a Body Corporate with continual succession, and be able to purchase, receive, and enjoy lands:—

When any of the Governors, except the Vicar, shall die, or dwell above *two miles* out of the Parish for *one year*, the rest of the Governors are to nominate another in his place within *eight weeks* after such vacancy,—If the election be deferred beyond eight weeks, the Archbishop of York, or *(sede vacante)* the Dean of York, with the consent of *five* of the Governors, to appoint:—

That they shall have a Common Seal,—and be able to plead, and be impleaded:—

Power is given to the Governors under their Common Seal to constitute a discreet and fit person, who hath taken the degree of Master of Arts, to be Schoolmaster,—and so from time to time as the place shall become void, within *sixty days* to present some other meet man for knowledge, religion, and life unto the Archbishop of York; or *(sede vacante)* the Dean of York, who shall allow him to be Schoolmaster, to continue so long as he shall be found by the Governors to be diligent and faithful in his office and fit for the same, both for his religion, knowledge, and conversation, and no longer:—

The Governors may, upon one quarter's warning, *displace* the Schoolmaster, and elect another,—And, if they shall not present a fit Schoolmaster within sixty days after a vacancy, the Archbishop of York, or *(sede vacante)* the Dean of York, to elect a fit person with the consent of *five* of the Governors, who shall then be admitted under the Common Seal:—

Power is given to the Governors to nominate an Usher or Under Teacher from time to time within one month after a vacancy, and to displace him for negligence or unfitness:—

Power is also given to the Governors to make Statutes and Ordinances in writing under their Common Seal, to be kept under *two locks*,—the Master to have one key, and one of the Governors by the consent of the rest to have the other:—

The Governors, Master, and Usher, before they enter upon their offices, are to take an *Oath* before a Justice of the Peace of the County of York, to be faithful and careful for the good of the School in all things appertaining to his office and charge, and also the Oaths of Obedience and Supremacy:—

The Governors are further empowered to keep lands already given to the School, and to purchase and take any lands and possessions, not exceeding the clear yearly value of 100 marks:—

The Archbishop of York for the time being is constituted VISITOR of the School.

The Governors have hitherto been Gentlemen of the greatest respectability in the Town and Neighbourhood.

It is not possible at present to state, what was the original Endowment, as, many years since, some changes of the property appear to have taken place.

The present rental arises from lands and buildings, and annual rents issuing out of Freehold estates, all within the Parish of Bradford.

But the Revenue is likely soon to be much increased,

from the intention of The Governors to apply to Parliament, to enable them to grant building leases, and to make such other disposition of the School property as will be greatly for the benefit of the Establishment.

There are no STATUTES.

The School is open to boys of the Parish indefinitely, free of expense; and there are generally about 55 in the *Grammar* School, exclusive of boys in the *Writing* School which was some years since very beneficially established by The Governors, from the then improved state of the Revenues.

Boys are admitted, when qualified to begin the Latin Accidence, and no period of Superannuation is prescribed. They are admitted on application to the Head Master.

The ETON Grammars are used; and the system of Education is left to the discretion of the Head Master.

This School is entitled to send a Candidate for the Exhibitions under the Will of Lady ELIZABETH HASTINGS. See, *Leeds*.

The present Head Master is, The Revd. JAMES BARMBY, M. A., late Fellow of University College, Oxford, and Rector of Melsonby, in the North Riding of the County of York, whose Salary is £160. *per annum*. But the Salaries of all the Masters, it is expected, will, for the reasons already given, be in a few years considerably augmented.

Neither the Head, nor Second Master, takes Pupils.

Among the Eminent men who have been educated here, may be mentioned,—

JOHN SHARP, D. D., Archbishop of York.

RICHARD RICHARDSON, M. D., of North Bierley, who died on the 21st of April, 1741, the friend of Sir HANS SLOANE,—an eminent Botanist, and a considerable Contributor to THE PHILOSOPHICAL TRANSACTIONS.

JAMES SCOTT, D. D., late Fellow of Trinity College, Cambridge, Rector of Simonburn, in Northumberland, well known in the days of "*Wilkes and Liberty*" as Writer of the Political Letters in THE PUBLIC ADVER-

TIZER, signed "*Anti-Sejanus,*"—by which he obtained that Living through Lord SANDWICH, then first Lord of the Admiralty,—the Patronage being in The Governors of Greenwich Hospital, as part of the estate of the Earl of DERWENTWATER, after his attainder for the rebellion in 1715. It is so great and extensive a Living, that on the death of Dr. SCOTT, it has been divided into *Four,* furnishing a handsome provision for Four Chaplains in the Royal Navy.

The present School is unpleasantly situate on the West side of the Church-yard. The date of it's erection cannot be ascertained, but it appears to have been built at different periods, or to have undergone great alterations and repairs; and although not absolutely now in a ruinous state, yet it is an indifferent edifice. It is, therefore, the intention of the Governors to erect a new School in a better situation; and, as soon as their funds will permit, a Residence also for the Head Master, for whom there is none at present belonging to the School.

Round the handle of the Seal, which is of silver, is engraven "*Ex dono* PETRI SUNDERLAND *Armigeri.*"

CAWTHORNE, near BARNESLEY.

THE FREE SCHOOL at CAWTHORNE was founded in consequence of a Decree of the Duchy Court of Lancaster, dated the 25th of June, 1639, in which it is ordered,—

That £5..4..0. be paid annually to the Master by the Receiver of the Honour of Pontefract out of the Revenues of the Duchy,—

That the Master be nominated and elected by the Chancellor of the Duchy Court,—

That the Inhabitants of Cawthorne should pay to the Master the sum of £8..2..8. for his better maintenance and encouragement,—

And that they should from time to time, at their own costs and charges, keep and maintain a commodious School-house, with all needful reparations.

The Inhabitants have erected not only a spacious School-house, but also a convenient Dwelling-house for the Master, with a place for his cow, worth upwards of £4..4..0. *per annum*, and make him an allowance of £5..5..6. a year out of the Town's rates.

There are SIX Scholars belonging to Cawthorne taught to read, free of expense. The number of boys, and girls, on an average amount to 40, and are admitted at any age.

The system of Education is reading, writing, arithmetic, mensuration, and geometry. The *Classics* are not taught.

There are no Exhibitions.

The present Master is, Mr. GEORGE BACKHOUSE, who does not take Pupils to board.

COXWOLD, near EASINGWOLD.

THE FREE GRAMMAR SCHOOL at COXWOLD was founded in 1603, by Sir JOHN HARTE, Knight, Citizen and Alderman of London,—for the support and maintenance of which, he charged his Manor of *Nether Silton* alias *Silton Pannel*, in the County of York, and the rights, members, and appurtenances thereof, with the payment of £36..13..4. in manner following,—

> "To the Master of the same School yearly £20., for his pains, and 26*s*..8*d*. for his livery.
>
> "To the Usher of the same School yearly for the time being £10. for his pains, and 13*s*..4*d*. for his livery.
>
> "To a Schoolmaster yearly for the time being, to teach the *Petties* or Young Children in Coxwold, to read *English*, 53*s*..4*d*.
>
> "To a Preacher yearly for the time being, for three Sermons to be there made, 20*s*.
>
> "To the Visitors (The Master and Fellows of Sidney Sussex College, Cambridge) yearly, for a *drinking* or repast 20*s*.
>
> "And also to repair the same School-house from time to time, as need shall require."

This last expense is an *onus* upon the present most honourable and conscientious Patron, DAVID BURTON FOWLER, Esq.

The present Master is, The Revd. THOMAS NEWTON, M. A., Vicar of Coxwold, who was appointed by the Patron in 1806.

This School is now in a flourishing state,—Latin, Greek, and English being regularly taught by the present learned Master all under the same roof.

DONCASTER.

THE GRAMMAR SCHOOL at DONCASTER is in the lower apartments of the Town-Hall,—where the sons of Freemen have a right to be taught *Latin*, free of any expense to their parents,—for which purpose The Corporation allow the Master, who must be a Clergyman, a Salary of £50. *per annum.*

According to Dr. MILLER, the Corporation, when they appointed the late Revd. Mr. CROCHLEY, Master, who had been one of the Tutors at Westminster School, promised to give him the Living of Rossington, *provided he had* FIFTY *Scholars when that Living became vacant.* The Freemen of Doncaster, *generally thinking the knowledge of the Latin tongue of but little consequence in the education of their children,* so few of them took the advantage of this privilege, that the Master was never able to procure a greater number than *forty-five.* Thus, Mr. CRICHLEY never obtained the Living,—"and although a good Scholar, an excellent Pulpit Orator, and a respectable Poet, *died nearly broken-hearted in distress and misery!*"

There is a SCHOLARSHIP of about £10. *per annum* at JESUS COLLEGE, Cambridge, for a Scholar from the Free Schools at Doncaster *or* Arksey.

No answer has been received to the Author's Letter.

DRAX, near SELBY.

THE FREE GRAMMAR SCHOOL at DRAX was founded in the 21st year of the reign of CHARLES the Second, 1669, by CHARLES READ, Gentleman, of Darleton in the County of Nottingham, who was born in this Parish.

He erected a School-house and Dwelling for a Master, as also Six Alms-houses, in the Town and Parish of Drax,—and designed the same School-house for a Free School and a Master for ever, to teach the youth of the Parish to read, write, and accompt, and also the Latin, Greek, and Hebrew languages.

The original endowment was £30. *per annum* to the Master, which yet remains the same, but an advance of Salary is expected to take place at Midsummer, 1818.

"If any of the boys for their ingenuity or towardliness in Learning be deemed fit for the University, they shall be sent to either Cambridge or Oxford."

The present Master is, The Revd. JOHN NICHOLSON, who has recently been appointed.

DRIGHLINGTON, near LEEDS.

THE FREE GRAMMAR SCHOOL at DRIGHLINGTON, in the Parish of Burstal, owes it's origin to the benevolence of JAMES MARGETSON, Archbishop of Armagh, a native of this Village,—who having built a School here, but not having endowed the same in his life time, by his Will, dated the 31st of May, 1678, gave all his lands, tenements and hereditaments in Drighlington and Newhall to his son ROBERT MARGETSON and the heirs of his body, with remainders over to others,—to the intent, to pay yearly for ever towards the maintenance of the School £60. out of the rents and profits of those lands,—

Of which King WILLIAM and Queen MARY having been informed, they, by their Letters Patent dated the 11th of Jany., in the third year of their reign, 1691, granted,—

That Sir JOHN TEMPEST, Bart., and other persons therein named, should be a Body Corporate, by the name of "THE GOVERNORS of THE FREE SCHOOL of JAMES MARGETSON, late Lord Archbishop of Armagh," with perpetual succession, and be able to receive the said yearly sum of £60., and take a conveyance thereof for the benefit of the School,—and to purchase and receive lands and possessions,—to plead and be impleaded, —to have a Common Seal,—and to make Statutes and Ordinances in writing:—

That there shall be for ever *Nine* honest and discreet persons who shall be GOVERNORS for life, unless removed for just and reasonable cause by such of the Governors as shall be then living:—

That, when any of the Governors shall die or be removed, the remaining Governors shall elect one other honest and discreet person inhabiting within *Twenty miles* of the School in his room, to continue for life,—first taking his Oath for the due execution of the Office before the Governors, or any *Two* of them.

The right of nominating the Head Master of the School was granted by the Will of The Founder to The Master and Senior Fellows of PETER-HOUSE, in Cambridge.

In the distribution of the Endowment, £40. *per annum* were to be given to the Head Master,—£13..6..8. to an Usher,—and £6..13..4. to a Master for teaching English. The Usher, and English Teacher, were to be appointed, as often as necessary, by the Head Master with the consent of the Governors.

The *Register Book* appears to have been kept in the most *careless* manner,—for the name of a single Scholar cannot be discovered in it, and only that of *one* of the Head Masters,—neither are any particulars respecting the School recorded,—for more than *fifty* years past.

The number of Governors having a few years since been reduced to *One*,—the Survivor, in 1811, chose *Eight* others,—the greater number of whom accepted the office, and were afterwards duly sworn to perform the duties of it. They found that they were empowered by the Letters Patent to make such REGULATIONS and ORDINANCES, as they might deem most conducive to the welfare of the Institution,—They accordingly adopted some, which promise to be of use to the Neighbourhood for whose benefit the School was, doubtless, originally intended,—

The most prominent of them are,—

The limiting the number of Free Scholars,—the fixing the age of their Admission, and the time of their Superannuation,—and, permitting them to be taught English, writing, arithmetic, or *Classics,* according to the ability of the Scholar, and the desire of their Parents,—giving the whole of the £60. to the Head Master.

The present Head Master is, The Revd. HENRY BAILEY, who was appointed in the Autumn of 1814. He resides in a House adjoining the School-room, in which are conveniences to accommodate Boarders,—and, it is stated, that one of his Predecessors had as many as *Thirty* Pupils in his house, besides a large family.

Since the year 1814, a CHAPEL in the Village of Drighlington has been consecrated by His Grace the Archbishop of York, and Mr. BAILEY has been nominated the Perpetual Curate of it,—but the Curacy is not necessarily connected with the School.

GIGGLESWICK, *in* CRAVEN, near SETTLE.

THE FREE GRAMMAR SCHOOL at GIGGLESWICK was founded by King EDWARD the Sixth, by Letters Patent dated the 26th of May, in the Seventh year of his reign, 1553, at the Petition of JOHN NOWELL, Clerk, then His Majesty's Chaplain and Vicar of Giggleswick, and of other Inhabitants of the Town and Parish,—by which it was ordained,—

That there should be a Grammar School in Giggleswick, to be called "THE FREE GRAMMAR SCHOOL of King EDWARD the Sixth of GIGGLESWYCKE,"—to consist of one Master, and one Under Master or Usher :—

That *Eight* of the most discreet and honest Inhabitants, whereof the *Vicar* to be one, should be GOVERNORS,—who should be a Body Corporate, with perpetual succession, and be able to hold lands and possessions :—

That, when any of the Governors, except the Vicar, shall die or dwell out of the Parish, the Survivors there residing, or the major part of them, are to elect another of the Inhabitants in his place :—

That the same Vicar, with one other of the Governors, shall have power to call together the rest of the Governors when necessary :—

The King granted to the Governors several small rents,—A capital messuage and lands in *North Cave*, lands called "*Forbyland*,"—A close, called "*Espyng Close*," in North Cave,—Two Oxgangs of land in *South Kelthorp*, and *North Kelthorp*,—And all his messuages and premises in the tenure of divers persons in *North Cave*, and *Brampton*,—A capital messuage and lands in *Ryse*, and *Aldburgh*,—The tythes in *Edderwycke*, within the Parish of Aldburgh,—Which messuages and lands then amounted to the clear yearly value of £23..3..0.,—To hold in fee, rendering to the Crown 63*s*. yearly :—

The Governors to have a Common Seal,—and to be able to plead and be impleaded :—

The Governors and their Successors were likewise empowered

to elect a Master, and Under-Master, so often as the same shall be vacant:—

And that they, with the advice of the Bishop of the Diocese, shall make Statutes touching the Governors how they shall behave in their offices, and for what causes they shall be removed, —and concerning the election of the Master, and Under-Master, and the order and government of them and the Scholars, and their Stipend and Salary, and other things concerning the same School:—

If the *Vicar* shall infringe and not fulfil the Statutes, the rest of the Governors, for that turn, may elect another of the most discreet and honest Inhabitants to the office of Governor, in the place of the Vicar:—

License is also given to the Governors to have and purchase for the support of the School, lands not exceeding the clear yearly value of £30., besides those before granted to them:—

And it is ordered, that all the issues and profits of the lands and possessions given and assigned to the support of the School, shall be from time to time converted to the support and preservation of the School, and not otherwise.

The Endowment was part of the possessions belonging to the Dissolved Monastery of Nether Acaster,—the value of which has so much increased, by the drainage and inclosure of *Walling Fen*, and other improvements, that it's present amount is nearly £1000. *per annum.*

There are Three Masters,—two of them for Classics, and one for Mathematics.

The number of Pupils is limited only by the want of room,—who are admitted "*from every quarter of the Globe*," if their moral characters be good, and are taught, *gratis.*

Boys may be boarded at different rates from £30. to £150. a year.

Dr. WHITAKER suspects the present School to have been the house belonging to *The Rood Priest.*

There are SIX SCHOLARSHIPS at CHRIST COLLEGE, Cambridge, founded by Mr. CARR, for Scholars educated at this School.

WILLIAM PALEY, D. D., author of the Elements of Moral and Political Philosophy, received his classical education here under his Father, who was Head Master nearly FIFTY years.

The Author regrets that he is not able to give a more full description of this wealthy Establishment.

Guisbrough, *or* Gisburn, in Cleaveland.

On the North side of the Church-yard towards the East, stand The Grammar School and Hospital which were founded by Letters Patent of Queen Elizabeth, dated the 19th of June, in the Third year of her reign, 1561, granted to Robert Pursglove, Clerk, the *last* Prior of Guisbrough.—

By which it was ordained, that he, or he being dead, his heirs, executors, or assigns, for the education and learning of boys and youth, and for the support and relief of the poor and aged, might establish a Grammar School or Alms-House or Hospital in Honour of Our Lord Jesus Christ, in the Town of Gisburn,—to consist of Two Wardens, one Preceptor or Master of the Scholars sufficiently learned in the Grammar art, and certain other poor, infirm, and aged Persons, according to the Ordinances and Statutes by the same Robert, his heirs, executors, or assigns to be made :—

And that the Two Wardens, Preceptor or Master of the Scholars and poor and aged persons, when the same School or Alms-House or Hospital should be established,—should be a Body Corporate, with perpetual succession,—and be able to plead and be impleaded,—and to have, use, and retain lands and possessions, to be given or purchased in aid of the said purpose,—Provided, the premises shall not exceed the clear yearly value of £60.,—And that they should have a Common Seal:—

License was given to the Founder during his life, and after his death to his heirs, executors, and assigns in his Will to be thereto specially appointed, to make Statutes and Ordinances for the good rule and government as well of the said Alms-House, Hospital or School, as of the Wardens, Preceptor or Master of the Scholars, Boys, Youth, Poor or Aged Persons and their Successors, and the same from time to time to change, amend, and reform.

The benevolent Founder accordingly endowed the Institution with his lands, tenements, and services at *Bolam*, in the Parish of Gainford in the County Palatine of Durham; and with 68a..0r..26p. in the Parish of *Smeaton*, in the County of York.

The original Endowment was £41..4..0.,—But, by a late division of the Common fields at *Bolam*, and some future additional grants to this Charity, it's revenues have been greatly augmented,—the lands now being 361 acres, and it's present rental £375..15..7½ *per annum*.

The School-house adjoins to The Hospital on the East, and consists of a spacious School-room upon the ground floor, and two chambers,—with a garden, and other offices, for the residence of the Master.

By the STATUTES of THE HOSPITAL and SCHOOL, which were drawn up by the benevolent Founder himself and dated the 11th of August, 1561, it is directed,—

"That no persons shall be chosen, or admitted to be Masters of the Scholars of the said School, except he be sufficiently learned and exercised in *Grammar*, honest in conditions and living, and a Priest in Orders at the time of his admission, and no *Scot*, or Stranger born,—But, if a *Priest* cannot be had and gotten within a reasonable time at every vacation, then a *Layman*, being *unmarried*, and of such qualities and conditions as is before said, may be chosen and admitted to the said office,—But, if after his admission he do *marry*, then immediately his said office shall be void, and the said Wardens shall remove and utterly put him from the same for ever.

"The Electors shall present the person whom they choose to be Master, to the Archdeacon of Cleaveland or his Official, and in their absence to the Dean of Cleaveland, to be examined by one of them touching his learning and living.

"The Master shall teach *freely*, all Scholars coming to the School, Grammar, honest manners, and godly living.

"He shall keep a Register of the names of all his Scholars, with the day and year of their first coming and admission, taking therefore of every Scholar 4*d*.,—and *never after any thing of duty*,—but, if any of the Parents or Friends of the Scholars *give him any thing of their free will*, he may take it thankfully.

"The School shall be divided into *Four* several Forms,—and in the first shall be placed young beginners, commonly called "*Petits*,"—whom the Master himself shall not be bound to teach so long as they continue there, but only assign so many of his Scholars in the third and fourth Forms, as may suffice to instruct them.

"No Scholar shall be suffered to continue in the School over one month, except he have books necessary for his Form, or else daily write his lessons with his own hand.

"The Scholars of the Third and Fourth Forms shall speak nothing within the School-house but *Latin*, saving only in the teaching of the lower Forms.

"The Statutes shall be read every year at the Feast of St. Michael the Archangel, or within eight days next after, openly in the School-house, in the presence of the Members of THE CORPORATION, and of Two other honest men of the Parish of Guisbrough.

The number of Boys upon the Foundation at present, is *Ten*. And there are about *Fifteen* other Scholars, who pay 5*s*. *per* Quarter.

The Revd. JAMES WILCOCK is the present Master, whose Salary is £50. *per annum*.

There are SIX old Men, and SIX old WOMEN now in THE HOSPITAL, who are supplied with clothing, and five shillings *per* week each ; together with a small dwelling, and £1..0..8 each *per annum*, for *coals*. This last sum is called LUMLEY'S money.

The present acting TRUSTEES are,—

—— LEE, Esq., of Pinchinthorpe.
Mr. JAMES HICKSON, of Guisbrough.
Mr. JOHN HUTCHINSON, of Guisbrough.

"In the Chancel of Tyddeswell Church, in Darbyshire, is the Pourtrayture of a Bishop in Brass in his Habit, and at his Feet this

INSCRIPTION.

Under this Stone as here doth ly, a Corps sometime of Fame,
In Tiddeswall bred and born truly, Robert Pursglove by Name,
And there brought up by Parents Care at Schoole and Learning trad,
Till afterwards by Uncle dear to London he was had:
Who William Bradshaw hight by Name in Paul's which did him place,
And there at Schoole did him maintain full thrice 3 years whole space;
And then into the Abberye was placed as I wis,
In Southwark call'd, where it doth ly, Saint Mary Overis;
To Oxford then, who did him send into that Colledge right,
And there 14 Years did him find, which Corpus Christi hight:
From thence at Length away he went a Clerke of Learning great,
To Guisburn Abbey streight was sent, and plac'd in Prior's Seat;
Bishop of Hull he was also, Archdeacon of Nottingham,
Provost of Rotheram Colledge too, of York eak Suffragan:
Two Gramer Schools he did ordain with Land for to endure,
One Hospitall for to maintain twelve impotent and poor.
O Guisburn thou, with Tiddeswall Town lement and mourn ye may,
For this said Clerke of great Renown lyeth here compact in Clay;
Though cruel Death hath now down brought this Body which here doth ly,
Yet Trump of Fame stay can he nought to sound his praise on high.

Qui legis hunc Versum crebro reliquum memoreris
Vile Cadaver sum, tuque Cadaver eris.

Round the Verge of the Stone is this:

† Christ is to me as Life on Earth, and Death to me is Gaine,
Because I trust through him alone Salvation to obtaine;
So brittle is the State of Man, so soon it doth decay,
So all the Glory of this World must pass and fade away.

This Robert Pursglove, sometime Bishop of Hull, deceased the 2nd Day of May in the Year of our Lord God 1579."

HALIFAX, *or* SKIRCOAT.

THE FREE GRAMMAR SCHOOL at *Skircoat*, in the Parish of HALIFAX, was founded by Charter, granted by Queen ELIZABETH, on the 15th of February, 1585, at the humble suit of the Inhabitants of the Parish and Vicarage of Halifax, "for the continual bringing up, teaching, and learning of Children and Youth of the said Parish and Vicarage of Halifax, and also of other Villages and Hamlets near adjoining unto the same, and of other Our faithful and Liege people *whosoever they be*, to be taught, instructed, and learned there;"—

And ordained, that it should be called "THE FREE GRAMMAR SCHOOL of Queen ELIZABETH, for the bringing up, teaching, and instructing of Children and Youth in Grammar, and other good Learning, to continue for ever,"—to have one Master or Teacher, and one Usher or Under-Teacher;—

And that the Lands and Possessions might be the better preserved Her Majesty granted, that there should be TWELVE "of the discreetest and honestest men, dwelling within the same Parish and Vicarage for the time being," to be called "THE GOVERNORS of the Possessions, Revenues, and Goods of

The Free Grammar School;" and to be one Body Corporate and Politick, with continual Succession;—

That whensoever it shall happen any one or more of the Governors to die, or otherwise to dwell out of the Parish or Vicarage, that then it shall be lawful for the Survivors and then dwelling within the Parish and Vicarage to choose and nominate any other meet person or persons, of the Parish or Vicarage of Halifax, being above the age of *Twenty-four years*, into the place or places of him or them so dead, departed, or removed. The election to be made within one month next following the vacation, and to be ended the same day on which it is begun: but if the Election be not so made, then one to be chosen, whom The Archbishop of York, for the time being, "*Sede Archiepiscopali plena*," or, "*Sede eadem vacante*," The Dean of the Cathedral Church of York, with consent of *Two* of the Governors, shall name, so that he who is appointed, dwell within the Parish and Vicarage of Halifax:—

The Governors to have a Common Seal, and to plead and be impleaded:—

And Her Majesty further granted, that whensoever it shall happen the place of Schoolmaster to be void, the Governors, or the more part of them, shall have for ever full power and authority, from time to time, to choose, and appoint, "and under their Common Seal to present a meet man, *learned and cunning*, which hath been Student in one of The Universities of this Realm of England the space of *Five years* at the least, and hath well profited in Learning, unto The Archbishop of York, *Sede Archiepiscopali plena*, or, *eadem Sede vacante*, to The Dean of The Cathedral Church of York, and he so presented, and whom the foresaid Archbishop, or Dean, *Sede vacante*, so shall judge to be fit, shall be the Master of the said School, so long as he behaveth himself well in that office:"—

The said Election to be made always within *Six weeks* after the office of the Schoolmastership shall happen to be void; but if it should occur that the election of the Master be not so made, then it shall be lawful for the Archbishop, *Sede Archiepiscopali plena*, and *eadem Sede vacante*, to The Dean, "to nominate and admit what meet person soever to be Master of the said School, so that he whom they appoint hath been Student at the least five years in one of the said Universities, and hath profited well in Learning, and be of honest condition;"—this course to be pursued so often as the School shall be void of a Master:—

The Governors, or the more part of them, are empowered to appoint and admit the Usher, provided they take to them the Master "to judge of the sufficiency in learning and aptness in the function of the said Usher," and so that the election be made within *one month* after the place of the Usher shall happen at any time to be void :—

The Governors are further empowered to make good and wholesome Decrees and Ordinances, in writing, for the government of the Master, and Usher, and of the Scholars, and Possessions of the School, the same to be allowed under the Seal of The Archbishop of York :—

And for the faithful keeping of these Statutes, it is directed, that every person who shall be nominated to the office of a Governor, or to the office of the Schoolmaster or Usher, before he be admitted to his office, shall take a corporal *Oath* to do and execute his office well and faithfully, before the other Governors of the School :—

Her Majesty further granted her special license to the Governors to receive any other lands or possessions whatsoever, provided that they do not exceed the clear yearly value of £40.

This Charter is said to have been procured by HENRY FARRER, Esq., of *Ewood*, at his own expense, and who was one of the *first* Governors of the School.

On the 14th of August, 1598, The Right Honble. GILBERT Earl of SHREWSBURY, EDWARD SAVILE, Esq., and Sir GEORGE SAVILE, Knt., gave by Deed the present School-house, and *Six* acres of land contiguous thereto, situate in *Skircoat*.

In 1634, the sum of £196..6..8. was collected, in order to purchase lands for the use of this School; and, besides other Legacies and Gifts, the following perpetual Benefactions have at different times been given to it, *viz.*,—

BRIAN THORNHILL, Esq., of *Fixby*, gave by Will, 20*s*. yearly.

ROBERT WADE, of *Fieldhouse*, gave £5. yearly out of *Fieldhouse*, in Sowerby, but the title being disputable, it was agreed, by the parties concerned, that £3..10..0. should be paid yearly.

GILBERT SALTONSTALL, of *Rookes*, in Hipperholme, gave 20*s*. yearly out of *Rookes*, in Fee, to be confirmed by his son SAMUEL, of Hunstwick.

EDWARD MAUD, Vicar of Wakefield, gave 10*s*. yearly out of a tenement.

In a Paper in the possession of the Trustees for CROWTHER and HOPKINSON'S Charity mention is made of £8. yearly to this School, out of a Farm in North Ouram, called "*Northfield-Gate*;"—£2..2..0. from a house and lands at *Swellwell-end*, in Ovenden;—40*s*. from Mr. ALLENSON'S heirs, and Mr. GREEN'S, in *Lightcliffe*;—also a Farm, called *Balsham*.

An old Church book at Halifax contains the following entry;—

"We find, by the information of THOMAS WILKINSON, that one House, and one Lathe or Barn, at a place in Halifax, called "*Back-Lane-End*," is given to The Free School of Halifax; and we find, that the same is assured to The Governors to the use of the said Free School for ever.

Item, we hear by WILLIAM WHITACRE, that ROBERT CUNLIFFE reporteth, that The Governors of The Free School demanded 8*s*. *per* year, which were given out of his lands in *Blackledge*, to the use of The Free School, and asserted that he bought the rent out for £8. of the Governors.

"*Item*, we find, that there is given out of the House of ROBERT HARGREAVES, in *Bury-Lane*, in Halifax, 4*s*. *per annum* for ever, for the use of The Free School of Halifax."

The Foundation Charter having been broken into, through the *neglect* of THE GOVERNORS, who had not filled up the vacancies in their number as directed, the Inhabitants of the Parish and Vicarage of Halifax petitioned King GEORGE the First for a Renewal of the said Charter,—Who, on the first of July, 1726, referred their Petition to his Attorney and Solicitor General, who found,—

"That, pursuant to the Letters Patent of Queen ELIZABETH, a School-house had been erected, a Master and Usher chosen, Lands purchased and acquired within the yearly value in the said Letters Patent limited, and that the School *had flourished* for a great many years next after it's Foundation, to the great benefit of the Inhabitants of the said Parish and Vicarage, 'till through the *neglect* of the last set of Governors, the places and offices of the said School became vacant by death or removal, and the same had not been filled up as directed by the said Letters Patent, so that there was at that time but *one Governor* living, and the School, through default of due order and government, *was fallen into great decay, and disrepute*, to the great prejudice of the Inhabitants of the said Parish and Vicarage;—

" That the Petitioners were advised the said Corporation, through such neglect of filling the vacant offices of Governors, was *dissolved*;—

" And that the said Parish was very large, and much more populous than at the time of founding the said School:—

" The Agent for the Petitioners also laid before them an Affidavit of HENRY GREAME, whereby it was sworn, that the Deponent, with three other persons therein named, were, by His Grace Dr. JOHN SHARPE, late Archbishop of York, elected Governors, to make up the then number of Governors *Twelve*; that for several years last past, all the said Governors had been dead except the Deponent, and that there had been no election of Governors since that of the said late Archbishop:—

" They also certified, that as to the allegations in the Petition, that the Corporation was dissolved through the neglect of filling up the vacant offices of Governors, the point was of great consequence to The Corporation with regard to their Revenues, which might be in danger of being *lost*, if the Body Corporate was extinct:—

" Whether it was extinct or not, depended on the construction of the clause in the Charter, whereby power was given to the Archbishop of York to fill up the vacant offices of Governors, in default of The Governors making elections within the time therein prescribed; if that power was not vested in the Archbishop singly, but was to be exercised by him with the consent of *two* of the Governors, as only *one* Governor then remained, that power could not be exercised; and as no Corporate Act could be done by *one* Governor alone, the Corporation was *dissolved*;—but if the power of nomination was vested in the Archbishop alone, and the words, " with the consent of *Two* of the Governors," be taken to relate to the *Dean* only, then the Archbishop might fill up the then vacancies, and the Corporation be continued.

" The words of the Charter they represented to be doubtful, and capable of being understood either way, but the construction most favourable to The Corporation, and tending most to preserve their being and revenues, was to understand the words above-mentioned as relating to *The Dean only*, and consequently, that the power given to the Archbishop was vested in him alone, unrestrained by those words:—

" Under these circumstances they were of Opinion, that if the Archbishop of York filled up the vacancies with persons qualified as the Charter directed, and His Majesty would be pleased to grant a *new Charter* of *Confirmation* to the Body so filled up, it would be the most probable method of preserving and continuing The Corporation, and avoiding all questions touching their dissolution, and the loss of their revenues. Signed, P. YORKE, C. TALBOT, 2d June, 1727."

In consequence of this Opinion LANCELOT BLACKBURN, then Archbishop of York, by a proper instrument, under his hand and seal, dated the 23d of October, 1727, nominated and appointed RICHARD STERNE, Esq., of Woodhouse, THOMAS BURTON, Clerk, Vicar of Halifax, and NINE others, GOVERNORS of the School and it's Possessions.

And, on the 30th of July, 1730, His Majesty GEORGE the Second also granted a Charter of Confirmation.

By the STATUTES which are said to have been drawn up by The Revd. Dr. HAYTER, successively Bishop of NORWICH and of LONDON, it is ordained,—

That none shall be chosen Schoolmaster of this School, who is not well affected to the present Settlement in Church and State,—has not been Student in one of the Universities of Oxford or Cambridge for *five years* at least, and during his stay there conducted himself with discretion and sobriety, diligently pursued his studies, and is well skilled especially in Grammar and the Latin and Greek tongues;—

The Master on his election, is to be presented to the Archbishop of YORK, to be licensed to teach School by His Grace;—

And shall take an *Oath* before The President Governor and Governors, that he will instruct the Youth of this School in Religion, Learning, and good manners, and will be faithful and careful for the good of the School in all things belonging to his office and charge, according to the Trust reposed in him;—

And for the improvement of his Scholars in learning, he shall in the most familiar manner teach them Grammar, and the Latin and Greek tongues, by reading to them all or some of the Classic Writers, which follow,—as in LATIN, *Phædrus' Fables, Cornelius Nepos, Cæsar's Commentaries, Terence, Livy, Tully, Ovid, Virgil,* and *Horace,*—and in GREEK, *the Greek Testament, Xenophon, Isocrates, Demosthenes, Hesiod, Homer,* and *Sophocles,*—And he is strictly charged, to make his Scholars, according to their age and capacity, perfect Grammarians, and not to carry them on too hastily from *Prose* to *Verse,* or from *Latin* to *Greek,* and especially to be constant and strict in the examination of their Exercises;—

" These duties by the Master thus performed, yet lies there upon him at least the duty of informing his Youth in GOOD NATURE and GOOD MANNERS, which are of themselves an ORNA-

MENT to GOOD LEARNING,—We adjudge it, therefore, a part of the Master and Usher's duty, respectively to instruct their Scholars to reverence their betters in all places, to be courteous in speech to all men, in their apparel always cleanly, and in their whole carriage joining decency with modesty, and good manners with good learning;"—

No one shall be admitted as a Scholar, upon any pretext whatever, unless he be able to read *English* tolerably well, and be promoted to the *Accidence*,—And for the admission and teaching of every Scholar of the Town and Parish of Halifax, "*of what condition soever, nothing shall be demanded*;—

And for the admission of all *Foreigners* 10*s*. only shall be demanded by the Master, and for their teaching no more than 10*s*. *per* quarter,—And the quarterly payments for their teaching shall entirely belong to him under whose care they are, whether Master or Usher.

The original Endowment which is in land, is situate in the Parish of Halifax. The annual amount is uncertain.

Mr. STAINCLIFFE who received his education at this Seminary, left £100. to repair the School.

The School is open indefinitely to the children of the Parish of Halifax, free of expense, for learning the *Classics only*. There are generally from 40 to 50 Extra-Parochial Scholars.

Both the ETON and WESTMINSTER Grammars are used.

BRIAN CROWTHER, of Halifax, by his Will dated the 9th of September, 1606, bequeathed to The Governors, to the use of THE FREE GRAMMAR SCHOOL, an Annuity of £20., issuing out of lands and tenements, within the Manor of *Armyn*, to be paid half yearly, for ever, by even portions.

THOMAS MILNER, Clerk, Vicar of Bexhill, in Sussex, formerly Fellow of St. Mary Magdalen College, in Cambridge, by Will and Codicil, bearing date in 1722, gave to the said College, a Reversionary Grant of £1000., for the maintenance of THREE BACHELOR SCHOLARS, 'till Masters of Arts or Fellows, to be chosen from the Schools of Heversham, Halifax, and Leeds.

And, in the year 1736, Mrs. MARY MILNER, his Sister,

added £200. to his Benefaction, to be applied by The College to the same uses.

A Scholarship is now about £20. a year.

The present Head Master is, The Revd. ROBERT WILKINSON, B. D., who takes Boarders at Thirty-five and Forty guineas *per annum* each, according to their age.

He has the appointment of his ASSISTANTS; who do not take Boarders.

Among the Eminent Men, who have been educated at this School, may be enumerated,—

JOHN MILNER, B. D., the learned Divine. Dr. GOWER, Lady Margaret's Professor at Cambridge, gave the following character of Mr. MILNER to Mr. THORESBY, —"Great learning and piety made him really a great man; he was eminent in both, and nothing but his humility and modesty kept him from being more noted for being so. I had the happiness of much of his conversation, but still desired more. He was a Blessing to the whole Society, by the example he gave in every thing good. He died in St. John's College, Cambridge, on the 16th of Feby., 1702, in his 75th year, beloved and much lamented here, and his memory is honourable and precious among us, and will long continue so."

Dr. CYRIL JACKSON, the late venerable Dean of Christ Church.

WILLIAM JACKSON, D. D., his brother, late Lord Bishop of Oxford.

The Revd. EDWARD ELLIS, M. A., the present Second Master of Westminster School.

The Revd. Mr. SHARPE, the present Vicar of Wakefield.

HARTFORD, near RICHMOND.

OF THE FREE GRAMMAR SCHOOL at HARTFORD the Author is not able to give a description, as no answer has been received to his Letter.

HEMSWORTH, near PONTEFRACT.

THE FREE GRAMMAR SCHOOL.

THE FREE GRAMMAR SCHOOL at HEMSWORTH was founded in or about the last year of King HENRY the Eighth, 1546, by ROBERT HALGATE *otherwise* HOLGATE, a native of this place, and then Archbishop of York, and President of the King's Council established in the Northern Parts of England, —by virtue of His Majesty's Letters Patent, dated the 24th of October, in the 38th year of his reign,—

By which full power was given to His Grace or his Heirs or Assigns to found and establish THREE FREE and PERPETUAL SCHOOLS, "for the good education and instruction of Children and Boys of our Kingdom of England as well in good Morals, as in Grammar or other liberal Sciences,"—*viz.*,

One within THE CLOSE of THE CATHEDRAL or METROPOLITAN CHURCH of YORK, or within the City of York in the County of the same,—

Another in HYMSWORTH, in the West Riding in the County of York,—

And the third within the Village of OLD MALTON, in the North Riding in the County of York,—

Of which there should be Three several Preceptors or Masters, skilful in the art of Grammar or the other liberal Sciences, and their Successors, for ever,—

To be called "THE FREE SCHOOLS of ROBERT HALGATE *otherwise* HOLGATE, Archbishop of YORK,"—

And the same Three Schoolmasters to be Three several Incorporations,—to plead and to be impleaded, by the names aforesaid,—to have Three Common Seals, every of them one,—and to continue for ever in Succession according to such Statutes, Ordinances, and Constitutions as should be devised and made by the said Archbishop,—

And further, to give lands and tenements to the Masters of the said several Schools, and to their Successors for ever, to the yearly value of £56., over and above all charges and reprizes,— *viz.*, To the Master of the said School of the City of York £12.,— to the Schoolmaster of Hemsworth £24.,—and to the Schoolmaster of Old Malton £20. yearly.

The Three Free Schools were founded accordingly, and endowed with lands and tenements, it is presumed, at or about that value respectively,—And the entire Patronage of, and Nomination to, the same vested in THE ARCHBISHOP of YORK, and his Successors for ever.

The present reserved Rental of that part of the property which is now attached to Hemsworth, is about £150., besides incidental Fines on renewals of Leases, which are let for the term of 21 years, customarily renewable every 7 years, as in several Church, Prebendal, and College lands. This property is situate at Sinnington in the North Riding, and at Bilborough and Hemsworth in the West Riding of the County of York.

No subsequent Endowments have been made.

By the STATUTES which were drawn up by the munificent Founder himself, it is ordained,—

That the Master shall "teach Grammar and other Knowledges and Godlye learninge in the same Schole *freely*, without taking any stipend, wages, or other exaction of the Schollers or any of them thither resortinge to learne and know the same:"—

The Archbishop of York to appoint a Master within 20 days after any avoidance,—and in default thereof, then the Dean and Chapter of the Cathedral Church, in like manner within 20 days,—and if neither party fill the office within 40 days, then the Householders of the Parish of Hemsworth, or so many of them as shall repair to the Church when warned by the Parson, Vicar, or Curate or by two honest persons of the Parish, shall nominate *Nine* honest Householders, who, with the Archdeacon, Parson or Curate then resident, shall for that time have the grant of the office to such person "as shall be apte and able thereunto:"—

The Master to have continually under him one person to be an Usher, "to teach such Children and Scholars of the lowest Forms, as to him shall be appointed" by the Master,—his Stipend to be £4. to be paid at the Feasts of Pentecost and St. Martin, by even portions, or within 20 days after each, "uppon paine of deprivation of and from his office and room of Schoolmastershippe:"—

The Usher to be nominated by the Master,—and not to be deprived of his office, but for reasonable cause to be allowed by

The Archbishop of York, or by the other persons to whom the gift of the Mastership is appointed, or by *Six* of them at the least :—

On a vacancy in the office of Master, if the Usher be able to teach the School, it shall be given to him, " *and to none other,*"— But if he is " *not able or apte thereunto,*" then to give the same to one of the Ushers of the Free Schools in the City of *York*, or in *Old Malton*, which shall be most competent,—And if neither of them be meet for the place, then the Usher of this School shall keep and teach the Scholars, as Master, until there be a Master put into the office to exercise the same, according to the Ordinance and Foundation of the School :—

Prayers to be strictly observed both Morning and Evening :—

And to the intent, that all the lands, tenements, and hereditaments which shall be given to the Master of the School, and his Successors, for their living and maintenance of the School and effect of this Foundation, shall be kept in good order and well maintained without wasting or decay,—And that also the rents thereof may be well and truly paid to the Master, and his Successors, at the days appointed,—" And alsoe the Farmers and Tenants thereof to be able to lyve and pay the same accordingly,"—

It is, therefore, ordained that neither the Schoolmaster, nor his Successors, shall devise or let the lands, tenements, and hereditaments to any person for a longer term than 21 years,— Unless it be to some of the Founder's Kinsmen or Servants then living, and to them not above the space of 31 years,—Nor shall make any new lease, so long as any old lease doth continue,— Nor shall raise the rents, above the yearly rents then paid,— Nor shall make any lease with remainder only without the assent of the Archbishop during his life,—and after his death, to make no other lease than is already expressed, upon pain of forfeiture of the office of Mastership.

Some other clauses in the Statutes are, however, in a great measure *obsolete*, from laying down and directing customs and modes of Classical education and studies which are quite incompatible with modern times.

The Latin, Greek, and Hebrew languages *only*, are taught *free*.

But from a custom, which has at some former period crept in, probably to render the School in later times of more diffusive benefit, Children of Hemsworth and other places indiscriminately are taught at the School, *English*, *writing*, and *arithmetic*, for which they pay a Quarterage,—the highest rate being 10*s*. The number of Scholars is usually 60 or 70, and sometimes more,—and it is most gratifying to add, "*that the School flourishes, and is highly useful to the Community.*"

The ETON Grammars are alone used.

There are no Exhibitions, nor other University advantages, belonging to this School. But the Master has the presentation to the Vicarage or Perpetual Curacy of Sinnington, the emoluments of which Benefice are about £80. *per annum.*

The present most worthy Master is, The Revd. JOHN SIMPSON, who was nominated to the School, in the year 1800, by Archbishop MARKHAM.

No Common Seal was found to be in use, or in existence, at that time.

Many persons who have proved useful and valuable Members of Society, have received the rudiments of their Education at this School.

HEMSWORTH.

THE HOSPITAL.

THE HOSPITAL in the Village of HEMSWORTH was founded by the same benevolent Archbishop of York, ROBERT HOLGATE,—

Who, by his Will dated the 26th of April, 1555, constituted Sir WILLIAM PETRE, Knt., Mr. THOMAS GAUDYE, Serjeant at Law, Sir THOMAS GARGRAVE, Knt., EDWARD WOTTON, Doctor of Physic, JOHN BROXHOLME, Gentleman, JOHN GOLDING, Clerk, and THOMAS SPENCER, his Executors,—And thereby gave to them, their heirs and assigns for ever, The scite and precinct of the then late Priory of *Old Malton*, and all the demesne lands, possessions, and hereditaments in *Old Malton*, *Wykeham*, and *Howhouse*,—And the scite, precinct, and demesne lands of *Yeddingham*,—And all his lands, possessions, and hereditaments in *Huggate, Hemsworth, Felkirk, Badsworth,* The City of *York, Bishopthorpe, Pickering Lythe,* and elsewhere in the County of York,—And in *Newcastle upon Tyne,*—as are particularly specified in his Will,—which was proved on the 4th of December, 1556, in the Prerogative Court of Canterbury by JOHN BROXHOLME and THOMAS SPENCER, Gentlemen, and Sir THOMAS GARGRAVE, Knt., three of the Executors therein named, and entered in the book marked "*Kitchin,*"—

To the intent, that his Executors or the Overseers of them should within two years after his decease found, and cause to be incorporated One HOSPITAL, of one Master and Twenty Brethren and Sisters (*Ten* of each sex), in Hemsworth, to continue for ever,—

And willed, that the Master should be a Clerk and within the Holy Order of Priesthood at the time of his appointment,—That the poor people should be chosen out of the poor Parishioners of the Parish of Hemsworth, and of Felkirk, South Kirkby, and Wragby next adjoining,—

That the Master should yearly have Twenty marks, and each of the Brethren and Sisters 53*s*..4*d*. towards their support,—

That if his Executors should have after his decease, goods and chattels or lands or revenues, sufficient to fulfil his Will, and to make the said 20 marks £20., then he willed, that the Master for the time being should yearly for ever have £20., and every one of the Brethren and Sisters should have £4. yearly for ever.

The Hospital was accordingly founded, and Letters Patent for it's Incorporation obtained, dated the 17th of March, 1557.

Great abuses in the distribution of the rents by the Trustees having afterwards happened, who had "*combined together to defraud the Master, Brethren and Sisters of their lands and hereditaments,*"—and in the granting of Leases,—Bills in Chancery were at different times filed,—the last being in April, 1805, at the relation of WILLIAM WOOD WATSON, Esq., then Tenant of the estate at Old Malton,—which Suit was long protracted,—but, on the 29th of November, 1816, a Decree was pronounced amply to the honour and satisfaction of the present Master, The Revd. JOHN SIMPSON, whose fidelity and resolution, in steadily pursuing the rights of the Hospital, deserve the highest commendation.

In the prosecution of this business, Mr. SIMPSON had an able Coadjutor in Mr BOWNS, his Solicitor, who was a most affectionate friend as well as a most zealous and honourable Assistant in all his arduous trials relative to the concerns of this Hospital,—but who unfortunately died a few weeks since, in consequence of a fall from his horse,—and whose fair fame and reputation the Author gratefully and with melancholy, endeavours to record, for an elaborate description of this Establishment which was nearly the last act of his well-spent life.

The Estates belonging to the Hospital are all situate in the Three Ridings of the County of York, and are as follow,—

At Old Malton, and Pickering Marshes, 900 acres, being part of the Dissolved Monastery at Old Malton.
How-House, at Old Malton, about 32 acres.
Thorp Audlin, near Pontefract, 16 acres.
Sand Hutton, near York, about 230 acres.
Huggate on the Wolds, 574 acres.
Two tenements in the City of York.
In Hemsworth and Felkirk, some Farms amounting nearly to 200 acres.
Nine Chief or Quit rents in Hemsworth, South Kirkby, and Badsworth.

The present reserved rents are nearly £2000. *per annum*,—and as there are yet some Leases of small Farms, that have been hitherto holden at very inadequate rents and fines, when they have all expired, the *reserved Rents* of the Hospital will be something more than £2000. a year.

The Master's share of all the revenues is *One-fifth*,—and the remaining *four-fifths* are equally divided amongst the Ten Brethren and Ten Sisters, who are each to be not under *Sixty* years of age when elected, except in case of blindness or other great infirmity.

THE ELECTORS are always SEVEN, *viz.*, The Rector of Hemsworth, and the Two Churchwardens, for the time being, with Four of the "most honest" Parishioners of

Hemsworth. These are merely *Elective* Trustees, and have no further control over The Hospital.

The Lord Chancellor is the VISITOR.

The *first* SEAL of the Hospital which was made soon after the year 1555, was *lost* during the times of turbulence. The present seal is of *silver*.

HEPTONSTALL, near HALIFAX.

THE FREE GRAMMAR SCHOOL in HEPTONSTALL was founded by CHARLES GREENWOOD, Clerk, Rector of Thornhill;—who, by his Will, dated the 14th of July, 1642, bequeathed a messuage and tenement, with the appurtenances, situate near the Chuch-yard, which he had made into a School-house, "and the two messuages, tenements, and farms, and all the lands, closes, and grounds therewith, now or commonly demised, used, or occupied, with the appurtenances, in *Colden*," then of the annual value of £20..10..0., for the maintenance of a sufficient School-master, who hath well profited in learning, for teaching of Children and Inhabitants of the Town and Parish of Heptonstall, for ever. The present rental is £70. *per annum*.

The benevolent Testator also left rents for the founding of Two FELLOWSHIPS, and Two SCHOLARSHIPS in UNIVERSITY COLLEGE, Oxford, of which he had been Fellow,—but they were unfortunately *lost* by the mismanagement of his Executors.

No Answer has been received to the Author's Letter.

HIPPERHOLME, near HALIFAX.

THE FREE SCHOOL in HIPPERHOLME was founded by MATTHEW BROADLEY, Esq., of London;—who, by his Will, dated the 15th of October, 1647, gave to his Brother ISAAC BROADLEY, of Halifax, his tenements, "with all the appurtenances, situate in the Township of Hipperholme, to him and his heirs for ever, provided he pay out of the same yearly, the sum of £5. *per annum* towards the maintenance of a FREE SCHOOL, to be erected near Hipperholme aforesaid, where my Executor shall appoint:"—

"*Item*, I give towards the erecting of the said FREE SCHOOL the sum of £40.:—

"Also, I do give unto MATTHEW BROADLEY (who was sole Executor, and son of SAMUEL BROADLEY), the sum of £1000., for which Sir WILLIAM WATERS, and Sir THOMAS CHAMBERLAIN, Knt., and RICHARD SPENCER, Esq., stand bound, provided that upon receipt thereof he bestow £500. thereof, partly upon settling a convenient yearly means for the aforesaid FREE SCHOOL, and partly in providing 52*s*. in bread yearly to be given by 12*d*. each Sunday, at *Coley Chapel*, to the Poor of Hipperholme Town and The Lane-Ends."

On the 22d of May, 1661, an Indenture tripartite was made between SAMUEL SUNDERLAND, of Harden, Esq., of the first part; MATTHEW BROADLEY, of London, Gentleman, Executor of the Testator, of the second part; and WILLIAM FARRER, of Midgley, Esq., and others, of the third part,—reciting, that MATTHEW BROADLEY had received £1000., and being willing to perform the will and good intention of the Testator, he had, with the advice and consent of some of the principal Inhabitants of Hipperholme and Halifax, agreed with the above named SAMUEL SUNDERLAND for the purchase of certain lands and tenements within the Township of Hipperholme, with the sum of £500., agreeably to the Will of the Testator,—the issues and profits thereof to be applied by the Trustees yearly, for ever, as well for the payment of the annual sum of 52*s.* at the Chapel of *Coley*, as for the support and keeping in repair of the School-house for THE FREE SCHOOL, to be erected in or near the Town of Hipperholme,—and to employ all the residue of the rents, together with the annual sum of £5., for the maintenance of one learned, able, and sufficient person, being a Graduate of the Degree of Bachelor of Arts at the least, of either Oxford or Cambridge, to be Master of THE FREE SCHOOL, " to educate, and instruct in Grammar, and other Literature and Learning, the Scholars and Children of the Township and Constablery of Hipperholme *cum* Brighouse only, *gratis*, and *without any other reward, and allowance*:" to be paid to him half yearly, by equal portions:—

If the rents became raised to a greater yearly value, such increase was to be employed for the better maintenance of the Master for the time being, " *and to no other use, intent, or purpose*;" except that any Suits in law or equity, concerning the premises, should happen; in which case, the Trustees were empowered to deduct the expenses attending the same:—

When the place of Schoolmaster shall happen to be vacant, that then the Trustees, or the greater number of them, are empowered, within *One month* next after such avoidance, to nominate and appoint one other learned and fit person, qualified as aforesaid, to be Master of The Free School:—And if no Schoolmaster is by them within *Two months* chosen, it shall be lawful for the Vicar of the Vicarage of Halifax, to nominate and appoint a meet and fit person, qualified, and at the least of the Degree aforesaid, to be Master of THE FREE SCHOOL:—

THE TRUSTEES to make such Rules and Orders for the good government of the School, the Master, and the Poor People, as should seem meet and convenient:—

When only *Three* Trustees shall be living or resident within the Township of Hipperholme, or Vicarage of Halifax, they are, together with the Non-residentiaries, to convey and assure the premises, to *Nine* other sufficient persons inhabiting in Hipperholme, or the Vicarage of Halifax, so always that there be at least *Six* of the Trustees inhabitants in Hipperholme.

As it appeared that there were several defects in the Testator's Will, to the remedy of the same, this Indenture was made; but notwithstanding the agreements therein contained seem to be good and necessary, yet as doubts might be entertained of their legality for want of proper parties, and because not strictly warrantable by the Will, for the greater security of the Trustees named in the Indenture, application was made to a Commission for Charitable uses at Halifax, on the 29th of August, 1662, when the whole of their proceedings were confirmed.

On the 30th of June, 1671, SAMUEL SUNDERLAND, Esq., of *Harden*, gave, by Indenture, to RICHARD HOOKE, D. D., Vicar of Halifax, and Six other Feoffees, a messuage or tenement (part of which had been converted into a School-house) and the lands and buildings thereto belonging in Hipperholme,—and also another messuage or tenement, with the lands and buildings belonging to the same, at *Norwood-Green*, to the use of the Master, and upon the condition that out of the rents and profits of the same he should pay £6. *per annum* to an Usher of the School, who should be from time to time nominated and appointed by The Feoffees.

The present rental is £114. *per annum.*

No Answer has been received to the Author's Letter.

HORTON in Ribblesdale, near Settle.

The Free Grammar School at Horton was founded about the year 1725, by John Armitstead, Gentleman, who resided at *Dubcoat*, in this Parish,—and endowed with land, and money, with which estates were purchased by the then Trustees. One of these estates is situate in the Parish of Horton, and the other in the Parish of Giggleswick The present Rental is £180. *per annum*, but is capable of increase.

The School is open to the boys of the Parish indefinitely, free of expense. They are admitted at any age, and may remain until they have finished their Classical education. About 70 attend.

The Westminster Grammars are used; and the system of Education is such as is pursued in other Grammar Schools.

There are no Exhibitions, nor other University advantages, belonging to this School.

The present Master is, The Revd. George Holden, LL.D., Vicar of Horton, whose Salary and Emoluments are from £250. to £300. *per annum;* out of which he has to pay an Assistant, to teach writing, arithmetic, &c.

Neither of the Masters takes Pupils: but Boarding may be obtained in the Village at about 10*s*..6*d*. or 12*s*. *per* week. The terms for Education are at the discretion of the Master.

Many most respectable Gentlemen, both in the Church and State, have been educated here.

KINGSTON *upon* HULL.

THE FREE GRAMMAR SCHOOL at KINGSTON *upon* HULL was founded and endowed in 1486, by JOHN ALCOCK, a native of Beverley, and successively Bishop of Rochester, Worcester, and Ely;—who built the School-house in a garden which belonged to him, on the South side of Trinity Church.

It continued without interruption until all the Chantries and other Religious establishments, in the reign of EDWARD the Sixth, were granted to the King,—when it's revenues were seized,* and the School suppressed.

On remonstrances, however, from this and several other Towns, Commissioners were soon after appointed for the re-establishment of Schools and other purposes,—upon which it's estates were restored, and it was ordered that the late Schoolmaster, JOHN OLIVER, should be replaced and receive the Salary of £13..2..2½. formerly paid

This was confirmed in the following reign, and exemplified by the Barons of the Exchequer under their Seal, and that

---

* £10. *per annum*,—issuing out of Two tenements at

Keelby, in the County of Lincoln, -	£4..10.. 4
One tenement at *Bigby*, in the County of Lincoln,	0..16.. 8
Nine tenements at Hull, - -	4.. 1.. 6
Sundries elsewhere, not named, - -	4..17..10
	£14.. 6.. 4

Out of which 40*s*. *per annum* were to be paid to the Clerk of Trinity Church, for teaching the boys to *sing*,—and 6*s*. each to 10 of the best Scholars, if the revenue was sufficient. The Priest of Bishop ALCOCK's Chantry in the Church to be Master, and to teach the poor free boys, *gratis*.

Stipend was directed to be paid half yearly by the Receivers of the Revenues of the Crown, in the County of York, and Town of Kingston *upon* Hull.

In 1563, Mr. John Smith, Mayor, agreed with and obtained of the Vicar of Trinity Church, and of Mr. John Dixon, a piece of ground contiguous to the School, and belonging to the Vicarage, for a yearly rent, to enlarge the School-house garth.

And, in 1578, Mr. William Gee, Alderman, opened a Subscription for erecting a new School-house, himself subscribing Twenty Thousand *bricks*, and £80. in money for that purpose,—he soon after finished the present building, joining on the West end to the old School, which was thereupon converted into a Dwelling-house for the Master. The School-room is large and commodious, and is said to be one of the best in England.

The *School-house* appears to have been often in danger of being *sold* or *given away*,—and a portion of the *Garden* is stated to have been *alienated*,—it seems to be that which now belongs to the Vicarage House.

A Field, formerly used by the boys as a Play-ground, *without the Walls*, and always believed to be their property, *was sold* by The Corporation to The Dock Company, notwithstanding a strong remonstrance by the old Inhabitants, *and is now within the area of the Humber Dock!* The boys had no Documents to show, and the sum went into the com mon purse.

In 1620, The Revd. Andrew Marvel, father to the famous Patriot of that name, was Master of this School. It does not appear, who succeeded him,—but, in 1647, seven years after his death, Mr. Robert Steel was chosen to be Head Master by the Corporation, who was to have and enjoy the following benefits and gratuities,—

1. The School-master's house adjoining the School, with the great *garden* belonging to the same, rent free, paying only to the

Sheriff of the Town 2*s*..4*d*., which is the Fee-Farm owing yearly to the King.

2. That whereas there was an annual Salary of £13..2..2½ belonging to the School, which was paid by the King's Receivers,—he should, in lieu thereof, have £20. *per annum* paid to him out of the Town's Chamber, at four quarterly payments, without any further trouble,—the Town to receive the £13..2..2½ towards the £20. paid to him.

3. That he should receive £6. a year, issuing out of certain houses in the *Butchery*, left to him by Mr. GEE, in 1603. N. B. *Nothing can be found of this at present.*

4. That he should receive 20*s*. a year, quarterly, of every Scholar in the Head Master's seats under him, and of all *Strangers* for their Children, as much as he and they should agree for.

It was at the same time agreed, that Mr. STEEL should not undertake any Church duty, *lest it should be a hindrance to his School,*—And that the Usher of the School should have 10*s*. a year for every Scholar under his care.

Mr. BALDWIN who, by the force of genius and industry, rose from the humble station of a *Bricklayer* to that of a learned and eminent Critic, was a great benefactor to the School Library.

In 1666, Dr. THOMAS WATSON, formerly a Pupil of this School, afterwards Fellow of St. John's College, Cambridge, and Bishop of St. David's, was a Benefactor to it.

The Usher is appointed by the Corporation.

The School is open to all sons of Burgesses, on the payment originally of 14*s*., then of 20*s*., and lastly of 40*s*. *per annum*, for *Classical Instruction only*,—of which class there are *none* at present. The present Master has added writing and arithmetic, for which he charges £4..4..0. *per annum* to the Free boys, all of whom avail themselves of this privilege,—and £8..8..0. to sons of Non-Freemen, by consent of the Corporation. There are now about 30 Free boys, and 30 other Scholars. They are admitted at any age, and there is no prescribed time of superannuation.

The ETON Grammars are used.

There is ONE EXHIBITION of £40. *per annum*, payable

by The Corporation, to any College in Cambridge, founded by a person of the name of BERRY or BARY.

There is also ONE SCHOLARSHIP, founded by ALEXANDER METCALFE, of 12*s*..9*d*. *per* week and rooms at Clare-Hall. This was forgotten or unknown until two or three years since, when it was discovered by the Cambridge Calendar, and it is believed that the same youth now has both the Exhibition and Scholarship.

The present Master is, The Revd. GEORGE JOHN DAVIES, M. A., appointed in 1810, whose emoluments are,—

Salary paid by The Corporation*	-	£63..0..0
Paid by the King's Receiver	- -	13..2..2½
Rent of a tenement adjoining the School,,		6..0..0
		£82..2..2½

This Gentleman takes Pupils at about Sixty guineas *per annum*. He is also *Reader* in the Holy Trinity Church, for which he receives about £5.

The *Lectureship* of the Holy Trinity Church has usually been enjoyed by the Master. Mr. SCOTT, the late Master, had permission to resign the School, keeping the Lectureship, —but The Corporation, it is understood, will not separate them again.

The Masters of the School who have been distinguished, were,—

In 1620. Revd. ANDREW MARVELL, M. A.
1665. JOHN CATLYN.
1720. JOHN CLARKE, the Translator of *Suetonius* and *Sallust*,—removed to Gloucester, where he died.
1767. Revd. JOSEPH MILNER, M. A., author of "*The History of the Church*,"—who was highly cele-

* The Corporation are in trust for certain Houses, and, it is presumed, pay the £63. out of that estate,—but no particulars are known.

brated all over the North, and produced many excellent Scholars.

1798, Revd. JOSIAH RODWELL, M. A.

1801, Revd. JOHN SCOTT, M. A., author of several Sermons,—resigned in 1810.

Among the Eminent men who have been educated here, may be mentioned,—

THOMAS JOHNSON, M. D., Editor of "*Gerard's* Herbal,"—supposed to have been killed at *Basing-House* in 1644.

ANDREW MARVELL, M. P. for Hull, the Patriot and Poet.

THOMAS WATSON, D. D., Bishop of St. David's,—died in 1714.

GREGORY SHARPE, D. D., Master of the Temple, and Chaplain in Ordinary to His Majesty.

The Revd. WILLIAM MASON, M. A., the Poet.

The Revd. DAVID BROWN, Chaplain at Calcutta, and Author of a volume of Sermons,—died in 1812.

WILLIAM WILBERFORCE, Esq., M. P. for Hull and the County of York,—removed to Pocklington.

The Revd. FRANCIS WRANGHAM, M. A., the learned Vicar of Hunmanby.

ISAAC MILNER, D. D., the present Dean of Carlisle.

The Revd. WILLIAM DEALTRY, B. D., Rector of Clapham.

There are a few good books in the LIBRARY, including STEPHENS's *Thesaurus*,—a List of Benefactors,—and a fine Portrait of WILLIAM GEE, 1568 *æt.* 45.

KIRK LEATHAM, near GUISBROUGH.

The Stately HOSPITAL at KIRK LEATHAM was founded in 1676, by Sir WILLIAM TURNER, Lord Mayor of London in 1669,—

Who, by his Will, bequeathed £5000. for founding a FREE GRAMMAR SCHOOL here, which was erected in 1709, by CHOLMLEY TURNER, Esq., his nephew, and is a large and handsome quadrangular building near The Hospital.

The Master's Salary is £100, and that of the Usher £50.; but both these offices are now *Sinecures*, the School having been entirely "*discontinued*," about thirty years since, by the late Sir CHARLES TURNER.

The Building contained apartments for the Master, and Usher, as well as the School-room; but *it is now occupied in tenements by various Mechanics*, &c., *Servants to Lady* TURNER.

Mr. JOHN IRVINE, the family *Steward*, holds the *Sinecure* office of *Master*,—and The Revd. JAMES SHAW, Minister of Kirk Leatham, that of *Usher*.

The Lord or Lady of the Manor of Kirk Leatham, who is sole Governor or Governess of THE HOSPITAL, is sole Trustee for THE SCHOOL also.

KIRKBY ON THE HILL, near RICHMOND.

THE SCHOOL and HOSPITAL of ST. JOHN the BAPTIST at KIRKBY ON THE HILL, in the Parish of Kirkby Ravenswath, was founded by JOHN DAKYN, LL. D., Rector of that Church.—(and who had been concerned as Commissioner in the reign of HENRY the Eighth, to take an account of the Religious Houses of Richmondshire,)—by License granted to him for that purpose, dated the 26th of October, in the 2d and 3d of PHILIP and Mary, 1566.

By the sixth Statute it is directed,—

"Et quod post mortem meam, quoties officium Ludimagistri prædicti per mortem, privationem, promotionem, aut alio quovis modo vacare contigerit, duo Gardiani prædicti, cum Rectore, Vicario, vel Parocho dictæ ecclesiæ parochialis de Kirkby Ravenswath, ac duobus ad minus Gardianis ejusdem ecclesiæ parochialis, simul conveniant de alio Ludimagistro collocuturi. Et illi omnes vel eorum major pars alium in demortui vel amoti locum substituant, nempe virum honestum, irreprehensibilem, in ordine sacerdotali constitutum, *non religiosum,** nullibi saltem cum curâ animarum beneficiatum, neque officiatum, doctum et in arte grammaticâ peritum, *qui pueros ipsius parochiæ de Kirkby Ravenswath, et alios ad se confluentes gratis docebit,* et in grammaticâ, rhetoricâ, et metro pro cujusque pueri ingenii capacitate instruet et informabit diligenter."

"Quod si dicti duo Gardiani et alii prænominati intra sexaginta dies a die mortis, privationis, seu promotionis hujusmodi illam substitutionem facere neglexerint, ex tunc substitutio hujusmodi ad Decanum et Capitulum Eboraci (modo ipsi intra triginta dierum spatium a tempore notitiæ id perficiant) pertinebit. Et si ipsi intra dictos triginta dies præmissa facere neglexerint, ex tunc provisio et ordinatio dicti Ludimagistri ad Episcopum Cestrensem (Sede plenâ), vel ad Decanum et Capitulum ibidem (Sede vacante), illâ tantum vice devolvatur."

"Dictusque Ludimagister novem libras quolibet anno ad quatuor anni terminos,—per æquales portiones per anums dicto-

* The same injunction occurs at Manchester.

rum duorum Gardianorum, de redditibus et proventibus dicti Hospitalis, pro salario sive stipendio suo percipiet et habebit."

Within seven days after his appointment the Master is to take an Oath,—

That he will "freely, without exacting of any money or other gains, diligently instruct and teach the Children of this Parish, and *all other that shall resort to him,* in Grammar and other humane Doctrine, according to the Statutes:"—

And that he will "not read unto them any corrupt or reprobate books or works, set forth at any time *contrary to the determination of the universal Catholic Church,* whereby they might be infected in their youth with any kind of Heresy or corrupt Doctrine, or be induced to an insolent manner of living."

In the Register of THE LOW CHURCH at Richmond is an entry, importing that "RICHARD SNELL was *brut,* i. e., *burned,* September 9th, 1558," supposed in Newbiggin.

Concerning this horrid matter, JOHN FOX, the Martyrologist, informs us, that "there were *Two* of the SNELLS taken up for their *Religion.* One, after his toes were rotted off by lying in Prison by order of DAKINS, the Bishop of Chester's Commissary, went upon crutches; *at last went to Mass,* having *a certain sum of money given him* by the people; but, in three or four days after, *drowned himself* in a river, called *Swail,* by Richmond.—The other SNELL was *burned.*"

The concerns of this Institution are now (1st of May, 1818,) in Chancery, as the Decree of Commissioners under the Chancellor's authority in 1803, is not yet regularly confirmed.

By that Decree, the Head Master, (The Revd. THOMAS JACKSON, appointed in 1795), has a Salary assigned him amounting nearly to a *Sixth* part of the whole rental, and the Usher to an *Eighteenth,* at that time £150. and £50. a year,—now by increase of rents about £210. and £70. respectively.

KNARESBOROUGH.

THE FREE GRAMMAR SCHOOL at KNARESBOROUGH was founded by Letters Patent, dated the 26th of October, in the 14th of King JAMES the First, 1617, which recite,—

That ROBERT CHALONER, S. T. D., a native of the Town of Gouldesborough, and then Rector of the Parish Church of Amersham, in the County of Buckingham, of his pious affection and good disposition for the education and instruction of boys and youth of the Parishioners of Knaresborough and Gouldesborough, and of others whomsoever, *as well poor as rich*, intended to found and erect a Free Grammar School in the Town of Knaresborough, and to endow the same with a yearly rent of £20., for the better support of the Master,—

And that PETER BENSON, one of the Inhabitants of Knaresborough, designed a certain house with a garden there, adjoining the Church-yard, commonly called "*The School House*," from thenceforth to be the Grammar School, and to be applied to the instruction and education of boys and youth therein,—which House Mr. BENSON intended to grant to The Governors of the School,—

And that Mr. CHALONER, and the Inhabitants of the Towns aforesaid, had prayed that the School so designed might have perpetual succession,—

His Majesty, therefore, willing to promote good education and instruction of boys and youth, ordained,—

That the house aforesaid should be a Grammar School, for the education and instruction of boys and youth whomsoever, *as well poor as rich*, as well in Grammar as in the accidence and other inferior books,—to be called, "THE FREE GRAMMAR SCHOOL of King JAMES in KNARESBROUGHE of the Foundation of ROBERT CHALONER, S. T. D."—with one Master,—

That there shall be within the Parish of Knaresborough and Town of Gouldesborough, or either of them, SIXTEEN Men of the most discreet and honest Inhabitants, whereof the Rector of Knaresborough for the time being to be one,—who shall be GOVERNORS, and be a Body Corporate for ever, with perpetual Succession,—and be able to receive, purchase, and possess lands and premises, not exceeding the clear yearly value of £100.,—to plead and be impleaded,—and to have a Common Seal,—

That, when any of the Governors shall die, or dwell with his Family out of those Towns for *one year*, the rest of the Governors shall elect another of the Inhabitants in his place,—

The Founder during his life, and, after his decease, the Governors shall nominate the Master, so often as a Vacancy shall happen,—and have power to remove him upon reasonable cause,—

If, upon a vacancy, The Founder during his life, or the Governors after his decease, shall not elect another Master within *Three months*, The Archbishop of York is then to appoint,—

ROBERT CHALONER during his life to make Statutes and Ordinances in writing, for the government o the Master and Scholars,—

Power is given to Mr. CHALONER to grant by Deed inrolled or not inrolled to the Governors, an annual Rent of £20. issuing out of a messuage and lands in *Wavendon*, in the County of Buckingham, for the better support of the School and the Master,—

The Governors are likewise empowered to receive and purchase lands and possessions, not exceeding the clear yearly value of £100.,—The issues, rents and revenues of all lands to be given and assigned to the support of the same School, to be from time to time converted to the maintenance of the Master, and to the support and maintenance or erection of the School-house,—and for defence of the lands and possessions,—or to instruct the boys *to sing or write*,—and not to any other uses or intents.

A further Benefaction of £150. was made by the Will of ROBERT STOCKDALE, Esq., of Knaresborough, who died on the 2d of February, 1816,—but, by the Legacy duty, &c., it is reduced to about £130.

There are no STATUTES or ORDINANCES, except those which are contained in the Charter.

The School is open to the boys of the Parish of Knaresborough and of the Village of Goldsborough indefinitely, and *gratuitously*,—but, notwithstanding such liability in the Master, he is always *paid* by the Parents of the Children, *as if there was no Endowment*. There is no prescribed age of admission, or superannuation. The Governors have a right to nominate the Scholars, but they never exercise that privilege.

The system of education is at the discretion of the Master.

There are no Exhibitions, nor other University advantages.

The present Master is, The Revd. WILLIAM HENRY POWELL, who is a Bachelor, and resides in lodgings: and consequently, no Scholars are taken to board.

LEEDS.

The first Endowment of THE FREE GRAMMAR SCHOOL at LEEDS, which has since been so eminently useful, is contained in the Will of Sir WILLIAM SHEAFIELD, Priest, dated the 6th of March, in the fifth year of the reign of King EDWARD the Sixth, 1552, by which he vested in Sir JOHN NEVILE, Knight, and Sixteen others, as Co-Feoffees, certain Copyhold lands situate near *Shipscar Bridge*, "for finding sustentation and living of one honest, substantial, learned man to be a Schoole Maister, to teach and instruc- freely for ever all such yonge Scholars, Youths, and Children as shall come and resort to him from time to time, to be taught, instructed, and informed in such a School-house as shall be founded, erected, and builded by the Paryshioners of the said Town and Parish of Leedes." Upon condition, that if the Parishioners should not found a School-house, and also purchase unto the Schoolmaster for the time being a sufficient living of other lands, together with his gift, to the clear yearly value of £10., for ever, within four years after his decease, then the Feoffees should stand seized to the use of the poor Inhabitants of Leeds. The Testator directed, that his Feoffees and their Heirs for ever should have the nomination, election, and appointment of the said Schoolmaster; and gave them power to put him out for reasonable cause, at their discretion; "The best man's voice to take no more place than the honest poorest man of them."

Subsequent Endowments, in houses and land, were made, as will be particularized in the Report hereafter mentioned.

The original School being in a very inconvenient situation was removed by the munificence of JOHN HARRISON, Esq., Alderman of Leeds, to a pleasant field of his own, which he inclosed with a substantial brick wall, and in the midst of the Quadrangle erected the present Edifice.

To this building an addition was made by GODFREY LAWSON, Esq., in 1692; the Lower apartment being allotted to the Scholars; and the Room over it being appropriated to a "*growing Library;*" which, it is to be lamented, has suffered diminution, although it still contains some valuable Books.

Application having been made to The Court of Chancery to permit the appropriation of part of the Funds of this Charity, to procure Masters for *French, German,* and to other Establishments with a view to *Commerce,*—" THE ATTORNEY-GENERAL *versus* WHITELEY,"—The Case was argued and determined, on the 20th of July 1805, and is reported as follows, in VESEY'S Chancery Reports, *vol.* XI. *Part* II. *pp.* 241—252.

By the Decree, pronounced in this Cause, on the 11th of December, 1797, an inquiry was directed, among other things, as to what Estates were derived under the respective Donations to the Charity; what Salaries were paid to the Master and Usher of THE FREE GRAMMAR SCHOOL of LEEDS; how many Boys there then were in the School, and from time to time had been for the last Five years; whether it would be proper to make any and what additional Salary to such Master or Usher in future; and whether it would be proper and for the benefit of the Charity to have any other Master or Masters to teach Writing, Arithmetic, and other Languages besides the Greek and Latin; and it was ordered, that the Master should consider of a proper scheme for carrying the Charity into execution.

The Master's Report stated the first Donation, by the Will of WILLIAM SHEAFIELD, dated the 6th of March, 1552, as before mentioned.

The Report also stated a surrender of Copyhold premises on the 13th of May, in the Second year of PHILIP and MARY, by RICHARD BANK and his Wife, to the use and sustentation of The Free Grammar School in Leeds:—A Feoffment by Sir WILLIAM ARMYSTEAD in the same reign, with a declaration, that the Feoffees should employ the profits towards the finding of one *Priest* sufficiently learned to teach a Free Grammar School within the Town of Leeds for ever, for all such as should repair thereto, without taking any money more or less for teaching of the said Children or Scholars, saving of 1*d.* of every Scholar to enter his name in the Master's book, *if the Scholar have a penny;* and, *if not,* to enter and continue freely *without any paying:*—And a surrender of Copyhold premises by JOHN MOORE and others, in the Thirty-seventh year of Queen ELIZABETH, to the use, and for the support and maintenance of a Free Grammar School in Leeds.

That, by an Inquisition, on the 28th of April, in the Eighteenth year of King JAMES the First, it was found, that LAWRENCE RAWSON surrendered Copyhold premises to the sustentation, reparation, and free use of the Grammar School of Leeds, and other premises, as well to the same use, as of a Master, Usher, and Scholars, of the said School:—That certain persons took of Queen ELIZABETH other premises to the use of the School, and the King's Highways in Leeds; but that the Rents are solely applied to the use of The Free School:—That WILLIAM ROBINSON surrendered other premises, towards the keeping and maintaining of The Free Grammar School of Leeds; and that all the last mentioned premises were purchased with money belonging to The Free Grammar School of Leeds.

By another Inquisition, in the Thirteenth year of King CHARLES the First, it was found, that other lands were devised towards the maintenance of the said School; and that Sir THOMAS SHEAFIELD devised several Houses, the rent whereof was to go to the maintenance of The Free School of Leeds:—That JOHN HARRISON by his Will, in 1653, directed as to a House, then used as a Grammar School, that it should be for a Master and Usher to teach Scholars in for ever.

The Master then certified, that it did not appear to him, that there was any substantial difference between the uses of the several Donations; but *they are all meant to be applicable for the benefit of The Grammar School* in Leeds, originating under the Will of Sir WILLIAM SHEAFIELD.

He farther stated, that it appeared to him by the Affidavit of the Relators, Members of The Committee for the management of the Funds of The School in question, that the Tuition of the Scholars *was confined* to the *Greek* and *Latin* Tongues *solely*; and *did not extend to any other branch of Education whatever*; and particularly, that the teaching of *Writing* and *Arithmetic*, or of the *French* and other living Languages, formed *no part* of the present system of the School:—That the Town of Leeds and it's neighbourhood had of late years increased very much in trade and population, as well in respect of it's Inland trade, which was very considerable, as of a very extensive Foreign trade, carried on in a direct manner to most parts of Europe, independently of and without the intervention of the Merchants or Markets of London; and, therefore, the learning of *French* and other modern living Languages was become a matter of great utility to the Merchants of Leeds, and to such of the Inhabitants as were concerned in the Trade thereof; and the teaching of such living languages was become a proper and very useful part of the Education of Youths intended for trade:—That for the reasons aforesaid, and other reasons, arising out of the circumstances and situation of the Town of Leeds and the inhabitants thereof, the plan of Education, then practised in the said Grammar School, was in the judgment of the Deponents become inefficient for the purpose of giving the necessary and most suitable qualifications to the rising generation of that Town and it's Neighbourhood; and it would be proper and for the benefit of the Charity to have Masters appointed to teach *Writing* and *Arithmetic,* and the *French* and *German,* and such other living, languages, as were usually considered to form the basis of a mercantile or commercial Education: and that such an extended plan of Education in the School would be very useful to the inhabitants of the Town of Leeds, and would be the means of greatly increasing the number of Scholars, which had much decreased notwithstanding the extended trade and increased population of the Town; and, after a sufficient maintenance was provided for the Defendants, the Master and Usher, there would be a surplus arising from the Funds of the Charity; which might be usefully applied in Salaries of such additional Masters, as might be employed in the extended plan of Education above suggested.

The Master then farther certified, that a Salary of £126. a year is paid to the Master, and a Gratuity of about £75. at *Christmas;*—and a Salary of £63. a year to the Usher, and a Gratuity of £42.; that at the date of the Decree, the 11th of December 1797, there were 49 boys in the School; and there had been for the preceding five years about 44; and it appearing, that there is nothing in the original Institution and Endowment of this Charity, which necessarily excludes the teaching of any useful kind of learning, and that from the present situation and circumstances of the Town of Leeds (for the benefit whereof the Charity was instituted) it will be very beneficial to the inhabitants to employ part of the Funds towards teaching those things, which may be useful in Trade and Commerce, he approved of adding to the present establishment one *German* Master and one *French* Master, to teach those languages, and a Master for teaching *Algebra* and the *Mathematics;* but it appearing to him, that there are a variety of Schools in Leeds already for teaching *Writing* and *Arithmetic,* where boys may be instructed at a very small expense in those branches of Education, and that a greater proportion of prejudice may arise to such Seminaries, than of benefit to the Inhabitants of the Town of Leeds, to have Writing and Arithmetic free of expense, he therefore approved only of those three additional Masters: to be elected in like manner, as the Master and Usher from time to time have been.

The Report farther stated, that as it was uncertain, what number of Scholars there may be upon this plan, the Master gave no opinion upon the propriety of any additional Salary to the Master and Usher; and for the same reason it should be left open to the Relators and their Successors to give reasonable Stipends to the additional Masters from time to time, and to vary the Salaries of the present Master and Usher from time to time, according to the increase and decrease of the Scholars.

An exception was taken to this Report by the Defendant, THE MASTER: on the ground, that this School was intended for a Free *Grammar* School only: *not* for *Algebra*, the *Mathematics*, or the *modern* languages: that it does not appear, the persons, who endowed the School, intended that more than one Master, and one Usher, should be appointed and endowed; and therefore, no more ought to be appointed; especially as no complaint is made, that they are not sufficient to instruct the number of boys, who attended or wish to attend a Free Grammar School in Leeds; and, as the estates, belonging to the School, are chiefly Copyhold, a considerable part of the Rents must be set apart to pay Fines and for Repairs; and the Residue will not constitute unreasonable Salaries for two men of Learning; who are to derive no other benefit from the School than their Salaries: that the utility of teaching the *French* and *German* languages in future must depend upon accident, and political and commercial circumstances; and, therefore, is not proper to be made a permanent part of an Institution like the present; and, in case the Master and Usher are not entitled to the whole of the Rents and Profits, after setting apart sufficient for the Fines, &c., their salaries ought to be augmented; and they ought not to be left to the discretion of The Committee; but specific directions should be given upon that head.

Mr. RICHARDS and Mr. BELL, in support of the Exception, contended, that this was the first attempt to divert a Charitable Foundation from it's original design; and, that it is of the utmost importance to keep up Foundations of this nature, and to secure to the Master a respectable situation.

THE ATTORNEY GENERAL and Mr. MARTIN, for the Report.

THE LORD CHANCELLOR, after reasoning upon the Case, then proceeded to direct:—

Taking upon me now to correct the omission of this Decree, and to declare, what this Foundation is, I am of opinion upon the evidence now before me, that The Free School in Leeds is a Free Grammar School, for teaching Grammatically the Learned languages, according to Dr. JOHNSON's definition; upon circumstances, without variation in fact since the year 1553; to which I cling, as better interpreters of the real nature of the Charity than any criticism I can form, or construction upon the Instruments; for, with the exception of the Highway, the original Founder proposed to the Inhabitants the benefit of this

Donation by his Will for a Free School: it appears, that there has been a Free School in Leeds; and to this time every Charity, given by these instruments, has been by Inquisition and Decrees upon them applied in fact for the benefit of The Free School in Leeds; in which nothing has been taught but the Learned languages; and under such facts the result of the Evidence is, that The Free School in Leeds is a Free Grammar School for teaching grammatically the Learned Languages. The reason of my opinion is, that I do not apprehend, it is competent to this Court, as long as it can find any means of applying the Charitable Fund to the Charity, as created by the Founder, upon any general notion, that any other application would be more beneficial to the Inhabitants of the place, to change the nature of the Charity. A Case may arise, in which the Will cannot be obeyed: but then the Fund will not go to the Heir; upon the principle, that an application is to be made, as near as may be; growing out of another principle, that you are to apply it to the object intended, if you can. It must, therefore, appear by the Master's Report, that the Court must despair of attaining that object: or the Court cannot enter into the Question, in what other way the Fund is to be applied:—

"Declare, that the Charity intended to be established by the first Donation, mentioned in the Master's Report, is the sustentation and maintenance of a Free Grammar School for the teaching the Learned languages: that the Free School in Leeds is a Free Grammar School for the teaching grammatically the Learned languages; and that it appears to the Court, that the free teaching thereof is the Charity intended to be established by the several Donations, mentioned in the Report, so far as the same relate to the School. With that Declaration let the Master review his Report as to any plan they may think proper to lay before him; and it will be open to him to consider, what is proper and necessary, not for the benefit of the Inhabitants of Leeds, but for the benefit of the Charity, declared to be such upon this Record. I send it to the Master in that large way; for, though it is determined, that the Charity is a Charity for the purpose of teaching the Learned languages, yet it is open to consideration, what arrangement as to the management and the Salaries and Gratuities to the Masters, may upon the whole be proper for promoting that Charity. But it goes much farther; for it is right to make that Declaration in the Decree."

No alteration has been made in the system of Education, so long and so beneficially observed in this eminent School.

In the year 1780, an excellent House near the School was erected by The Trustees, for the use of The Master.

The School is open to all Boys in the Borough or Parish of Leeds, free of expense. There are at present about 70 boys in the School. Boys are admitted by qualification, not by age; and there is no prescribed time for Superannuation. The form of Admission is, by public examination holden half yearly by The Masters, and which The Trustees may attend.

The ETON Latin and Greek Grammars are used. THE LOWER SCHOOL begins with the rudiments of Latin, and carries on the education of it's Scholars until they are perfect in the rudiments of Greek, when they are examined once a year, and if deemed fit, are advanced to THE UPPER SCHOOL.

By a Codicil to the Will of Lady ELIZABETH HASTINGS, the daughter of THEOPHILUS Earl of HUNTINGDON, dated the 24th of April, 1739, she bequeathes,—

" *First,* I give and devise all my mannors, lands, and hereditaments in *Wheldale,* otherwise called *Queldale,* in the West Riding of the County of York, with all the Quit Rents or Chief Rents, and Royalties belonging to the same, to THE PROVOST and SCHOLARS of QUEEN'S COLLEGE, in the University of Oxford, for ever,—subject nevertheless to a term of *Ninety* and *Nine Years,* determinable upon the lives of one or more Annuitants as the case shall be, and as is more fully explained in a former Codicil for charging Annuitys for lives, pursuant to a power reserved by my Will,—

" And to the end that The Provost may have true and speedy information of the state of the Annuitants, the Bailiff for the time being, who collects the rents of the said Premises, shall at the end of every year send a list of the names of the Annuitants, then alive, to The Provost of the said College, signed by the Bailiff and one or more of the Trustees,—As also upon the death of the last Annuitant, as soon as he receives information of it, immediately send notice thereof to the said Provost in writing, signed also by himself and one or more of the Trustees,—

" And I will, that, after the expiration of the said term of 99 years determinable as aforesaid, ONE HUNDRED and FORTY POUNDS, out of the clear rents and profits of the same Premises, shall from time to time be applied for EXHIBITIONS towards the maintenance of FIVE poor SCHOLARS of the said College, to be nominated and elected in manner hereinafter directed; Each of which poor Scholars shall be entitled to a yearly payment of £28., but shall receive for the *Four* first years (to be computed from the Pentecost preceding the Election) only £20. each year by Quarterly or Half yearly payments,—my will being, that the remaining £8. out of each sum of £28. be laid up and deposited yearly in the College Chest, and that out of this deposited money, £20. shall be paid at the middle of the *Fifth* year, and £20. more at the end of the said year (over and above the first mentioned yearly payments) to each of the said Exhibitioners that shall have taken their Batchelor of Arts Degree, and shall strictly and religiously conform to the directions, limitations, and conditions hereinafter given, made, or expressed,—

"And in regard to the qualifications, nomination, and election of poor Scholars, who shall be entitled to such Exhibitions, my Will is, that EIGHT of the principal Schools in the County of York, *viz.*, those of LEEDS, WAKEFIELD, BRADFORD, BEVERLY, SKIPTON, SEDBERGH, RIPPON, and SHERBURN,—and Two more, in the County of Westmoreland, *viz.*, APPLEBY, and HAVERSHAM,—and Two more, in Cumberland, *viz.*, ST. BEES, and PENRITH,—shall each of them have the priviledge or liberty of sending ONE POOR SCHOLAR every *Five* years to the place of nomination hereinafter appointed,—

"Provided, the Head Master of each School send along with such Scholar a Certificate, that he hath distinguished himself above the rest of the same rank in his School for his Morals and Learning,—That such Scholar is well grounded in the Principles of the Church of England as by law established.—That he hath competent parts and remarkable industry, and that he hath applied himself to the reading of Greek Authors at least *Four* years,—

"And Provided also, that each Candidate brings a Certificate of his age from the Register, signed by the Minister and Churchwardens of the Parish he was born in. It being required, that every Candidate shall be entered upon the *Nineteenth* year of his age, and none be allowed to stand after his *One* and *Twentieth* is compleated,—

"I will also, that fair copys of this Codicil be writ out in parchment, and sent to every one of the said respective Schools there, to be safely kept by the Master for the time being, who is desired to read the same or cause it to be read to the Scholars, Candidates for the Exhibitions, four times or oftener in the Two last years antecedent to the Election,—

"And I make it my earnest request, that the RECTORS of BERWICK SPOFFORTH, and BOLTON PERCY, and the VICARS of LEEDS, LEDSHAM, THORP-ARCH, and COLLINGHAM, in the County of York, will in the year wherein the Exhibitions shall commence (if the year be not too far advanced, for giving notice as is hereafter directed), and so likewise at the expiration of every FIVE years for ever after, meet together at the best Inn in ABBERFORD or ABBERFORTH, in the same County, *viz.*, on Thursday in Whitson-week before Eight of the clock in the Morning,—

"Also all the boys to meet at the said best Inn at ABBERFORTH the night preceding the day of nomination, in order to be ready to begin their Exercises the next morning,—

"And I intreat the Rectors and Vicars aforenamed will be there half an hour after Seven, that they may choose the Boys' Morning Exercise, and put them upon beginning the same by Eight of the clock,—

"And my Will is, that their Exercise be a part of an Oration in TULLY not exceeding eight or ten lines to be translated into *English*, and part of an Oration in DEMOSTHENES about the said number of lines to be translated into *Latin*,—And two or three verses of the Latin Testament to be translated into *Greek*,—And four books of each sort being provided, immediately put them upon beginning the Translations, *four* of the boys being imployed in one kind of translation, *four* in a secound, and *four* in a third,—And then changing the books, 'till they have gone through the *three* several translations,—

"And whilst the boys are making their Morning Exercise, the said Rectors and Vicars, or the greater number of them, shall proceed to chuse the Afternoon's Exercise (which shall be upon *Two* subjects),—one, of Practical Divinity out of the Church Catechism, upon which each boy shall give his thoughts in Latin, in not fewer than *eight* lines nor more than *twelve*,—the other subject, some distinguished sentence of a Classick Author, upon which each boy shall write *Two* Distichs of verses,—All which translations and compositions are to be written out fair upon one sheet of paper, and signed by the name of each boy they belong to, and then shewed to every nominating Rector and Vicar, who are desired impartially to weigh and consider, and return TEN of the best of the said Exercises (each of which Ten to be signed by the greater number of the Rectors and Vicars present) to The Provost and Fellows of Queen's College, in the University of Oxford,—

"And when the said Provost and Fellows have received the same, they are hereby required to meet together as soon after as conveniently may be, to examine into them carefully and impartially, and choose out of them EIGHT of the best performances which appear the best, which done the names subscribed to those EIGHT shall be fairly written each in a distinct paper, and the papers rolled up and put into an Urn or Vase by The Provost, or, in his absence, by the Vice-Provost or Senior Fellow, and, after having been shaken well together in the Urn, shall be drawn out of the same by some person whom he or they shall appoint,—And those FIVE, whose names are first drawn, shall to all intents and purposes be held duly elected and intitled to the whole profits each of his Exhibition, for the space of *Five* years as before provided from Pentecost then next preceding the Election,—

"And though this method of choosing by *lot* may be called by some Superstition or Enthusiasm, yet as the advice was given by an Orthodox and Pious Prelate of the Church of England as leaving something to Providence, and as it will be a means to save the Scholars the trouble and expense of a journey to Oxford under too great an uncertainty of being elected, I will this method of ballotting be for ever observed,—

"Provided also, and my will is, that no more sons than one of the same person shall be nominated or elected to or for any of the said Exhibitions,—

"And, as my intention in continuing the Exhibitions to each person for five years, is to take away from them all necessity of entering precipitately into Holy Orders, and to give them an opportunity of laying in some sort a sound foundation of Divine as well as Human Learning, so my desire is, that the *four* first years they apply themselves as they shall be directed in their College and University chiefly to the Arts and Sciences,—but that the *fifth* year be employed wholly in Divinity, Church History, and the Apostolical Fathers in the original tongues,—

"And, it is farther required, that, from their first admission into the College, they be obliged to spend one hour every Morning in the study of the Holy Scriptures, and to write their own explications of such particular places and passages of Holy Scripture as their Tutors shall think proper to appoint them, and which their Tutors are required to call for at proper times, —And that in a convenient time, before the expiration of their *fourth* year, each of them shall be obliged to translate into English such a portion of ST. CHRYSOSTOM's book "*De Sacerdotio*" (published by Mr. HUGHES, or any other better edition if such shall hereafter be published), as the Provost or their Tutors shall appoint, or, if it be thought feasible, to make an abstract of the whole,—And I beg of the Provost to recommend this in a particular manner to their Tutors,—

"It is also enjoined, that as soon as any of them shall have taken the Degree of Batchelor of Arts, they shall forthwith apply themselves to the Provost or their Tutors for their particular directions in their Theological studies to qualify them for Holy Orders, and be obliged to make proper abstracts or observations in writing from the several Authors they are appointed to read, which at the end of each Term, or at least every half year, shall be carried by them to the Provost, that he may be a witness of their proficiency, or punish them for their neglect,—And I most earnestly beg the Provost to insist upon their so doing,—

" Also my will and meaning is, that none of the said Exhibitions shall be continued to one and the same person above the space of *Five* years, from the time of his admission,—

" And, that if any such Scholar or Exhibitioner shall before the said five years are completed, either marry or accept of any Ecclesiastical Benefice, Curacy, or *School*, or enter into Holy Orders, from thenceforth his place shall become vacant,—

" Provided also, and my will and desire further is, that in case any of the said Rectorys or Vicarages shall happen to be vacant at the time of such meeting of the nominating Rectors and Vicars, or any of the said Rectors or Vicars shall be absent from such meeting, such of the said Rectors and Vicars as are present at such meeting, in case they are *five* in number, shall proceed to examine, nominate, and certify in such manner as is before directed,—

" And, in case it shall appear to the Vicar of LEDSHAM (who is desired to have previous information for a month before, what persons will be present and to move every one concerned by Letter, or otherwise, for his personal attendance), that only *four* of the Rectors and Vicars can be at the Meeting, he is hereby further desired to request the Rector of METHLEY or the Vicar of PONTEFRACT to make up the *fifth*,—And if only *Two* can be present, to desire the Vicar of ABBERFORD, and both the said Rector of METHLEY and Vicar of PONTEFRACT to appear and act,—

" And, in case the said Rectors and Vicars shall neglect to nominate as aforesaid, or shall be equally divided in their choice, The Provost and Fellows of the said College are hereby empowered to appoint in the *last* case one person as an Umpire,—And in the *first* case, *Five* proper persons residing as near as may be to the place of Meeting to fill up the vacancys within Three Calendar months after the time hereby appointed for the nomination,—Provided, they observe the qualifications, rules, and restrictions herein before prescribed,—

" Provided also, and my will further is, that every such Exhibitioner shall regularly observe and strictly conform himself to the rules and orders of the said College, upon pain of forfeiting the benefit of such Exhibition for such time, as the said Provost shall think fit,—

" And, that it shall be lawful to and for the Provost and greater part of the resident Fellows for the time being of the said College, in case of notorious obstinacy, immorality, or neglect of duty, after three admonitions in a public convention called by the said Provost, to deprive such Scholar of his Exhibition,—

"Provided also, that every *fifth* year notice be sent, that the term of five years is near expiring, by the Provost and Fellows of the said College or their Agent to the said Vicar of LEDSHAM, for the time being, Three months at least before the Thursday in Whitsun-Week, who is required immediately to give notice of meeting on the said Thursday to the Rectors and other Vicars, and to the Schoolmasters of all the Schools for the time being, who have any right to send boys,—

"Provided also, £10. be allowed and paid every five years out of the premises by The Provost and Fellows of Queen's College for ever to the Vicar of LEDSHAM and his Successors, £1. thereof being to the said Vicar for his trouble in giving notice, and the other £9. towards the defraying of the expenses of the Meeting of the said Rectors and Vicars, and poor Scholars, at the time and place beforementioned, and towards defraying the travelling expenses of the poor Scholars, each Scholar from every School in Yorkshire that, for the time being, has the privilege of sending, being allowed 5*s*., and each Scholar from all the Schools in Westmoreland and Cumberland that, for the time being, hath the same privilege, being allowed 10*s*.,—

"Provided also, if any one or more of these Twelve Schools herein mentioned, shall so far come to decay as to have no Scholar or Scholars returned by the Rectors and Vicars, to take their lot by ballotting as before appointed, in *four* successive elections, I desire The Provost and Fellows of the said College to place, constitute, and appoint one or more other School or Schools in the County where the School is, which has come to decay, in the room and stead of any one or more of these Twelve Schools herein mentioned,—

"And I will, that the new appointed School or Schools shall have all the benefit and advantages, and be subject to the same rules, restrictions, and conditions as the other Schools,—

"And to the end it may be known whether any School has so far come to decay, the Provost and Fellows of the said College are hereby required to enter into a Book, set apart for this purpose, the names of all the boys returned as well as elected, together with the names of each School they are returned from in a column over against the name of every boy respectively,—

"And to the intent that all doubts may be removed, and all disputes avoided at the time of nomination with regard to the directions and appointments herein made and given, as also that proper books at the time and place of Examination may not be wanting, I do hereby direct, order, and appoint, that a fair copy of this Codicil, as also a fair and perfect Greek Testament, an Exposition of the Church Catechism by the late Archbishop WAKE, the Orations of TULLY and DEMOSTHENES, HOMER'S ILIADS, and VIRGIL'S Works, together with three Dictionaries, Three Lexicons, Three Latin Grammars, and Three Greek Grammars, be always and constantly provided by the Vicar of LEDSHAM for the time being as often as there shall be occasion, and deposited in the hands of the Vicar of ABBERFORTH, for all which Books as well as Codicils, the said Vicar is to be allowed and reimbursed by the Provost and Fellows of the said College,—

"And I do hereby earnestly request the said Vicar of ABBERFORTH, and his Successors, from time to time, to take the care and charge of the said Codicil or Codicils and Books, during the intervals between the meetings, and at the time of the meetings to deliver them to any one of the said Rectors or Vicars for the use and benefit of the said Rectors and Vicars Examiners,—

"And, as to the overplus of the rents and profits issuing out of the premisses after all deductions are made, and after all the Exhibitions are answered,—and as to all sum or sums of money that may arise by death, marriage, or misbehaviour of any of the said Exhibitioners, or by getting of *Coals*, (which are supposed to be in the estate), or by any other contingencies,—for the further encouragement of residence, my will and mind is, that as soon as the said overplus and the said money arising by death, marriage, misbehaviour, coals, or other contingencies, shall amount to 60. the Provost shall pay it to any one of the Exhibitioners, whom he thinks in all respects most deserving of it,—Provided he has already taken his degree of Batchelor of Arts, is not married, and has enjoyed his Exhibition *five* years, to be computed from the time of election, and consents to stay another whole year in the College without accepting any *School* or other Preferment whatsoever, that may be a means to hinder him from pursuing his studies in Divinity,—

"And, in case the said overplus and money arising by the said contingencies shall amount to two or more £60., the said Provost shall dispose of it to two or more of the said Exhibitioners that have taken their Batchelor of Arts Degree, and enjoyed their Exhibitions *five* years under the limitations and conditions before mentioned, with regard to residence, marriage, and preferment,—

"And, in case there are not a sufficient number of Exhibitioners so qualifyed to take the said overplus, or that are willing to take it upon the last mentioned limitations and conditions, that such part of it as remains undisposed of be kept in the College Chest 'till there are Exhibitioners one or more that have taken their Batchelor's Degree, and have enjoyed their Exhibitions *five* years, and that will accept of it under the said limitations and conditions, no such person having in the year more than £60., and no one being entitled to it or any part of it after *seven* years from his election are compleated,—

" And, in case the rents of the Estate should so increase as to produce yearly £25., be it more or less, over and above what is sufficient for FIVE EXHIBITIONS at £28. by the year each, for five years, in the manner before directed, and over and above what is sufficient to answer the other expenses of meeting and buying books, as is before provided, my will is, that the said increase of rents after all deductions made, shall be divided into as many shares as there are Exhibitions, and two-thirds of each share added to and paid with each Exhibition by quarterly or half-yearly payments, and the remaining third part of each share put into the College Chest, yearly to be paid along with each sum of money saved and reserved for the fifth year to each Exhibitioner by two half-yearly payments, as before directed,— For experience shews, *as the value of Land increases the value of Money decreases.*"

The TATLER has done the highest honour to the memory of this benevolent Lady; Where, No. 42, she is depictured under the title of " *The Divine Aspasia.*"

This School has also a claim in it's turn to the FELLOWSHIP, and TWO SCHOLARSHIPS, founded at Emanuel College, Cambridge, by JOHN FRIESTON, of *Altofts*, in the County of York, in case the same are not filled up from The Free School at Normanton.

There are likewise THREE SCHOLARSHIPS of £20. *per annum* each, at Magdalen College, Cambridge, for Scholars from Leeds, Halifax, and Heversham Schools. See, *Halifax.*

The present Head Master is, The Revd. GEORGE PAGE RICHARDS, M. A., whose Salary is £500. *per annum*, and a very good House.

Neither the Head nor Second Masters take Pupils at present.

THE MASTERS, of whom it may be proper to give a continued Catalogue since the second Endowment by Mr. HARRISON, have been—

In 1624. SAMUEL PULLEN, D. D., afterwards Archbishop of Tuam.
1630. JOSHUA PULLEN, his Brother.
1651. JOHN GARNET, M. A.
1662. MICHAEL GILBERTS, M. A.
1690. EDWARD CLARKE, M. A.
1694. MILES FARRER, M. A.
1698. THOMAS DWYER, B. D.
1706. THOMAS DIXON, M. A.
1712. THOMAS BARNARD, M. A., a very pious and learned man.
1750. RICHARD SEDGEWICKE, M. A.
1755. JOHN MOORE.
1764. SAMUEL BROOKE, M. A., distinguished for the point and neatness of his Epigrams, Latin and English.
1778. THOMAS GOODINGE, LL. D., a very elegant Scholar, now Rector of Counde, in the County of Salop.
1790. JOSEPH WHITELEY, M. A.
1815. GEORGE PAGE RICHARDS, M. A., Fellow of King's College, Cambridge.

Among the many distinguished men who have been educated at this School, may be enumerated,—

Sir THOMAS DENNISON, One of the Judges in The Court of King's Bench.
CHRISTOPHER WILSON, Bishop of Bristol.
SAMUEL KIRSHAW, D. D.
THEOPHILUS LINDSEY, Vicar of Catterick.
JOHN BERKENHOUT, M. D., the Naturalist.
THOMAS BARNARD, S. T. B.
JOSEPH MILNER, a pious and learned Divine, Vicar and Head Master of The Grammar School at Hull.
ISAAC MILNER, D. D., now Dean of Carlisle, and Master of Queen's College, Cambridge.
JOSEPH JOWET, LL. D., of Trinity Hall, late Professor of Civil Law in The University of Cambridge.
JAMES FAWCETT, B. D, Norrisian Professor in The University of Cambridge.
JOSEPH PROCTOR, D. D., Master of Catherine Hall.
RICHARD FAWCETT, M. A., the present worthy Vicar of Leeds.

The Authorities, which have been used in the description

of this School, are THORESBY's *Ducatus Leodiensis*,—WHITAKER's *Loidis* and *Elmete*,—VESEY's Chancery Reports,—and the obliging Communications of the Author's ever loved and valued Friend and Schoolfellow, THOMAS BUCKLE, Esq., of Leeds.

LINTON, near SKIPTON.

THE GRAMMAR SCHOOL at LINTON has an Endowment of £30. *per annum*, for *Two* Masters.

There are FOUR EXHIBITIONS of £12. *per annum* each at ST. JOHN'S COLLEGE, Cambridge, for Scholars from this School.

OLD MALTON.

THE FREE GRAMMAR SCHOOL at OLD MALTON was founded by ROBERT HOLGATE, D. D., Archbishop of York, in 1546, and endowed with lands and tenements of the value of £20. *per annum*. See, *Hemsworth*.

By Statutes 1, 2, and 3, he orders, that the Master shall teach the Learned languages to all Scholars to him "resorting, without taking any wages, stipends, or other exaction,"—nominates the first Master, and makes him and every Successor, a Body Corporate.

By Statutes 4, 5, and 6, he gives the nomination of the Master to the Archbishop of York,—and, in case of his neglect, to others.

By Statute 7, he orders, that the Master shall "have understanding" in Latin, Greek, and Hebrew.

By Statute 8, 9, 10, and 11, he orders, that there always be an Usher, to whom the Master shall pay £4. *per annum* for his maintenance.

By Statute 12, 13, and 14, he fixes the School hours,—appoints what Prayers shall be read,—and directs how the Master and Scholars shall be employed at Church.

By Statutes 15, 16, 17, and 26, he directs for what offences, and in what form, the Masters shall be deprived.

By Statute 18, he orders, "That (to the intent the Lands may be maintained without decay, the Rents may be duly paid, and *the Farmers may so pay the same*, and *have a competent Living thereof towards the finding of their Families*) the Master shall not let the lands to any person or persons for above the space of 12 years, except to some of his (the Founder's) kinsmen or servants, and not to them for more than 31 years."—"Nor shall the Master inhance or raise the rents" above what they were at the time of the Foundation.

By Statute 19, he directs, that such Fines only shall be taken when new Leases are made, as are appointed in a "Rental or Schedule" said to be annexed to these Statutes.

And also by Statute 19, and 31, he orders the Fines to be laid up in a Strong Box, for the "Reparation of the School-houses, and for the necessary Suits, Defences, and Causes of the Lands and Tenements." And that after £10. is so raised, the Surplusage shall be employed in the repairs of the High-ways and Relief of the Poor.

By Statutes 20, 21, 22, 23, 24, and 25, he directs, that there shall be an Organist at Malton, and one at Old Malton,—to the former of which the Master shall pay £4. Salary,—to the latter £2.—And, for want of such Organists, the £4. and £2. *per annum* shall be paid to the Poor of the respective Parishes, by Statute 34.

By Statute 27, he makes it deprivation for the Master, Usher, or Organists, to violate any of these Statutes.

By Statutes 28, 29, and 30, he orders how rebellious Scholars shall be treated,—directs that every Master shall publicly take an Oath to observe these Statutes,—and appoints at what time he shall break up School.

By Statutes 32, and 33, he reserves to himself power to alter these Statutes,—And says, the Master may be married or unmarried, a Layman or a Clergyman.

By Statute 35, he orders, that neither the Master nor Usher shall be obliged to teach any, that cannot read.

In witness whereof he signs and seals four original Instruments of Foundation, on the 4th of May, 1547, in the presence of many Witnesses, to remain to perpetuity in such hands as are there directed.

The Master is appointed by The Archbishop of York.

Anciently it appears that there were *lands* belonging to the School; but now instead of them, there are certain *money* payments amounting to about £100. *per annum*, with a good house and a garden attached to it.

Although the School is "*free to all the World*," yet no boys are now sent, except *Boarders*, and the Children of *a few Labourers* in Old Malton. The School is divided into two parts,—so that none of the Children have access to the Head Master, *except his own Pupils*.

The last Master, The Revd. WILLIAM JOHNSON, taught many boys from *New* Malton, *gratis*,—And the present Master professes himself ready to instruct gratuitously, *any* boys who may require it.

There are no University advantages belonging to this School.

The present Master is, The Revd. JOHN RICHARDSON, who takes a few "*very young*" Children, as Boarders, at about £40. *per annum*. He keeps an Assistant, who teaches only the English Grammar, and a little Arithmetic.

NORTHALLERTON.

THE origin of THE GRAMMAR SCHOOL at NORTHALLERTON is uncertain.

There is, however, in the *Liber Præsentationum et Literarum Prioris et Conventus Eccl. Dunelm. in Bibl. Cotton.*, the register of the Presentation of WILLIAM DE LEEDS to the Mastership of the Grammar School at Northallerton, in 1385; to which are annexed the following words, "*Consimilem habet Chartam Johannes Podesay v. a. Octob.* 1327."

It seems to be a Royal Foundation, as £5..1..8. *per annum* are now paid by the King's Receivers, who deduct 5*s.* for poundage, 2*s.*.6*d.* for debenture money, and 8*d.* for acquittance.

There is a further endowment of a house, a garden, and a small close, worth about £20. a year; but when made, and by whom, is unknown.

The House and Garden are situate in the Town, and adjoining to the School-room. The close is distant about a mile North from Northallerton, on the road leading to Darlington.

There are no STATUTES.

The School is *free* only to FOUR boys, for whose education JOHN ESHALL left 20*s.*, to be paid yearly out of certain lands at *Catto*, in the North Riding of the County of York. The average number of boys educated here of late years, is about 40. No particular age is assigned for admission, nor for superannuation.

The WESTMINSTER Latin and Greek Grammars are used; but the system of Education for many years past, has been confined *chiefly* to reading, writing, and arithmetic.

The only University advantages belonging to this School, are FIVE SCHOLARSHIPS at Peter-House, in Cambridge of

£10. *per annum* each, founded by JOHN COSIN, D.D., Bishop of Durham; who gave such Scholars as should be educated in this School a right to them, immediately after those of Durham School.

The present Master is, The Revd. JAMES WILKINSON, Rector of Rokeby, whose only source of emolument, besides those above-mentioned, is the payment of his Scholars, which is *7s..6d. per* Quarter each.

Among the Eminent men who have been educated at this School, may be enumerated,—

Dr. WILLIAM PALLISER, sometime Archbishop of Cashel in Ireland.

GEORGE HICKES, D.D., Dean of Worcester.

JOHN RADCLIFFE, M.D., the Founder of the noble Library at Oxford.

JOHN KETTLEWELL, an eminent Divine.

THOMAS RYMER, Author of the *Fœdera.*

THOMAS BURNET, LL.D., Master of the Charter-House.

PENNISTON, near BARNESLEY.

THE FREE GRAMMAR SCHOOL at PENNISTON is endowed with £100. *per annum*,—and also the Interest of £200., for the education of *eight* poor *Girls*.

No answer has been received to the Author's Letter.

POCKLINGTON.

THE FREE GRAMMAR SCHOOL at POCKLINGTON was founded by JOHN DOLMAN *or* DOWEMAN, LL. D., Archdeacon of Suffolk, who died in 1526,—and endowed with lands, situate in several parts of the East and West Ridings of the County of York, for the maintenance of a Master and Usher, now yielding an annual Rent of from £1000. to £1200.

It was at first entrusted to The Master, Wardens, and Brethren of The Guild there,—but, on their Dissolution, it was by an Act of Parliament passed on the 8th of April, 1552, so far transferred to THE MASTER and FELLOWS of ST. JOHN'S COLLEGE, in Cambridge, that the nomination of the Schoolmaster belongs to them,—and who is to be appointed within *Two months* after a vacancy, otherwise the appointment, for that turn, lapses to The Archbishop of York.

The Master and Usher were incorporated by the same Act.

There are no STATUTES. But by the Act, the Master is to be "*a discreet, and well learned man*,"—and the Usher is to possess the like qualifications.

The School is open to the Boys of the Parish of Pocklington, and indeed to any other boys, without limitation; but it has not been considered that they are entitled to their education, *free* of expense, although the School is designated The *Free* Grammar School.

In the time of the late Master, The Revd. Mr. BASKETT, there were between 40 and 50 boys at once in this School. But at present, it is "*believed*" that *two* or *three* Town boys only attend, and "*no Aliens*." It has been publicly stated, that "*the Lower School-room is made use of as a Saw-pit and Barn,—that the Master has not attended for the last Twelve months,—and that the Usher, being deaf, the Children have necessarily been sent to other Schools*."

The Founder appropriated FIVE SCHOLARSHIPS at ST. JOHN'S, for Scholars educated at this School.

The present Master is, The Revd. THOMAS SHIELD, B. D., of St. John's College, Cambridge, whose emolument is *two-thirds* of the Endowment.

The Usher who is appointed by the Master, and the two Church-wardens of Pocklington, has the remaining *one-third* of the Endowment for his Stipend.

All the Documents relating to the School, are in the possession of the Master.

WILLIAM WILBERFORCE, Esq., the benevolent Abolisher of the Slave Trade, was educated here under the late Mr. BASKETT.

The name of the Founder is supposed to have been written formerly DOVEMAN; for, within memory, there was a piece of carved work fixed upon one of the beams in the School, bearing three *Doves* with the letters M. A. N. under them, evidently meaning the word *Doveman*.

The Manor of Pocklington, and a considerable Estate there, continued in the family of the DOLMANS 'till within about the last thirty years, when it was purchased by ROBERT DENISON, Esq., of Kilwick Percy.

The Inscription upon the Seal is,—*Sigillum Commune Fraternitatis Nominis Jhesus, Beatæ Mariæ, Sancti Nicholai de Poklington.*

No answer has been received to the Author's Letter.

PONTEFRACT.

THE KING'S FREE GRAMMAR SCHOOL at PONTEFRACT was originally founded by King EDWARD the Sixth, in the Second year of his reign, 1549, and endowed with the small Salary of 59*s*. to the Master.

In this state it continued until the Fifth year of Queen ELIZABETH, 1563, when complaint was made of the inattention and negligence of the School-master, to The Chancellor of the Duchy of Lancaster; and, in consequence, the right to present a suitable Master was vested in The Mayor and Aldermen of Pontefract.

No addition was, however, made to the endowment until the 25th of ELIZABETH, 1583; when, on the petition of BONIFACE SAVAGE and others, several small endowments of Schools, which had been wholly neglected, were appropriated to the School at Pontefract, that a Master in every degree qualified to teach and instruct the rising generation might be obtained.

From this period the School continued to flourish, or otherwise, according to the talents and industry, or inattention and neglect, of the various Masters who were appointed. The grant obtained by the Petitioners took from the Mayor and Comburgesses the right of appointing the School-master, and such right remained with the Chancellor of the Duchy. But the Master was only to be properly qualified for his office; nor was he in the least bound or restricted to any particular branches of instruction.

In the lapse of a Century the School again fell into decay, and for some years, no School-master applied for the appointment. The inhabitants, however, desirous to restore this foundation, and to render it permanently useful, again petitioned The Duchy Court, and engaged to re-build the School, and to purchase or erect a House for the residence of the School-master.

Their Petition was graciously received, and, on the 13th of February, in the 32d of King GEORGE the Third, 1792, the School was re-founded; and a Charter was granted, to the following effect, for it's better government in future.

By this Charter, The Free Grammar School is re-founded, and it is ordained, that it shall for ever hereafter be called "THE KING'S SCHOOL;" for the teaching and educating of *Seventeen* Boys, all of whom (except the boy to be appointed from the Charity School,[a] in the Town of Pontefract) at the time of being elected and appointed to be of the said Foundation, shall be Children of resident Inhabitants, legally settled within the Township of Pontefract or the Township of Tanshelf, or of any deceased inhabitants, who were legally settled therein at the time of their decease;—that a fit and discreet person, as soon as conveniently may be, and for ever hereafter upon the happening of any vacancy within Three Calendar months from the happening of such vacancy, shall be nominated and appointed in the name of His Majesty by the Chancellor of The Duchy of Lancaster, by Letters Patent under the Seal of the said Duchy, to be Master of the said Free Grammar School during the good-will and pleasure of His Majesty; which person, as a necessary qualification for such appointment, shall have taken upon him, previous to such appointment, the state and degree of a Master of Arts, or Bachelor of Laws, at one of the Universities of Oxford or Cambridge, and also shall have had Ordination as a Priest or Deacon of the Church of England; and who, at his appointment, or at any time afterwards, during his continuing Master of such School, shall not have any benefice, within Fifteen miles of the Town of Pontefract, the Lectureship of the said Town, or Preacher of the Sunday Afternoon Sermon, in the said Town only excepted:—that of the *Seventeen* Boys, *two*

[a] When THE KING'S GRAMMAR SCHOOL was re-founded, the Trustees of this Charity appropriated £150. from it's funds towards the erection of the School: and were, in consequence, authorised to appoint *one* Boy, to be educated, *free of all expense*.

shall be nominated by The Chancellor of The Duchy of Lancaster; *fourteen* boys, who shall also be *seven* years of age at the least, at the time of appointment, shall be of the nomination of The Curators of the said Foundation; and the *one* other boy, to be elected from the Boys nominated and educated at "*The Charity School*" within the Town of Pontefract, called "THE TOWN SCHOOL," by The Trustees of the said Charity School: the Mayor, Recorder, and Aldermen of the town of Pontefract, and the Vicar of the Vicarage within the Parish of Pontefract, for ever hereafter, to be The Curators or Guardians of the said School; and the Chancellor of the Duchy of Lancaster to be the Visitor of the said Free Grammar School, with full power to decide upon appeals.

In consequence of this Charter, the following CONSTITUTIONS and ORDINANCES were made by The Attorney General of the Duchy of Lancaster, for the regulation of the said Foundation and School, and of the Master and Scholars of the same:—

"CONSTITUTIONS, RULES, STATUTES, and ORDINANCES, to be kept, maintained and observed, by The Master and Scholars of THE FREE GRAMMAR SCHOOL of the Town of PONTEFRACT, of the Foundation of His Most Excellent Majesty King GEORGE the Third, duly made, and signed by JOHN ORD, Esq., His Majesty's Attorney General of the Duchy of Lancaster, pursuant to powers for that purpose to him given, in and by His said Majesty's Letters Patent, under the Seal of the same Duchy, bearing date the 13th day of February, in the Thirty-second year of his reign, and in the year of Our Lord, 1792. That is to say,—

First, That the Boys educated at The Free Grammar School in the Town of Pontefract, by virtue of His Majesty's said Letters Patent, shall be assembled and instructed in the School-room erected for that purpose, and not elsewhere; at such hours of the day as the Master shall think fit, in the Latin and Greek Grammars; and, at suitable periods, in the Latin and Greek Classics. The Master of the said School shall have the appointment and regulation of the periods, at which such Books and Authors shall be taught and explained to the Boys upon the said Foundation; and of the several Hours of the day when such Boys shall be assembled together and taught; and of the distribution, and order of reading or teaching such Books, and of every regulation touching the teaching and instruction of such Boys, subject to the control herein-after mentioned, That is to say:—

That the Master shall put down in writing, the Scheme and Plan of instruction which he means to pursue, and lay the same before the Curators, who shall be summoned to take the same into consideration; and the said Curators, or the major part of them, of whom the Vicar or Recorder of Pontefract shall be one, shall have full power to alter, vary, or new model, such plan of instruction and teaching, and every thing relating thereunto; and when such plan of Instruction shall be approved by the said Curators, or the major part of them (of whom the Vicar or Recorder of Pontefract shall be one) the same shall be fairly transcribed, and signed by the Curators, allowing and approving the same; and such Plan of Instruction shall from thence-forward be continually used at the said School, by every succeeding Master, subject to such alterations as may be made therein at any time, by the Curators or Guardians of such Foundation, or the major part of them.

2. That the discipline of the School, so far as relates to the censure, punishment or reward of the Scholars, shall be left wholly to the discretion of the Master; but, in case of any cruelty, or immoderate punishment of any kind, upon the complaint of the Parents, Guardians, or any other person who may have the superintendance of the education of any Boy upon the said Foundation not having any Parent or Guardian, to the Mayor; or, in his absence, to the Senior Alderman of Pontefract, then resident in the said Town; which said Mayor, or Senior Alderman, shall, within two days from the time of such complaint, summon a Meeting of the Curators, or so many of them as shall be within a reasonable distance, to meet within Twenty-four hours, and shall hear the complaint in the presence of the Master, and of the Parent, Guardian, or person standing as aforesaid in the place of Parent and Guardian; who shall have notice in writing of the time and place of such meeting, and examine into the circumstances, and shall determine whether such complaint is well or ill founded generally, without stating any special circumstances; and shall cause to be put down in writing, and signed by the Curators present, or the major part thereof, such their resolution, and preserve the same until a general meeting of the Curators shall be had; and such resolution shall be laid before such general meeting; and if the complaint shall be resolved to be well founded, the said Master may be admonished and reproved by the Mayor, in the name of the Curators, and an entry shall be made in a book, and preserved of such admonition; and the Curators, if they shall think fit, shall represent the same to the Visitor of the School, for his judgment therein.

3. That the Master shall have no power to expel any offend-

ing Boy of the said Foundation; but that upon any offence committed by any of the said boys, which shall in his discretion be worthy of punishment, or notice to that extent, the master shall, with all convenient speed, apply to the Mayor for the time being; or in his absence to the Senior Alderman, then resident in the said Town, and request in writing, that he would summon a meeting of the Curators, or so many of them as may live within a reasonable distance, within two days from the time of such request, to consider of the offence of such boy, during which interval, and until such meeting shall be had, the Master shall be at liberty to suspend the education of such boy, and to prohibit his coming to be taught at the School; And, at such meeting of the Curators, the said Boy and the Parent, Guardian or person having the direction of the education of such boy, if he hath no Parent or Guardian, shall have notice in writing, signed by the Mayor, or the Senior Alderman then resident, to be present; and such order shall be made, for the admonition, punishment, suspension or expulsion of such boy, as to the Curators present, or the major part of them, (the Vicar or Recorder being one, joining in the making of such order) shall seem just, and such admonition or punishment shall be carried into effect with all convenient dispatch, publicly in the School-room, in the presence of the other Boys upon the same foundation, as far as the same may be consistent with the right of the Visitor therein.

4. There shall be paid (except by the Boy chosen out of the Charity School, as aforesaid), to the Master, *One* Guinea a year, by Quarterly payments; and for such of the said Boys who shall learn Writing and Arithmetic, (except such one Charity Boy), *One* Guinea more a year, by such Quarterly payments, and it shall be at the option of the Parent, &c., of such boy, to chuse whether he shall, or not, be instructed in Writing and Arithmetic. But the Boy elected to the said foundation, from the Charity School, shall be taught Writing and Arithmetic, and nothing shall be paid for such his instruction, nor for any other instruction he shall receive upon the Foundation.

5. That the Master shall be obliged to receive the sons of any of the inhabitants of the Towns of Pontefract and Tanshelf, and instruct and educate them in the same manner, and in the same Authors, and with the like discipline, and subject to the same Rules as those herein-before specified relating to the said *Seventeen* boys, upon the said Foundation, (except that of expulsion, which shall be at the discretion of the Master, as to such boys as are not of the said Foundation) upon being paid for the education of each boy, *Two* Guineas a year by quarterly payments; and, in case any of such boys shall be taught Writing and Arith-

metic, which shall be at the option of the Parent, &c., there shall be paid by Quarterly payments, *One* Guinea a year and no more. Over and above the Fees of Salary paid to the Master for the education of the said boys, he shall be paid for the Latin and Greek books necessary for their instruction, and for the Paper, Pens, and Ink used by them, a fair and reasonable price, to be ascertained and settled by the Curators, or any three of them, the Mayor and Vicar being two, in case of any difference or dispute about the price or charge for such articles made by the Master.

6. No Boy, whether of the Foundation, or not, and whether he be the son of an Inhabitant of the Town of Pontefract and Tanshelf, or not; shall be taught by, or under the direction or permission of the Master of such School, Writing and Arithmetic, or either of them, unless he is also instructed in the Latin and Greek languages, or one of them, in the same manner with the boys upon the Foundation.

7. That the Master be permitted to take into his House Boarders and Lodgers, and instruct any other Boys, although they may not be the sons of Inhabitants of the Towns of Pontefract and Tanshelf, upon such terms as he shall think fit, so that such Boys be educated at the same times, and in the same Authors, and in the same School-room as the boys of the Foundation, and be mixed with them, according to their ages of proficiency in learning; but the Master shall, on no account, be permitted to take any boys to educate privately, and separate from the other boys, or any of them, nor shall any distinction be made between the boys upon the said Foundation, and the other boys educated by the said Master; either by any badge or mark, or by the place of their sitting in such School-room, or by any other mode of treatment, except so far as relates to the expulsion, which, as to such boys who are not upon the said Foundation, shall be left to the discretion of the Master.

8. That an annual Meeting shall be held by the said Curators upon Tuesday next after Easter day, in the School-room; at which Meeting the Master shall, without any notice for that purpose, lay before the Curators present at such meeting, the number of all the boys under education at his School, and the number of Assistants or Ushers which he, then, and for Six months before hath had constantly in employ, and for the teaching of what branches of education; and, in case the Curators, or the major part of them, at such Meeting, shall resolve that the number of such Assistants or Ushers is insufficient for the teaching the said boys, then the Master shall, upon the order or request in writing, signed by the said Curators, or the major part thereof, add so many Assistants or Ushers, within

one Calendar month from the date of such request, as such Curators shall direct; whose Salaries shall be paid by the said Master.

9. That no Boy shall be taken and educated at the said School, whether he be of the said Foundation, or not, unless he be of the age of *Seven* years complete, at the time of his first coming to be educated; nor shall any boy upon the said Foundation, be permitted to stay at such School beyond the full age of *Sixteen* years, unless it is intended to send any of the boys to any of the Universities of Oxford or Cambridge, and, in such case, upon the representation of such intention by the Master, and upon the request, in writing, of the Parent, &c.; or, in case of the said Charity Boy, upon the request of the Trustees of the said Charity School, in writing, signed by themselves, or the major part of them and given to the Curators at their annual Meeting; such boys or boy, upon the special permission, in writing, signed by the said Curators of such meeting, or the major part of them, may be continued at the School to the full age of *Eighteen*, and no longer.

10. That every election of the *Fourteen* boys to be elected by the Curators, to be upon the foundation of the said School, be made by ballot, whereof every Curator shall have eight days notice, in writing, exclusive of the day of giving such notice, and of the day for such ballotting; and no one boy shall be elected without having, on the ballot, a majority of the Curators present in his favour.

11. That on every vacancy amongst the Fourteen boys, a notification thereof in writing, within two days, shall be given by the Master to the Mayor, or in his absence to the Senior Alderman resident in the said Town, and that the said Mayor, or Senior Alderman, shall, within seven days summon a Meeting of the Curators, to be held at the School-house, to ballot for and elect another boy to supply such vacancy; and that on every vacancy made by either of the two boys, nominated and appointed by the Visitor of the said Foundation, the like notice in writing, shall be given by the Master to the Mayor, or in his absence to the said Senior Alderman, and the Mayor or Senior Alderman, then resident, shall give notice thereof in writing, to the Visitor of the said Foundation, who shall, by the said Mayor or the said Senior Alderman, be respectfully requested in writing, to fill up such vacancy; and upon the vacancy of the boy appointed from The Charity School of the said Town, the like notice shall be given to the Trustees of The said Charity School, or such of them as shall be then in England, and capable of acting in the said Trust, of such vacancy, and a request shall be made by the Master, in writing, to them, to fill up the vacancy.

12. That over and above the aforesaid Fees and Allowances to the said Master, for the instruction of the said boys, elected to be upon the Foundation, and of such other boys as shall be the sons of Inhabitants living and residing within the Town of Pontefract and Township of Tanshelf; there shall be paid to the Master yearly, for each boy, (except for the said Boy, chosen from The Charity School) after the Christmas Holidays, beginning after Christmas next, after each boy's coming to School, *Two Shillings* each, for the expense of a *fire* in the said School-room, and the further sum of *One Shilling* each, for *repairing* the School-room and School-House; and the Master shall regularly account for, and deposit such monies in the hands of the Town Clerk of Pontefract, and the same shall be kept by him, as a fund for repairing the said School-room and School-house, and shall be applied for those purposes as the Curators, or the greater part of them, shall at any time direct; But the boy nominated by The Trustees of the Charity School in Pontefract, shall pay no part of such expense of fire and repairs, or any other expense of education whatsoever.

13. That all the Children during their education in the said School, shall be instructed in the PROTESTANT RELIGION, according to the Rites and Ceremonies of the Church of England, as by law established; and every Scholar, unless impeded by bodily indisposition, shall regularly, as well on Sundays as on such other of the days set apart by the Church for Public Worship, as shall be specially directed by the Master, resort to the Parish Church of Pontefract, or some other Parish Church in the neighbourhood thereof, to be allowed by the Master; and there abide orderly and soberly, during the time of Common Prayer and Preaching the Sermon."

Signed, F. RUSSEL, Register.

There are now about *Twenty* Scholars in the School.

JOHN FRIESTON, of *Altofts*, in the County of York, and who died in the year 1594, gave some lands in the Town of Pontefract to University College, Oxford, for the maintenance of one Fellow or Exhibitioner, to receive out of the same Ten pounds *per annum;* besides the use of a Chamber and Exemptions from all decrements.

This benevolent Gentleman also built and endowed a Free School at Normanton, and left £500. to purchase £25. *per annum*, for the maintenance of ONE FELLOW and TWO SCHOLARS in EMANUEL COLLEGE, Cambridge; the said Fellow and Scholars to be sent out of Normanton, and for want of such there, then out of the Free Schools of Pontefract, Wakefield, Leeds, and Rotherham, or any part of the County of York.

About the year 1790, the Gentlemen of the Town, willing to obtain for the Master of this School a suitable residence, and large enough for him to take a few Boarders, generously exerted themselves to accomplish such a laudable design. The Corporation gave the sum of £250., and other Gentlemen of the Town handsomely contributing, a good spacious house and garden, adjoining the School, were purchased, and invested in Seven Trustees; who possess the power of admitting the Schoolmaster to enjoy the premises according to their discretion.

The present Master is, The Revd. ARCHIBALD COLIN CAMPBELL, M. A., the whole of whose emoluments are under £100. *per annum.* He does not take Boarders.

There is no Usher. A Writing-Master attends at stated hours.

RICHMOND.

THE FREE GRAMMAR SCHOOL at RICHMOND, situate in the Church-yard of THE LOW CHURCH, was founded and endowed by THE BURGESSES,—who appear to have petitioned Queen ELIZABETH for her Royal License to erect "unam Scholam Grammaticalem ad bonam educationem et instructionem puerorum et juvenum ibidem et circa partes vicinas habitantium et commorantium."

By Letters Patent from the Queen, reciting the Petition, and dated at St. Alban's, on the 14th of March, in the Ninth year of her reign, 1568, it was ordained, that there should be "una Schola Grammaticalis in Richmond - - - - de uno Magistro seu Pedagogo pro perpetuo continuatura - - - - - quæ vocabitur Libera Schola Grammaticalis Burgensium Burgi sive Villæ de Richmond pro educatione, institutione, et instructione puerorum et juvenum in Grammaticâ perpetuis temporibus duratura."

And that Her Majesty's intentions might take the better effect, and that the lands and revenues to be granted for the support of the School might be the better governed, she directed, —that, from thenceforth the FOUR BAILIFFS of the Borough and Town, at that time CUTHBERT HUTCHINSON, RALPH UBANK,

WILLIAM HIGHINTON, and JOHN JOHNSON, should be Guardians and Governors of all it's Possessions, with perpetual Succession,—should be a Body Corporate and Politic,—might plead and be impleaded,—and have a Common Seal:—

The Governors were further empowered, with the *assent* of The Burgesses, or the major part of them, on any vacancy in the Office of Schoolmaster, to nominate and appoint "another fit and learned person," within *Two* months,—and from time to time to make good and wholesome STATUTES in writing, concerning the Revenues of the School and the direction of the Master and the Scholars, &c.:—

The Governors had also authority to hold, purchase, and receive any other possessions, provided they are not holden immediately *in capite,* and do not exceed the clear yeary value of £40.:—

And, finally, that *all* the issues and profits of the estates should be converted to the support of the Master and the maintenance of the premises, and to *no other* use whatever.

On the renewal of the Corporation Charter, in the 20th of King CHARLES the Second, 1668, the right of nominating the Master, and of being Guardians and Governors of the School and it's Revenues, devolved upon THE MAYOR and ALDERMEN, who are indisputably the Successors of THE BAILIFFS mentioned in the Letters Patent.

What the original Endowment was, is not known,—but the present gross amount is fully £330. *per annum.* It is situate in the Parish of Richmond, and is all in land, with the exception of an Out-payment of 13*s*..4*d.* from HUTCHINSON'S Charity, and Quit-rents to the amount of £3..4..0. from certain Estates belonging to Lord DUNDAS in this Town and Neighbourhood.

Since the year 1722, the Masters have possessed every benefit belonging to The Foundation. At present, after certain lawful payments and a small *per* centage to the Chamberlains for the trouble of collecting, the Rents are fairly enjoyed by The Master. And it is gratifying to observe, that the Governors in all cases act with the strictest honour and liberality.

By the STATUTES (nearly copied from those in 1750)

which were subscribed on the 11th of October, 1796, by Mr. TATE, it is directed,—

That no Scholar shall be admitted into the School, 'till he can read the *Bible,* and is capable of being instructed and taught in the *Accidence*:—

That, for the instruction of the Scholars in Literature, the Master shall teach them the Latin and Greek tongues by such Grammars, and such Latin and Greek authors, as he, in his discretion, shall think meet:—

And, for preventing all disputes touching what Children are to be deemed entitled to be taught at the School *as free thereof,* it is ordered and directed, " That all Children *Natives in the Borough,* and the Children *of all Burgesses* and other persons *inhabiting* in the said Borough and *exercising any trade, mystery,* or *manual occupation therein,* shall be admitted and be entitled *to be taught free* in the said School:"—

That, if the Scholars shall increase to *Twenty* (*Forty,* in 1750), the Master shall *at his own expense* provide such an *Usher* to assist in teaching the same, as the Mayor and Aldermen, or the major part of them, with the consent of a majority of the Common Council, shall approve.

The number of boys upon the Foundation seldom exceeds TWENTY. There is no prescribed time of Superannuation.

The average number of Boarders and Free Scholars has lately amounted to betwixt 50 and 60 in the whole.

The ETON *Latin* Grammar is used;—and the *Greek* Grammar of Professor MOOR, of Glasgow, though infected with several of the old errors, for it's simplicity, neatness, and brevity, has been adopted by the present Master.

JOHN BATHURST, of London, Doctor of Physic, by his Will dated in 1659, gave a rent charge of £12. *per annum,* payable out of the House now known by the sign of "The King's Head," and several acres of land lying in different parts of "The Gallow Field," to charitable uses,—of which, £8. a year were to be applied to the maintenance of Two poor SCHOLARS at the University of Cambridge, who shall be found pious, virtuous, and competently learned, until they commence Masters of Arts, —but to cease to such as shall discontinue above one quarter of a year together, or to such as shall be employed out of the University in any other capacity. The two Exhibitions which are generally enjoyed in one, with such accumulations as arise when no claim is made, have been declared appropriate to Free Scholars *on the Foundation only.*

WILLIAM ALLEN, M. A., Rector of Swanington and Vicar of Wood-Dalling in the County of Norfolk, by his Will dated the 9th of November, 1730, after certain reversions, gave all his estate " in Bures St. Mary in Suffolk or Villages adjacent," to The Master, Fellows, and Scholars of Trinity Hall in Cambridge, and their Successors for ever, " for the founding Two SCHOLARSHIPS of £10. *per annum* each more or less, desiring that Two of his nearest kindred may have the preference of being elected into the said Scholarships before all others,—and, for want of such kindred, then that Two Scholars from The Free Grammar School of Richmond, in Yorkshire, may have the next propriety to the same,—and, for want of such, then that Two Scholars from any other School, in Yorkshire, may have the third propriety to the said Two Scholarships,—and, for want of such, then that Two Scholars out of the Diocese of Norwich may have the fourth propriety to the same,—and, for want of such, then that Two Scholars out of the Town or County of Cambridge may have the fifth propriety to these Two Scholarships." They are now worth about £17. *per annum* each. The estate is under lease of 21 years, which wants some years of expiring; but, at it's termination, no doubt exists of a considerable increase. They are by custom holden for *four* years. As there has been no person claiming to be Founder's Kin,—or, from Richmond School,—for a long time;—these Scholarships are now always given, according to merit, among the Under-Graduates of the remaining classes. One of them will be vacant at Christmas, 1818. Mr. GELDART, as a third Claimant under the Will, now occupies one of the Scholarships. Mr. ALLEN's Will was proved in the Consistory Court at Norwich, on the 12th of July, 1733.

The Revd. THOMAS KAY, formerly Fellow of University College, Oxford, and Rector of Melsonby, near Richmond, by his Will dated in 1782, and who died on the 23d of January, 1787, founded an Exhibition of £30. a year to Worcester College, Oxford,—(as his own College could not consistently accept a very handsome bequest, from the nature of the terms attached to it; and so the whole passed on, by his Will, to Worcester)—for a native of that part of the County of York, commonly called " *Richmondshire,*" if *Two* candidates from thence offer themselves,—if only *one,* then for a native of the County at large, if they think proper. No Scholar from Richmond has ever enjoyed this Exhibition; nor, perhaps, from the rest of Richmondshire.

This is one of the Schools which has become entitled to

send Candidates for Lady ELIZABETH HASTINGS's valuable Exhibitions at Queen's College, Oxford. See, *Leeds*.

The present Master is, The Revd. JAMES TATE, M. A., late Fellow of Sidney Sussex College, Cambridge, whose Salary is about £310. *per annum* clear. This Gentleman takes Pupils at One Hundred Guineas a year each, for board and education,—of whom the number is limited, and does not now exceed that of his own children.

The Usher, a Graduate of the University of Cambridge, who is engaged at a Salary of 100 guineas a year by the Master, takes *Ten* Boarders at Forty-six guineas *per annum* each. The annual charge for their instruction, varies from twelve guineas, according to the Pupil's advancement in the higher classes of the School.

To other Boarders and Oppidans, classical education, under certain circumstances, is differently charged.

No house of residence belongs to the Master.

The following is a List of THE MASTERS,—

In 1696. JOHN PARVEING.
1706. WILLIAM THOMPSON.
1722. ROBERT CLOSE, M. A., of St. John's, Cambridge.
1750. ANTHONY TEMPLE, M. A., of Sidney Sussex, Cambridge.
1796. JAMES TATE, M. A.

Among the many able Scholars who have proceeded from this Seminary of sound Learning and religious Education, may be mentioned,—

THOMAS CHAPMAN, D. D., Master of Magdalen College, Cambridge, and author of the "Essay on the Roman Senate."

CONYERS MIDDLETON, D. D.,—so reported by the late Mr. KAY,—author of "The History of the Life of M. Tullius Cicero."

WILLIAM ALLEN, M. A., the Founder of the Two Scholarships.

The Revd. THOMAS KAY, Rector of Melsonby, and Founder of one of the Exhibitions.

JOHN BAYNES, M. A., third Wrangler, Second SMITH's Prize man, and Senior Medallist, at Cambridge, in

1777;—who, if he had lived, might have risen to the highest eminence in the Law by the force of uncommon talents. *Vide*, WHITAKER's Craven, *p.* 321.

JAMES TATE, M. A., the present most worthy Master, who, as a native of this Town, was a free Scholar, and enjoyed Dr. BATHURST's benevolence,—and under whose able instruction, several Pupils have already been known and distinguished at Trinity College, Cambridge.

THE SEAL represents ST. JAMES, styled THE GREAT, and the Proto-Martyr of THE APOSTLES. His Festival was first instituted in the year 1089, and his emblems are a Pilgrim's Staff and a Gourd Bottle. The Spaniards have the highest veneration for ST. JAMES, whom they call their Patron Saint, not only from the pretence of his having *first planted Christianity* in that Country,—but on account of their having the honour of possessing *his remains*, which are alleged to have been brought from Jerusalem, and deposited at *Compostella*, the Capital of Galicia.

In the application of this Seal to the School, it may be observed that there was anciently a CHAPEL (of which there are still some remains) in this Town, dedicated to *St. James;*—part of the possessions of it given to this Establishment, were alienated, in 1803, to defray expenses incurred by the School on the inclosure of the Common fields.

An apology is scarcely necessary for the insertion of the following beautiful—

" Lines written in the Church-yard of Richmond, Yorkshire, by HERBERT KNOWLES, who died, Æ. xix. 17th Feb. 1817.

" *It is good for us to be here:*
" *if thou wilt, let us make here three Tabernacles;*
" *one for thee, and one for Moses, and one for Elias.*"

MATT. xvii, 4.

Methinks it is good to be here:
If thou wilt, let us build—but for whom?
Nor ELIAS nor MOSES appear,
But the shadows of eve, that encompass the gloom,
The abode of the dead, and the place of the tomb.

Shall we build to ambition? oh, no!
Affrighted he shrinketh away;
For, see! they would pin him below,
In a small narrow cave, and begirt with cold clay,
To the meanest of reptiles a peer and a prey!

To beauty? ah, no!—she forgets
The charms which she wielded before—
Nor knows the foul worm, that he frets
The skin which but yesterday fools could adore,
For the smoothness it held, or the tint which it wore.

Shall we build to the purple of pride—
The trappings which dizen the proud;
Alas! they are all laid aside—
And here's neither dress nor adornment allow'd,
But the long-winding sheet and the fringe of the shroud!

To riches? alas! 'tis in vain—
Who hid, in their turns, have been hid—
The treasures are squander'd again—
And here in the grave are all metals forbid,
But the tinsel that shone on the dark coffin lid.

To the pleasures which mirth can afford—
The revel, the laugh, and the jeer?
Ah! here is a plentiful board!
But the guests are all mute as their pitiful cheer,
And none but the worm is a reveller here!

Shall we build to affection and love?
Ah, no! they have wither'd and died,
Or fled with the spirit above—
Friends, brothers, and sisters, are laid side by side,
Yet, none have saluted and none have replied!

Unto sorrow?—The dead cannot grieve—
Not a sob, not a sigh meets mine ear,
Which compassion itself could relieve!
Ah! sweetly they slumber, nor hope, love, or fear—
Peace, Peace, is the watchword, the only one here!

Unto Death, to whom monarchs must bow?
Ah, no! for his empire is known,
And here there are trophies enow!
Beneath, the cold dead! and around, the dark stone!
Are the signs of a sceptre that none may disown!

The first tabernacle to Hope we will build!—
And look for the sleepers around us, to rise!
The second, to Faith, which ensures it fulfill'd—
And the third to the Lamb of the great sacrifice,
Who bequeath'd us them both, when he rose to the skies!

Herbert."

Richmond, October 7th, 1816.

RIPON.

The Free Grammar School in Ripon was founded and endowed in the year 1555, by King Philip and Queen Mary.

By an abstract of the Charter it appears, that their Majesties, upon the Petition, as well of Anthony Frankish, Gentleman, as of the Inhabitants of the Town and Neighbourhood of Ripon, did, by their Letters Patent, under the Broad Seal and the Seal of the Duchy of Lancaster, bearing date at Westminster on the 27th of June, in the Second and Third years of their reign, found, ordain, and erect a Free Grammar School in Ripon, at all times thereafter to endure, and to be called, "The Free Grammar School of Queen Mary," having one Master and one Usher, for the Instruction of Children and young Men :—

And, that their intent might have the better effect, and the lands, tenements, rents, revenues, and profits, to be granted and appointed for the support of the said School, might be better governed and applied, from thenceforth there should be Ten men of the Town and Parish of Ripon who should be called "The Governors of the Possessions, Revenues, and Goods of the said School," and elected and named John Norton, of Norton, in the County of York, Thomas Markinfield, William Mallorie, and Richard Arthington, Esquires; Ninian Staveley, Robert Walworth, Anthony Frankish, Miles Newton, Marmaduke Middleton, and Ninian Parnell Gentlemen, to be the first Governors, and the same Governors, and their Successors, are thereby incorporated and made Corporate and Politic of themselves for ever, by the name of "The Governors of the Possessions, Revenues, and Goods of the Free Grammar School of Queen Mary in the Town of Ripon," with power to receive and purchase to themselves and their Successors of the said King and Queen, and the heirs and successors of the said Queen, the lands, tenements, meadows, pastures, rents, reversions, and hereditaments thereunder specified, and any other lands, tenements, and hereditaments of the said King and Queen, her heirs, or successors, or of any other person or persons whatsoever, or of any other body or bodies Corporate or Politic:—

And that when one or any of the said Ten Governors should happen to die, that it should be lawful for the others of the said Governors surviving, or the major part of them, to elect and name another convenient person dwelling and having his Family for the most part in the said Town and Parish of Ripon, into the place of the person or persons so dying, to succeed in the said office of Governor or Governors:—

And the said King and Queen, to effect their intent, granted to the said Governors and their Successors, all their messuages, lands, tenements, cottages, houses, buildings, barns, stables, gardens, shops, meadows, feedings, and pastures in the occupation of certain persons therein named, situate in *North Stainley*, *Studley Roger*, *Allhallow-Gate*, *Crosgate*, *Skell-gate*, *West-Gate*, and *Ripon*, in the said County, to the then late Chantry of The Assumption of The Blessed Virgin Mary in Ripon belonging:—

Also all their messuages, cottages, houses, buildings, barns, stables, gardens, shops, lands, meadows, and pastures, in the occupation of certain persons therein named, situate in *Skell-gate*, *Allhallow-Gate*, *Horse-Fair*, *Finkle-Street*, *Blossom-Gate*, *Bondgate*, *Norton*, *Durton*, *Speltriggs*, *Long-furlong*, *Fisher-gate*, and *Ripon*, to the then late Chantry of St. James The Apostle in Ripon aforesaid belonging:—

Also all their messuages, tofts, cottages, houses, buildings, lands, meadows, and pastures, in the occupation of certain persons therein named, situate in *Ripon*, *Bondgate*, *Thorpe*, *Sharow*, *Waller-thwaite*, *Markington*, and *Helsey-Ings*, to the then late Chantry of St. John The Evangelist in Ripon belonging:—

And six messuages and tenements and all their lands, meadows, and pastures, in the occupation of the persons therein named, situate in *Allhallow-Gate*, and *Kirk-Gate*, in Ripon, to the then late Chantry of The Blessed Virgin Mary, in the Manor of *The Hall-Garth* in Ripon belonging:—

And also all other messuages, &c., in the several places before named and elsewhere, which belonged to the then late Chantries, in as ample a manner as they could or ought to have come to the hands of the said King and Queen, or of their Brother Edward the Sixth, then late King of England, by force of an act of divers Chantries, Colleges, Gilds, Fraternities, and Free

Chapels, dissolved and determined in the Parliament of their said Brother, holden at Westminster in the first year of his reign, which said messuages, &c., then extended to the yearly value of £16..14..9. To hold the same to the said Governors and their Successors for ever, to be holden of the said King and Queen, their heirs and successors as of their Manor of *East Greenwich*, in the County of Kent, by Fealty only:—

And the said King and Queen ordained, that the said Governors and their Successors, should dispose, and convert all the rents and profits from time to time arising from the said possessions, to the maintenance and support of The School-master and Usher, and to the other necessaries concerning the School, and the supporting, repairing, and maintaining thereof, and no other way, nor to any other use or intent:—

And that the Governors might have one Common Seal:—

And might plead and be impleaded:—

And that the Governors and their Successors, or the greater part of them, of which the said ANTHONY FRANKISH, during his life, should be one, should have power to nominate and appoint a School-master, and an Usher of the said School, as often and when the same should want either Master or Usher:—And with the advice of The Archbishop of York for the time being, might make lawful and wholesome Statutes and Ordinances in writing, touching the order, government and direction of the Master and Usher, and of the Scholars of the School, and of it's possessions, and of the Stipend of the Master and Usher, and appoint and set down all other things concerning the ordering, governing, preserving, and disposing of the revenues and to the maintenance of the School,—all which Statutes and Ordinances to be made should be inviolably observed:—

And that the Governors, and their Successors, might receive, and purchase, as well of the said King and Queen, as of the heirs and successors of the Queen, or of any other person, any manors, &c., within the realm of England, so that they do not exceed the clear yearly value of £20., besides the premises above granted, the Statute of Mortmain, or any other Statute to the contrary notwithstanding.

At a special Meeting of THE GOVERNORS in Ripon, on the 11th of November, 1814, the following STATUTES and ORDINANCES were made, with the advice of The Lord Archbishop of YORK, and testified by the Archiepiscopal Seal, and the Signatures of Nine of the Governors:—

1st. That the Appointment of The Head Master and Usher, the Amount and Payment of their Salaries, and the power of removing them from their Situations upon such grounds as may appear to the Governors just and sufficient, are vested solely and absolutely in the said Governors.

2d. That the Master at any time to be elected, shall be a Graduate of The University of Oxford or Cambridge, and well affected to the Established Church of England.

3d. That every Resident Inhabitant of the Town and Parish of Ripon is entitled to send his Sons as Day Scholars, upon paying the customary Entrance money: Provided that they are not under *Eight* years of age, and are able to read English.

4th. That the branches of Education of Free Scholars are to be Greek, Latin, and English Grammar, with Writing and Arithmetic, the two latter branches to be taught at the expense of the Parents.

5th. That all Payments of Entrance money, &c., shall belong to The Head Master.

6th. That the Head Master, for the time being, shall be responsible for the Library, Fixtures, &c., belonging to the Dwelling-House and School.

7th. That the Master shall deliver to the Clerk or Treasurer of the said Governors, a List of the Free Scholars once a year, previously to the annual Meeting of The Governors, distinguishing their several Classes.

THE TEN GOVERNORS of The School have always been chosen from the principal Gentlemen of Rank and Fortune in the Town and Neighbourhood. The present Governors are,—

The Right Honble Lord GRANTHAM, of Newby-Hall.
The Right Honble. FREDERICK JOHN ROBINSON, M. P.
Sir BELLINGHAM REGINALD GRAHAM, Bart., of Norton Conyers.
JOHN DALTON, Esq., of Sleningford.
CONYERS NORTON, Esq., of Sawley.
HENRY RICHARD WOOD, Esq., of Hollin-Hall.
CHARLES OXLEY, Esq., of Ripon.
GEORGE ALLANSON, M. A., Prebendary of Ripon.
ROBERT DARLEY WADDILOVE, D. D., Dean of Ripon.
Lieut. General STAVELEY, of North Stainley.

They appoint a Receiver; and the Revenues of the School which are under their management and direction, are administered in a proportionable increase of the Stipends of The Master and Usher, as improvements are made in the Rents.

The School Establishment seems to have been reduced

into regular form about the year 1622, when RICHARD PALMES was chosen Master.

The School is situate in *St. Agnes-Gate*, and consists of a good House and Garden for the use of the Master, and a commodious School for the Scholars.

The Classics are taught, free of expense. The number of Free Scholars is unlimited. There are above Thirty Boarders in the Master's House; and a few Boys are boarded in the Town. No age is fixed for the removal of the Free Scholars. There is no form of nomination.

Dr. VALPY'S Latin and Greek Grammars are used. The present Master has introduced into the system of Education, modern and ancient Geography, English and Ancient History, with the study of Chronology; and the principles of the Mathematics.

This is one of the Yorkshire Schools which have the right of sending Candidates for the valuable Exhibitions at QUEEN'S COLLEGE, Oxford, founded by Lady ELIZABETH HASTINGS;—these Scholars, *Five* in number, are to be taken from *Eight* Schools in Yorkshire, *Two* in Westmorland, and *Two* in Cumberland; and for their maintenance she gave the Manor of *Wheldale* or *Queldale*, in Yorkshire. This School has lost it's right: But the Master has lately been informed, that The Provost and Fellows of Queen's College are disposed to restore it's former privilege to the School. See, *Leeds*.

The present Head Master is, The Revd. WILLIAM PLUES, M. A., of Trinity College, Cambridge, whose Salary is £180. *per annum*, together with the School-House. This Gentleman's terms for Boarders are Forty guineas *per annum*, for Pupils under Twelve years of age; and Fifty guineas *per annum*, for those of the age of Twelve and upwards. Entrance Three guineas.

The Salary of the Second Master, The Revd. JAMES CHARNOCK, B. A., is £60. *per annum*. This Gentleman does not take Boarders; neither does the Writing-Master.

The following is a List of THE HEAD MASTERS, with the dates of their Appointments :—

In 1622. Richard Palmes, Clerk.
1650. Roger Holmes, Clerk, resigned.
1661. Charles Oxley, Clerk.
1676. George Loup, Clerk.
1681. Ralph Cottingham, Clerk.
1685. Thomas Thompson, Clerk.
1704. Thomas Lloyd, Clerk, resigned.
1721. John Barber, Clerk.
1730. Thomas Stevens, Clerk, resigned.
1737. William Scott, Clerk, chosen, but refused to accept the same.
1737. James Ropham, Clerk, chosen, but refused to accept the same.
1737. George Hyde, Clerk.
1772. Solomon Robinson, M. A.
1798. Isaac Cook, M. A.
1809. William Ewebank, M. A., resigned.
1812. William Plues, M. A.

Among the Eminent Men who have been educated at this School, may be enumerated,—

Beilby Porteus, late Bishop of London.

Thomas Balguy, D. D., Archdeacon of Winchester.

Admiral Gell.

Dr. Dering, Prebendary of Canterbury,—

and numerous most respectable Characters in the Neighbourhood, by whom it has ever been justly holden in great repute.

ROTHERHAM.

THE FREE GRAMMAR SCHOOL at ROTHERHAM was founded by LAWRENCE WOODNETT, Esq., formerly of Lincoln's Inn, and ANTHONY COLLINS, Esq., formerly of London;—who, by their Deed, dated the 1st of September, 1584, conveyed to certain Trustees and their Heirs, amongst divers messuages and lands in Rotherham, Masbrough, and Brinsworth in the Township of Rotherham, a building, called "*The Town's-Hall*," with the House adjoining; which, for time immemorial, have been occupied as a School-house and School, under the direction of the Trustees and Feoffees of other estates.

The School-house which has lately been rebuilt by the Feoffees, is worth about £12..12..0. a year, and is occupied by the Master, rent free.

Upon the inclosure of the Commons and Waste lands of Rotherham, in 1812, an allotment of about three roods was appropriated to the Trustees of the School, now let at £3. a year, and which the Master receives.

There is also a Crown payment of £10..15..4. *per annum* to the Master, which is paid at the Auditor's office at York.

And an annual sum of £2. is payable out of lands in the Township of Dalton in this Parish.

The School is open to the boys of the Town indefinitely, free of expense, for *Classics only*.

The ETON Latin Grammar, and the ETON and WESTMINSTER Greek Grammars are used.

This School has a claim in it's turn to the FELLOWSHIP and TWO SCHOLARSHIPS at EMANUEL COLLEGE, Cambridge, founded by Mr. FRIESTON, in case the same are not occupied from The Free School at Normanton.

There is a FELLOWSHIP also at LINCOLN COLLEGE, Oxford.

The present Master is, The Revd. BENJAMIN BIRKITT,

whose Salary is about £30. a year, including the house rent and the other small sums; besides which he has a gratuity from the Feoffees or Trustees.

ROBERT SANDERSON, D. D., Bishop of Lincoln, was educated here.

ROYSTON, near BARNESLEY.

THE FREE GRAMMAR SCHOOL at ROYSTON was founded by Letters Patent, in the Fifth of King JAMES the First.

The Endowment consists of a house, garden, and 24 acres of land, amounting to about £70. *per annum.*

A person now unknown, left the interest of £13. to the Master,—who also receives £4..6..11. from the Duchy Court of Lancaster.

The School is open to the boys of the Parish indefinitely, free of expense. There is no age specified either for their admission, or superannuation.

The ETON Grammars are used.

There are no University advantages belonging to this School.

The present Master is, Mr. WILLIAM COCKCROFT, whose Salary is £90. *per annum.*—And as there is not "a sufficient number of *Classic* Scholars, the Trustees *permit* him to teach *English.*"

SCORTON.

THE FREE GRAMMAR SCHOOL at SCORTON was founded by Mr. LEONARD ROBINSON, of Scorton, by Will dated in 1720, and endowed with a Farm in the Township of Scorton now producing upwards of £200. *per annum*, together with a dwelling-house and gardens.

The School is open to all, free of expense, for the *Classics;* but for the Stipend of the Usher, repair of buildings, writing, and arithmetic, a quarterly charge is made. There are *no* boys upon the Foundation. The number of Scholars fluctuates.

The ETON Grammars are chiefly used; and the principal object is to prepare young Gentlemen for the Universities, or some of the Learned professions.

There are no Exhibitions, nor other University advantages, belonging to this School.

The present worthy Head Master is, The Revd. WILLIAM BOWE, who takes Pupils at Fifty guineas *per annum* each, for board and education.

There are BOARDING-HOUSES also in the village, where boys are boarded on moderate terms,—particularly one very respectable House, at about £30. a year, for board and washing.

Scorton is a very pleasant and healthy place, as may be inferred from *Old* HARRY JENKINS who lived and died within a mile of it, at the extraordinary age of ONE HUNDRED and SIXTY NINE.

The Revd. JOHN NOBLE, who was educated at Queen's College, Oxford, where he took the Degree of B. A., soon after quitting the University, became the *first* Master of Scorton School,—which he opened in June 1736, and had the tuition of several young Gentlemen, who testified their regard to him, whilst living, by the institution of an annual *School-Feast* at Scorton,*—and, after his death, by placing a handsome Monument to his memory in the Church of BOLTON *upon Swale*, a Chapelry in the Parish of Catterick; the expense of which was defrayed by Subscription. He died on the 7th of October, 1767, at the age of Sixty-seven.

* Mr. NICHOLS observes, that this *Feast* was celebrated, on the 11th of June, 1766, in the Long room over the School, as "*there was a convenience of keeping the provisions warm, two fires below, and two above it.*"

SEDBERGH.

The Free Grammar School at Sedbergh was founded by Roger Lupton, D. D., Provost of Eton,—who directed, that The Master and Fellows of St. John's College, Cambridge, should always appoint the Master within a month after every vacancy certified to them,—and, upon their default, then the Governors with the consent of the Diocesan should elect for that turn.

To the honour of Sir Anthony Denny, Knt., who was a liberal Patron of Literature, it is recorded, that the buildings being fallen to decay, and the lands appropriated to the support of the Institution, being *sold* and *embezzled!*—he caused the School to be repaired, and not only recovered, but also settled the estate so firmly, as to prevent all future alienations.

Provost Lupton founded Two Fellowships, and Eight Scholarships, at St. John's College, Cambridge, for Students from this School.

Mr. Heblethwaite also founded One Fellowship at St. John's.

The annual produce of some Estates is applied to the relief of the poor Householders belonging to the Township, not receiving Parochial assistance,—towards Clothes for Twelve poor Children of the Township, above 7 and under 12 years of age,—to the purchasing of Bread to be given to poor people, at the Church yearly on *St. John's* day,—and for an Exhibition to a Sedbergh *born* Scholar, while educating at St. John's College.

This is one of the Schools which is entitled to send a Candidate for Lady Elizabeth Hastings's Exhibitions. See, *Leeds*.

Among the Eminent men who have been educated at this School, may be mentioned,—

ANTHONY ASKEW, M. D., esteemed one of the best Greek Scholars in England, and a Promoter of Learning.

JOHN BARWICK, D. D., successively Dean of Durham, and of St. Paul's.

PETER BARWICK, M. D., Physician in Ordinary to King CHARLES the Second.

ROBERT WILLAN, M. D.

No answer has been received to the repeated applications of the Author.

SHEFFIELD.

THE FREE GRAMMAR SCHOOL at SHEFFIELD was founded in the year 1603 or 1604, by THOMAS SMITH, of Crowland, in the County of Lincoln, who was an Attorney and supposed to have been born at Sheffield. The sum left by his Will was £30. a year,—out of which £20. was to be paid to The Head Master, and £10. to the Usher,—arising from lands situate in the Parish of Leverington, in the County of Cambridge: but these were afterwards sold by The Governors, and estates at *Wadsley*, near Sheffield, were purchased with the money. The present rental cannot be exactly stated; but, in 1787, it was calculated at £35..4..0. *per annum*.

Mr. SMITH having left the direction of his donation to the MINISTER and TWELVE of the most sufficient Parishioners of Sheffield, they were by Letters Patent, dated the second of King JAMES the First, 1605, incorporated,—and by which it was directed, that the School should be called "THE FREE GRAMMAR SCHOOL of JAMES King of England within the Town of Sheffield in the County of York,"—the Governors were to be in all respects and to act as a Body Corporate, and to have a Common Seal,—and it was ordered, that the Master must be a Master of Arts, or at least a Bachelor in Arts.

In 1606, an Assessment was made for the benefit of the School, which amounted to £103..18..3.

By an Indenture, dated the 3d of March, 1619, the Burgesses of Sheffield Church (who are also a Corporate Body, by Patent) granted to the School Governors the House, called "*The School House*," with the garden and croft adjoining, to be holden for eight Hundred years at 1*s.* rent.

The present School was built by Subscription in 1648.

JAMES HILL, of Sheffield, Schoolmaster, by Will dated in 1709, gave to the Governors all his lands at *Gilberthorpe Hill*, for the only use and benefit of the Master for ever, which, in 1787, were valued at £12..12. *per annum.*

On account of the insufficiency of the fund to keep the School and School-house in repair, a Subscription was begun amongst the Inhabitants of the Town and Parish of Sheffield, in 1776, when the sum of £805. was raised; with which the premises were repaired, and the remainder placed out on real security.

There are no STATUTES, except what are contained in the Royal Patent.

The School is open indefinitely, for boys inhabiting the Town of Sheffield and the Neighbourhood. There are at present 20 boys upon the Foundation, and 20 other Scholars. By some of the articles of agreement that were made between the Governors and the Master, the age of admittance was to be above *eight* years;—they may remain as long as they please. The right of nomination of Scholars is with The Governors.

The ETON Grammars are used.

There are no Exhibitions, nor other University advantages, belonging to this School.

The present Head Master is, The Revd. JOSEPH WILSON, whose fixed Salary is £60. *per annum.* He does not take Pupils. Neither does the Second Master.

SHERBURN, near FERRY BRIDGE.

THE GRAMMAR SCHOOL, and HOSPITAL, at SHERBURN were founded in 1619, by ROBERT HUNGATE, Esq., Counsellor, and endowed with £120. *per annum* for the clothing and maintenance of the boys in the Hospital, and £12. *per annum* to the Master, payable out of lands in this Parish, belonging to ROBERT OLIVER GASCOIGNE, Esq., of *Parlington*.

A subsequent endowment of £12. *per annum* was awarded to the Master on a late Inclosure.

There are EIGHT boys upon the Foundation, who are admitted at the will of Mr. GASCOIGNE. They are admitted at *eight* years of age, and are superannuated at *fifteen*. About 30 other Scholars attend, who pay a small Quarterage.

The ETON Grammars are used,—and besides the Classics, the English language and arithmetic are taught.

There are FOUR EXHIBITIONS of £7..10..0. each to ST. JOHN'S COLLEGE, Oxford.

This is one of the Schools which is entitled to send a candidate for Lady ELIZABETH HASTINGS'S exhibitions. See, *Leeds*.

The present Master is, The Revd. T. ALLEN, Clerk, whose Salary is £34. *per annum*. This Gentleman takes Boarders at £40. a year each.

The Assistant's Salary is £13..13..4. *per annum*.

SHIPTON, near YORK.

THE FREE GRAMMAR SCHOOL at SHIPTON is endowed with a Salary of £40. *per annum.*

No answer has been received to the Author's Letter.

SKIPTON in CRAVEN.

THE TOWN of SKIPTON has long enjoyed the benefit of a well endowed GRAMMAR SCHOOL, which was founded on the 1st. of September, in the second year of the reign of King Edward the Sixth, 1548, by WILLIAM ERMYSTED, Clerk, Canon Residentiary in the Cathedral Church of St. Paul, London,—who, having long been minded to found a School here, for instructing boys in Grammar, and to ordain certain Statutes for the government of the same,—

Granted to Sir INGRAM CLYFFORD, Knight, and others, all those messuages, lands, tenements, rents, and hereditaments in *Adyngham*, in the County of York, *viz.*,—One tenement with the lands and premises therewith demised of the yearly value of 38*s*..5d.,—one messuage and lands of the yearly value of 30*s*..7*d*.,—one messuage and lands of the yearly value of 8*s*.,—one messuage and lands of the yearly value of 17*s*.,—one messuage and lands of the yearly value of 6*s*.,—And also all those messuages, burgages, tenements and lands in *Skipton* and *Estbye*, which were of HENRY Earl of CUMBERLAND, *viz*.,—One messuage, tenement or burgage, and lands in the East part of *Bentley Bridge* of the yearly value of 36*s*..8*d*.,—a messuage or burgage and lands near *Walke Mylle*, called *Halcroft*, and another close there of the yearly value of 22*s*..8*d*.,—one Oxgang of land of the yearly value of 6*s*.,—another Oxgang of land of the yearly value of 6*s*.,—another Oxgang of land of the yearly value of 6*s*.—a messuage in *Estbye* of the yearly value of 12*s*.,—and one Oxgang of land in *Estbye* of the yearly value of 3*s*.,—to hold to them, their heirs and assigns for ever,—

To the intent, that they, and the survivors of them and their heirs and assigns, should yearly receive all the issues and profits thereof, and with the same perform all things which in a Schedule thereto annexed, for the erecting, continuing, support, government and good rule of a School in Skipton in Craven for boys resorting thither to be taught, are specified,—

That, whenever so many of the Feoffees shall die, that there shall not be above *Five* surviving,—the Survivors shall make an estate by their Deed to other discreet persons, to the number of *Thirteen* at the least, of the premises to the use aforesaid ;—

And the said WILLIAM ERMYSTED ordained, That there shall be a School in Skipton in Craven from time to time for ever, for the instruction of boys there in Grammar,—

That the said School shall be kept in a house in Skipton which he purchased of HENRY Earl of CUMBERLAND, on the 20th of August, in the first of EDWARD the Sixth, 1547, for the instruction of boys, as well in the first rudiments as in all the art of Grammar,—

That there shall be one Master,—

That he shall daily enter and teach in the same School (except Feast days), unless hindered by illness or other reasonable cause, immediately after *six* in the Morning, from the first of March to the first of October,—and shall there faithfully exercise himself in teaching the boys until *Eleven*,—and from *One* in the Afternoon until *six*,—And from the first of October to the first of March, shall begin at *seven* in the Morning, and shall instruct the boys there until *five* or *six*, as necessity shall require,—

That the said Master shall be a Chaplain or Priest,—And that he, and his Successors, shall teach the boys the Alphabet according to the proper pronunciation of Syllables, and shall afterwards proceed in order in the Grammar art and the rudiments thereof, with the frequent use in the Latin tongue according to their capacities from the advanced Scholars,—and that they compose epistles, orations, and verses,—

That the said Chaplain immediately after entering the School shall say the Psalm, "*Miserere mei Deus,*" which he shall not omit under the penalty of 20*d*. for each day,—And if he shall wilfully omit daily for a Month, he shall be removed.—That the said Chaplain shall be personally present in the Parish Church of Skipton every Sunday and Feast day, when there shall be Service,—

That the Chaplain if thereto disposed, and he shall not be hindered by any reasonable cause, shall celebrate in the said Church on Sundays and Feast days, and three days in every week before *seven* in the Morning,—

That he shall not absent himself from the said Church and School above 20 days at one time, or several, in any year under the penalty for the first offence of 20*s*,—then 30*s*,—and for the third, removal from his office,—

If the Chaplain shall dilapidate any of the buildings, or shall not faithfully observe all things incumbent upon him, or be convicted of any notable crime, or shall for his offence incur *any mutilation* whereby he shall be hindered from the execution of the Sacerdotal Order or the Instruction of boys, or that he shall not be able to perform the Service aforesaid and abide there, he shall be removed by the Vicar or Curate and Churchwardens there,—

That he shall have yearly for his support the issues and profits of all the premises, and shall possess the same service for life, if he well behave himself,—

The right of nominating a Chaplain to the said service of Master, to belong to the Vicar and Churchwardens,—If they shall omit to appoint within a month, the right of appointing shall devolve for that turn to the Rector or Master of Lincoln College, Oxford, and the Fellows of the same College,—And if they shall omit for a month after it comes to their knowledge, the right shall devolve for that turn to The Dean and Chapter of St. Paul's, London,—And if they shall omit for one month, then to return to the Vicar and Churchwardens,—

If the said Chaplain shall continue in any sickness, so that he cannot exercise his said office, he shall have the issues and profits of the premises for one year from the commencement of his sickness, so that he provide one of his Scholars or another sufficient man for the instruction of the boys in the School,—And after that year, the Vicar and Churchwardens shall provide another who shall instruct the boys there during such illness, or during his life if he continue ill, so that the Incumbent have *half* the profits for life, and the person exercising the office the other *half*,—and after the decease of the Incumbent such Instructor shall have the office and all the profits, if he be fit,—

That after the death of the said WILLIAM ERMYSTED the right of demising the premises shall belong to the Vicar and Churchwardens and the Chaplain of the School aforesaid, so that the emoluments arising therefrom, be expended in the support and repair of the said Schoolmaster and School,—

When any of the said Feoffees shall die, so that there shall be only *Four* surviving, the survivors shall enfeoff the most discreet and wealthy Parishioners of Skipton to the number of *Thirteen* of and in the said premises, and so for ever,—

That this Declaration, and all Writings and Muniments concerning the service aforesaid, shall for ever remain in a Chest in the Vestry of the Church of Skipton, under three Locks and three several Keys,—*one* to remain with the Incumbent of the School, the *second* with the Vicar of Skipton, and the *third* with the Wardens of Estby and Emsey for ever.

The whole rental which then amounted only to £9..15..4., is now about £600. *per annum.*

There is also an annual payment of £4..4..10. out of the Land Revenues of the Crown.

Boys are admitted, free of expense, indefinitely throughout the Parish.

The Grammars in use are,—*English*, ASH, LOWTH, and MURRAY,—*Latin*, WARD's edition of LILLY,—*Greek*, ETON, WESTMINSTER, and NUGENT's Port Royal,—*Hebrew*, ROBERTSON. The Master is required to explain to the Scholars, *Virgil*, *Terence*, *Ovid*, and the other Latin Poets,—and to teach them to compose epistles, orations, and verses.

Lady HASTINGS's Exhibitions at QUEEN's COLLEGE, Oxford, have been obtained by Scholars from this School, but no application has been made for several years past. See, *Leeds*.

WILLIAM PETYT, Esq., in 1707, gave £200. for the support of Two poor Scholars at CHRIST COLLEGE, Cambridge.

And his Brother, SYLVESTER PETYT, Esq., formerly of *Staple Inn*, Holborn, by his Will left £24,048. Old South Sea Annuities, now standing in the name of The Accountant General of The High Court of Chancery to the credit of a Cause, intituled, " ATTORNEY GENERAL *v.* ORD, *Petyt's* Charity," and a LIBRARY at Skipton,—the gross annual Income, in 1815, being £721..9..2.,—The objects of which Donation are, Persons, *wherever resident*, standing in need of immediate relief, according to the discretion of The Trustees,—and amongst whom the remainder of this sum is annually distributed, after paying £20. a year to Christ College, Cambridge, small Salaries to a Schoolmaster, and Librarian at Skipton, and for putting out annually about FOURTEEN poor Children apprentices in the County of York, and for buying books for the use of the School.

The present Master is, The Revd. THOMAS GARTHAM, M. A., late Fellow of Lincoln College, Oxford.

STEPHEN BARRET, a Classical teacher of considerable eminence, was educated at this School

THORNTON, near PICKERING.

THE FREE GRAMMAR SCHOOL at THORNTON was founded in the year 1657, by ELIZABETH Viscountess LUMLEY, and endowed with £30. *per annum*, for a Master "in Holy Orders" to teach the School, and to read Prayers in THE CHAPEL. The amount of the Endowment is now about £60. a year, consisting of ten acres of land at Thornton, and a stipulated Salary of £45., together with a house, garden, and School-house.

The School is open to all the children of the Inhabitants of Thornton, Farmanby, Sinnington, Marton, and Edstone. They are admitted when they can read the English Testament; and there is no prescribed time for their continuance at the School. The number of boys upon the Foundation is generally from *ten* to *twenty*; and of other Scholars the number has sometimes been from 15 to 25, but it is now small.

The ETON Grammars are used.

There are FOUR EXHIBITIONS of £10. *per annum* each, for Students from this School until they become Graduates, at either Oxford or Cambridge.

The present Master is, The Revd. MICHAEL MACKERETH, who takes pupils at about £40. *per annum*, but his terms vary according to the age and accommodation required.

There is no Second Master at present, nor is there any provision made for one by the Endowment.

Several excellent Classical Scholars have been educated at this School.

It was lately a matter of Litigation in the Court of Chancery, whether the School at THORNTON ought to be a *Grammar* School *only*, or a Free School for *reading*, *writ-*

ing, and *arithmetic*, as well as Classical learning,—when it was determined to be a *Grammar* School *only*.

There is a Free School at SINNINGTON, (for reading, writing, arithmetic, and mathematics,) which is a branch of this Establishment, and was erected there on account of the distance from Thornton.

There is an HOSPITAL also at Thornton, for 12 poor people (generally *Widows*), who have each a neat house of two apartments, with £10. or upwards yearly.

The CHAPEL is connected with the SCHOOL and HOSPITAL. The lands which support these Charities are partly at Thornton, and partly at Thirsk.

TICKHILL, near WORKSOP.

THE small SCHOOL at TICKHILL was endowed, near the close of the Seventeenth Century, by Mrs. JANE FARMERY, with a piece of land in this Parish, the rent of which pays for the Education in English of *Eighteen* boys, at 6*s*..8*d*. a year each.

When there are any vacancies, they are filled up by the Vicar and the Church-wardens.

A nett Payment of £4..8..8. *per annum* is also due at Michaelmas from the Duchy of Lancaster, and was so paid until the year 1815.

The present Vicar, The Revd. T. F. TWIGGE, has, for some years past, very benevolently expended a pretty considerable sum in the support of a SUNDAY SCHOOL,—and, if the Duchy payment should be renewed, he intends to apply it to the benefit of Mrs. FARMERY's Institution.

TOPCLIFFE, near THIRSK.

King EDWARD the Sixth, by Letters Patent in the second year of his reign, 1549, granted to an Assistant Curate to the Church of Topcliffe, and his Successors, £5. *per annum*, which was confirmed by Queen ELIZABETH, in 1559. This Pension the Feoffees have lately appropriated to the Schoolmaster. It is payable out of the Land Revenues of the Crown.

In 1588, JOHN HARTFORTH, of *Topcliffe*, gave a sum of money to THE FREE GRAMMAR SCHOOL which, with a sum added by the Parishioners, purchased a Cottage and *five* acres of land. The Cottage is now in ruins, and the land has been exchanged for about *three* acres.

WILLIAM ROBINSON, of London, Citizen, gave to this School £16. *per annum* for ever, to be paid by The Grocers' Company in London.

In 1674, HENRY RAPER, of London, Citizen, gave out of his lands at *Skipton* in the Parish of Topcliffe, £10. *per annum* for ever to The Hospital of Firby, and the residue of the profits of those lands to the Schoolmaster of Topcliffe and his Successors. The Master's annual share, which was then £5., is now £60.

The whole Income of the Master is at present upwards of £80. a year.

There are TWELVE FEOFFEES who are chosen out of the whole Parish, the Vicar being always one,—and who have a power of sending THIRTY poor Children at one time from the different Townships.

The Master should be capable of teaching *Latin* and *Greek*, and has always been in *Holy Orders*, until the election of the present Gentleman, Mr. THOMAS BELL, on the

22d of April, 1809, on the death of The Revd. RICHARD RAMSHAW.

In consequence of the Decree in Chancery, on the 16th of June, 1674, Mr. BOVILL was elected in the room of Mr. HESLINGTON, the late Master: when the concerns of the School were finally settled.

The School-house, which is a very good one, was re-built by Suscription in 1812.

WAKEFIELD.

THE FREE GRAMMAR SCHOOL at WAKEFIELD was founded by Queen ELIZABETH, by Letters Patent dated the 19th of November, in the 34th year of her reign, 1592, at the humble suit of the Inhabitants of the Town and Parish,—

By which it was ordained, that there should be one Grammar School in this Town, to be called "THE FREE GRAMMAR SCHOOL of Queen ELIZABETH at WAKEFIELD," for the teaching, instructing and bringing up of Children and Youth in Grammar and other good learning,—to consist of one Master or Teacher, and one Usher and Under Teacher:—

That there shall be within the Parish of Wakefield, or dwelling within *two miles* thereof, FOURTEEN honest men of the most wise, discreet, and religious persons, who shall be GOVERNORS, —shall be a Body Corporate, with perpetual succession,—and be able to purchase and receive lands and other possessions:—

That, when any of the Governors shall die or dwell with their Families *above two miles* out of this Parish *for a year*, the rest of the Governors are to take unto them the Schoolmaster, and to nominate another in his place within *six weeks* after such vacancy,—And, if the election be deferred above six weeks, The Lord President of the North Parts, or the Archbishop of York, with the consent of *Six* of the Governors, are to appoint:—

That they shall have a Common Seal,—and be able to plead and be impleaded:—

That, when the place of Schoolmaster shall be void, the Governors shall nominate, and within *Sixty* days after a vacancy present, a meet man for knowledge, religion and life, so the party be well reported of and hath taken the Degree of Master of Arts, to the Archbishop of York who shall allow him to be Schoolmaster there accordingly,—to continue so long as he shall be found by the Governors to be diligent and faithful in his Office and fit for the same, both for his Religion and Conversation, and no longer,—but upon one Quarter's warning to remove him, and to proceed to a new election,—But, if the Governors shall not present a fit Schoolmaster within Sixty days after a vacancy, The Master and Fellows of Emanuel College, Cambridge, to nominate a fit Master of Arts, with the consent of *Six* of the Governors, who shall be admitted under the Common Seal of the School:—

The Governors, with the help and assistance of the Schoolmaster, are to appoint a fit Usher and Under Teacher within a month after a vacancy,—with power to displace such Usher upon one Quarter's warning, if he be found negligent or unfit:—

Power is given to the Governors, *with the Schoolmaster's advice and consent,* to make Statutes and Ordinances in writing under the Common Seal, to be kept under two locks,—the Schoolmaster to have one key, and one of the Governors, by the consent of the rest, to have the other:—

The Governors, Masters, and Ushers thereafter to be made, to take an *Oath* before the Governors assembled for their election, on the day of their entry into Office, to be faithful and careful for the good of the School in all things appertaining to their office and charge:—

With license to purchase and receive lands and other possessions to the clear yearly value of 100 marks.

The School is situate on a well chosen site, and in a retired and silent quarter of the Town,—and built too, as appears from it's extent, with a foresight of it's popularity and of the numbers which were likely to resort to it.

Little more, however, can be said, respecting it's Foundation, as access has been "*refused to the original documents.*"

The School is open to the sons of the Inhabitants indefinitely, *free of expense*, who are desirous of a *Classical* education,—though the Head Master (and probably also the Second) is usually *complimented* with a small donation at Christmas. It is well conducted, and contains at present about 60 Scholars.

The Master does not confine himself to any particular Grammars.

There are Two EXHIBITIONS from this School,—one of them for the *Natives* only of Wakefield, which *ought* to be something considerable; but, it is believed, that the Scholar who is elected, has *only* allowed him about a guinea *per* week, during his residence in the University.

Mr. CAVE founded Two SCHOLARSHIPS at CLARE HALL,

Cambridge, of £1..11..6. *per* week each, appropriated to Scholars from this School.

This School has also a claim in it's turn to the FELLOWSHIP and TWO SCHOLARSHIPS at EMANUEL COLLEGE, Cambridge, founded by Mr. FRIESTON, in case the same are not filled from the Free School at Normanton.

The present Head Master is, The Revd. Mr. NAYLOR, who was the *Third Wrangler* of his year at Cambridge, and whose Salary is *now* £180. *per annum:* there is a House also, but he is not in occupation, nor receives the rent of it.

The present Second Master is, The Revd. Mr. SISSONS.

There is a good LIBRARY belonging to the School.

To this eminent Seminary the world is indebted for the scholastic erudition of RICHARD BENTLEY, D. D., and of JOHN POTTER, Archbishop of Canterbury,—the first a native of the neighbourhood, the second of the Town itself; To which may be added,—

JOHN RADCLIFFE, M. D., the Founder of the Library under his name at Oxford.

THOMAS ZOUCH, D. D., the learned Divine.

JOSEPH BINGHAM, M. A., Author of that laborious performance, "*Origines Ecclesiasticæ.*"

The Revd. THOMAS ROBINSON, a late eminent Divine at Leicester.

CHARLES HOOLE, a Schoolmaster of very considerable note in his day, and the Publisher of some School books not yet out of use,—

And, in conclusion, the Author may be pardoned the expression of his sorrow and esteem, in recording the name of a friend, whom death permitted him so shortly to know, The Rev. Dr. SWYRE, late Rector of Melsonby, near Richmond.

WORSBOROUGH, near BARNESLEY.

THE FREE GRAMMAR SCHOOL at WORSBOROUGH has a Salary of £5..4..2½ *per annum* for a Master, payable out of the Land Revenues of the Crown.

No answer has been received to the Author's Letter.

WRAGBY, near PONTEFRACT.

THE FREE GRAMMAR SCHOOL at WRAGBY has a Stipend of £16..16..4. *per annum* for a Master, payable out of the Land Revenues of the Crown.

No answer has been received to the repeated applications of the Author.

YARM.

THE GRAMMAR SCHOOL at YARM was founded by Letters Patent of Queen ELIZABETH, bearing date the 7th of July, in the 30th year of her reign, 1588; and endowed by THOMAS CONYERS, of Egglescliffe, in the County Palatine of Durham, Gentleman; who, by his Will dated the 10th of February 1589, left the sum of £9..4..0., payable out of his lands and houses at Yarm and Darlington, on the Feasts of Pentecost and St. Martin, "at the Schole of Yarome for ever."

By virtue of the Letters Patent, TWELVE GOVERNORS therein named, were authorized to elect a Master, and with the consent of the Archbishop of YORK as Visitor, to make Statutes for the regulation and management of the School.

But *these Twelve* all dying, and new Trustees not having been elected, the *Patent ceased.* And SIX of the Principal Inhabitants, who pay the rent charges, have from time to time elected the Master and nominated the *Six* Foundation Scholars, with the consent and approbation of the Minister for the time being, who generally acts as one of the Trustees.

In addition to the original Endowment, the late WILLIAM CHALONER, Esq., a native of Yarm, left, by his Will dated in 1801, to the Schoolmaster of Yarm for ever, the sum of £400. Three *per Cent.* Consols, for educating and instructing in reading, writing, and arithmetic, *Eight* poor Children of this Parish, to be nominated and elected by the Minister and Church-Wardens.

Mr. CHALONER also left £30., in Trust, to the Minister and Church-Wardens, for the repair of the Grammar

School: which was expended in the year 1802, and the School-house rendered comfortable and commodious.

There are no STATUTES in existence; neither is there a Common Seal.

The number of Boys upon the Foundation is FOURTEEN;—*viz.*, SIX on CONYERS's endowment,—and EIGHT on CHALONER's. They are admitted at 10 or 12 years of age, and remain three years. Being Children of Poor parents, their education is confined chiefly to English grammar, writing, and arithmetic. This Privilege is limited to boys within the Parish; and the form of admission is merely a note in writing, requesting the Master to "admit A. B., son of C. D., a free Scholar upon CONYERS's Foundation."

CHALONER's Scholars, as has been observed, are appointed by the Minister and Church-Wardens.

Besides the boys upon the Foundation there are about 30 others generally educated at this School; a few only of whom are taught the *Classics*. They are all Day-scholars.

The ETON Latin and Greek Grammars are used; and the ETON plan of Education is also followed.

The present Master is, The Revd. JOHN GRAVES, whose emoluments are about £90. or £100. *per annum*. This Gentleman is also the Officiating Minister of the Parish. He is the Author of an interesting "History of Cleveland," in one volume Quarto.

GEORGE PERROTT, Esq., late one of the Barons of His Majesty's Court of Exchequer at Westminster, received the first rudiments of his education at this School: his Father, The Revd. THOMAS PERROTT, being many years the Officiating Minister or Perpetual Curate of this Parish.

YORESBRIDGE, near BAINBRIDGE.

THE FREE GRAMMAR SCHOOL at YORESBRIDGE, in the Parish of Aysgarth, was founded in 1601, by ANTHONY BESSON, and endowed with a house, situate at York.

The School is open indefinitely to the Children of the four small Villages in it's vicinity, free of expense, for the *Classics only*. They are admitted when capable of learning *Latin*, and may continue as long as their Parents think proper. The number of Scholars who are free, and who are not free, is irregular,—being sometimes 70 or 80, and rarely under 50.

The ETON Grammars are used,—and besides the Classics, geography, history, arithmetic, merchants' accounts, with the various branches of the mathematics, are taught,—and "every prudential measure is adopted to encourage learning, good behaviour, and good morals,- and to discountenance idleness, rude behaviour, and immorality."

There are no University advantages, or Church Preferments, belonging to this School.

The present Master is, The Revd. ANTHONY WHARTON, whose emoluments are uncertain, and vary every year. It is but a very poor neighbourhood, and a great deal is humanely done for charity. This Gentleman's terms, for board and education, are 24 guineas *per annum*, and one guinea entrance. The domestic Scholars are taught two hours each day, in private. He is assisted by his Son.

It is gratifying to add, that Mr. WHARTON has educated many young men for the Church, several of whom have attained considerable Preferment, -besides numerous other boys, for mercantile and other useful departments of life.

Yoresbridge School is pleasantly situate upon the banks of the river *Yore*, nearly in the centre of *Wensley-Dale*, so justly celebrated for the beauty of it's scenery, the fertility of it's soil, and the salubrity of it's air.

At *West Witton*, in this delightful Dale, the Author received his humble Education under the late Revd. JAMES LAWSON.

YORK.

Holgate's Free School.

The Free Grammar School, within the Close of The Cathedral Church, was erected by Robert Holgate, D. D., Archbishop of York, in 1546, and endowed with £12. a year for a Master, to attend daily "to read and teach Grammar, and other good Authors and Works, generally to all Scholars thither resorting to learn the same."

His Grace obtained a Charter constituting Thomas Swan to be the first Master of it, and ordained that he and his Successors should be a Body Corporate,—that the Master should be called, "Master of The Free School of Robert Holgate," and by that name might plead and be impleaded, and have a Common Seal. That the Archbishops, his Successors, should be Patrons of the School for ever,—*sede vacante*, The Dean and Chapter;—if they do not present within Twenty days, then the Lord Mayor and Aldermen,—and if they do not present in the same time, the Patronage is left to the Archdeacon of York, and Twelve of the most substantial Housekeepers in the Parish of *St. John Baptist del Pyke*, to present as they please.

The rest of the Articles run upon the good behaviour of the Master, Usher, and Scholars. See *Hemsworth*.

No answer has been received to the Author's Letter.

YORK.

HORSE FAIR SCHOOL.

In a part of the City of York, commonly called "*Le Horse ayre*," stood a large HOSPITAL, which was founded and dedicated to ST. MARY MAGDALENE, by ROBERT *de* PYKERING, Dean of York, in 1330.

On it's suppression, the Hospital, with all it's possessions, was annexed to The Dean and Chapter of York,—who, by a Grant from King PHILIP and Queen MARY who had resumed the lands, founded a GRAMMAR SCHOOL, and perpetually endowed the Master with the same, to be from time to time by them presented.

In 1565, ROGER DALLISON, Chanter of the Cathedral Church of Lincoln, granted to the Dean and Chapter of York an Annuity of £4., issuing out of the Manor of *Hartlesholm*, in the County of Lincoln, which was appropriated to this School.

No information has been procured respecting the present state of this Establishment.